SKIING THE BEST

SKIING

A Guide
in the U.S.

 VINTAGE BOOKS   A Division of Random House
New York

THE BEST

to the Top 50 Ski Areas and Canada

MILES JAFFE
and DENNIS KRIEGER

To the two kids, Marcus Jaffe and Stephen Yeomans, who have at last (age 15) mastered the Plunge, and to my most tolerant law partners, who seem content not to try

Miles Jaffe

To Nicole and Eric,
and especially to Alice

Dennis Krieger

A Vintage Original, October 1978
First Edition
Copyright © 1978 by Miles Jaffe and Dennis Krieger
All rights reserved under International and Pan-American
Copyright Conventions. Published in the United States
by Random House, Inc., New York, and simultaneously in Canada
by Random House of Canada Limited, Toronto.

Library of Congress Cataloging in Publication Data
Jaffe, Miles.
Skiing the best.
Skis and skiing—United States. 2. Skis and skiing—Canada.
I. Krieger, Dennis, joint author. II. Title.
GV854.4.J25   796.9′3′097   78-55720
ISBN 0-394-72408-9

Manufactured in the United States of America

Cover photo: Sugarbush Valley, Vermont

CONTENTS

THE EAST

Introduction

The impetus for this book came from reflecting on the sheer number of questions we felt compelled to ask when, over the years, friends asked us a simple enough question: "Where shall we ski?" How well do you ski? Who are you going with? How many days do you have? What's your budget? Do you like the bumps? Do your kids ski? What do you like to eat? All these considerations seemed relevant in the intelligent making of what is for many people their major vacation decision.

Our research for this book has convinced us that even these questions are not exhaustive and that the factors in planning a ski vacation are both plentiful and subtle. Our purpose, then, is to provide an accurate, thorough, and critical view of what we regard as the fifty major ski resorts in North America. We have emphasized distinctions. Despite what you might have read in the past (airlines tend to be the worst offenders), not every area is "equally exciting for expert and novice alike" or "ideal for both the family and the swinging single." Also, we have discussed skiing and terrain in much more detailed fashion than we have seen elsewhere, because traditional descriptions of "wide-open slopes" and "exciting expert terrain" are insufficiently informative when it comes to deciding between resorts.

A WORD ABOUT US

We are two lawyers in our thirties who live in New York City. We are both expert skiers and have skied most of our lives. One of us grew up in New England and the other in the West, skiing California and the Rockies. We both have skiing children.

Over the years, we had already skied most all of the areas described in the book. During the last two seasons, however, we visited and skied each area again. Substantial amounts of time were spent with marketing personnel, ski school directors, ski patrollers, local residents, and tourists in order to get the most comprehensive view possible of the area. All expenses were paid out of our own pockets.

We do have our biases both as to skiing and ski resorts, and they should be made known. As to skiing, we are neither "bombers" nor "laid-back recreational skiers"; we ski aggressively and tend to judge mountains from that perspective. Thus we like tough terrain and we like the bumps. We like mountains where novice slopes are manicured and groomed, but where some variation in terrain is allowed to exist on intermediate trails. One of us is a powder freak and often prefers a helicopter to a chair lift.

Regarding ski resorts, other biases and predilections will surface. Accordingly, we detail here both how we chose these fifty areas and how we approached the information that we included.

THE CHOICE OF AREAS

The choice was based on an interplay of two factors: the quality of the skiing and the character of the area. As to skiing, the primary factor was the vertical drop of a given mountain, that is, the number of feet between the base of the mountain and its highest lift-served point. Examining this figure gives a good initial indication of the size and steepness of a mountain. With few exceptions, each area chosen has a vertical of at least 2,000 feet.

Choices made relating to the character of an area were obviously less quantitative. The appeal of a ski town often emanates as a "feel" rather than a statistic embodying the number of restaurants and lodges. While the feeling of the areas we have chosen often is radically divergent, running the gamut from frenetic Aspen to ascetic Grand Targhee, they all share certain qualities. We have chosen areas which honestly can be described as resorts. That is, we have established as a criterion the requirement that areas have a range of facilities and activities sufficient to satisfy skiers of all abilities who plan a stay of five or more days. Hence certain areas with verticals over 2,000 feet, such as Snow Bowl in Utah, Bridger Bowl in Montana, and Alpental in Washington, have not been included since there is little or nothing to do at these areas other than ski.

The book is regionally divided into the Far West, the Rockies, and the East. Geographic choices were made primarily on the basis of reliability of snow and thus resorts in places like West Virginia and North Carolina are not included.

THE INFORMATION INCLUDED

One of our purposes is to replace the general with the particular. If we think the night life is good, we undertake to tell you why; if we think the skiing is mediocre, we try to be as specific as possible. But certain generalities are helpful, and each chapter begins with our broad and often subjective impressions of the resort. Is it big and bustling or intimate and serene? Is the skiing tough, pleasant, or boring? The bases for these assertions are then set forth in some detail under the following categories.

Accessibility

This section lets you know where an area is and how long it will take to get there. Since resorts in the East and Far West draw most skiers from their immediate regions, we include the suggested auto routes and supply driving times from the nearest major metropolitan area. For resorts in the Rockies, which traditionally attract visitors on a less regional basis, the emphasis is on the ease or aggravation with which these resorts can be reached (usually by air) from more distant points.

THE SKIING

It is in this section more than any other that our standards need be described and our rationale explained. The goal of the section is to discuss, separately and in detailed fashion, the amount and quality of skiing available at each resort for each ability group of skier, i.e., novice, intermediate, and expert. In writing our descriptions and in making comparative judgments relating to the quality of skiing, we have applied certain standards and have looked particularly for certain qualities at each level.

In discussing novice trails, we isolated certain factors which we feel are important to the beginner both physically and mentally. For example, the degree of trail maintenance and the planning of novice runs in a manner that separates them from trails where experts will constantly be flying by both affect how easy a day the beginner will have on his skis. On the other hand, factors such as whether novices are relegated to the "bunny hill" at the base of the mountain or whether there is skiing for them up top, where they can meet up with better skiing friends and family, affect the beginner's psychological reaction to skiing and may regulate his desire to stick with it and improve.

Our leitmotif for analyzing intermediate skiing has been diversity, or, more appropriately, the lack thereof. Intermediate trails, particularly in the Rockies, tend to be cut from the same idealized mold. Moderate in length, modest in pitch, and mowed to billiard table smoothness, these trails proliferate in response to the demands of the recreational skier. And whereas there is absolutely nothing wrong with these trails, there is nothing much to say about them, either. While we describe Snowmass as being nearly perfect for the intermediate, there is not much more to say about its virtually indistinguishable trails. In reviewing intermediate trails, our interest was perked more by trails that deviated from the Snowmass norm by reason of either length, beauty, or interesting terrain. Thus our accolades were reserved more for seven-mile-long Olympic at Whistler Mountain, the beauty of the runs off the backside of Mammoth, and trails that offered the intermediate some challenge, as in the bumps on Storm Peak at Steamboat.

For expert skiers, by the use of a scale, we have attempted to compare, with some precision, the real difficulty of runs at the major areas. The most difficult—the ones where, if you fall, you don't stop till the bottom—are 10's. The top of the Starr at Stowe, the Headwall at Mt. Washington, the chutes at Jackson or Taos, the drops off the Central Ridge at Snowbird, and the West Face of KT at Squaw Valley are all 10's.

A 9 is a very steep expert trail, usually with bumps. In the East: the top of the National at Stowe, the Lift Line Chute at Mad River, Polly's Folly at Cannon. In the West: Limelight and Exhibition at Sun Valley, the Ridge of Bell at Aspen, Prima at Vail, Gunbarrel at Heavenly Valley, and the Plunge at Telluride.

An 8 is a challenging expert run that may be steep or bumpy but is not both, e.g., Regulator Johnson at Snowbird, the Headwall at Squaw Valley, and Bobby's Run at Waterville Valley.

A 7 is a run that may be marked expert but that good skiers can "cruise," i.e., ski without working hard. All of the expert trails at Mt. Bachelor fall into this category.

This rating system is not immutable. Weather, the amount of snow, and snow conditions (particularly in the East) all can change an intermediate trail into one only for the super-expert. This system, though, is more informative than traditional methods by which only percentages of novice, intermediate, and expert runs are given—a system which is both uninformative and misleading.

In discussing skiing, we often refer to the "ratio" of a given chair. This is the ratio between the overall length of the chair and the number of vertical feet it climbs. This ratio is a means by which to objectively judge both steepness and lift efficiency. A lift with a ratio of 3:1 or lower will necessarily service some demanding expert terrain, while a ratio of over 5:1 means that the skier must expect either long, flat runoffs or very gradual descents. In the East, for example, the chairs at Stowe, Sugarbush, and Mad River have 3:1 ratios, but such ratios are few and far between in southern Vermont. In analyzing lift efficiency, we looked to the vertical rise compared to the length of the ride. Thus lifts at Taos and Telluride are extremely efficient, rising 1,800 feet over a distance of 4,000 feet. In a word, this means that you get the most possible skiing for your lift line and chair ride.

In describing certain trails, we often make references to the "fall line." This is the direction down a trail that a stone would fall if dropped and represents the path a true expert will take down a run.

We also discuss the snow conditions and weather at the various areas. An Eastern skier may laugh at this, firm in the belief that ice is his permanent lot in life, but even in the East a discussion of these conditions is relevant and helpful. For instance, some areas in the East hold snow better than others, have less wind, or have more snowmaking capacity. In the West, annual snowfall may differ dramatically even between resorts only a few miles apart. Similarly, in both the East and West, conditions are affected by altitude and by which directions the slopes fall. It is essential to know that March days in Colorado are most often sunny and warm, while in neighboring Utah, March is one of the snowiest months. You probably don't need to be told that the Northwest is wet.

On lift lines, we try not only to single out those areas that are uncrowded but also to tell you how to minimize waiting time at even the largest, most crowded resorts (e.g., Squaw Valley and Aspen) by moving around and fully utilizing the mountain.

Integration of the Slopes

Here we discuss how easy or hard it is to get around on the mountain in order to maximize both skiing and meeting up with friends. This is of particular relevance at areas like Stowe and Winter Park, where skiing actually takes place on two or more separate mountains. We also often use this section to list the locations of the on-mountain eating facilities and comment on their convenience.

LIFE IN THE AREA

For many skiers planning a vacation of a week or longer, the nature of the resort will be even more determinative than the quality of the skiing. The skiing at Snowbird is perhaps the best in the world but the social life is certainly not. Similarly, Vail is an excellent mountain, but if you're looking for a quiet retreat away from the pressures of the city, it probably is not the right choice.

The nature of the resorts we have chosen vary dramatically as to most every major factor: accommodations, facilities, restaurants, child care, and general ambience. At each area, we have discussed and evaluated those factors we felt were critical in providing a full and complete picture of what a resort has to offer.

Accessibility to the Slopes

The distance from the mountain to available accommodations is important for several reasons. It affects the suitability of the area for children, it often determines whether a car is necessary, and it is significant for reasons of pure convenience. In this section, we point out these distances along with detailing methods and schedules of area-provided transportation between lodging and the mountain.

Accommodations

Lodging often represents the single most expensive item on a ski vacation. Prices varied widely over the territory we covered less by region (though the Rockies are generally the most costly) than by the glamour quotient of the resort. Not surprisingly, accommodations at resorts like Aspen, Vail, and Sun Valley are very expensive, while comparable lodging at Telluride, Crested Butter, and Okemo is often much cheaper.

The vast majority of accommodations we discuss fall into two categories. The first is what we have often called the lodge room. This is basically a motel or hotel room and, unless otherwise specified, meals or kitchen facilities are not included. The range in this type of accommodation is from elegant to substandard, and prices vary accordingly. The second type is the condominium unit. This is an apartment, ranging in size from studio to five bedrooms. Often preferred by families, these units have kitchen facilities. Prices vary widely, but generally the range is significantly higher than for the lodge room.

What we have looked for in recommending lodging is convenience, price, facilities, and taste. Often we refer to certain lodge accommodations as standard motel. This means in our parlance that you can expect to find a double bed (perhaps two), a bath or shower, and often a television set. When more facilities exist (e.g., game rooms, cocktail lounge, pool), we describe them. The convenience factor is related, of course, to the distance to the lifts, and in most cases we specify whether or not it is walking distance. Matters of taste are obviously subjective, but lodges like Sunriver at Mt. Bachelor, Top Notch at Stowe, and the Keystone Lodge at Keystone are so lovely that they, along with a few others, are singled out by us as being particularly gracious.

Condominiums show less variation in quality, though as a rule newer units are nicer than the older ones. Of primary interest to us in looking at condominiums was their range of facilities, and in each area we specify whether the condominiums have fireplaces, patios, pools, or Jacuzzis.

We have tried to consider the budget-minded. In areas where inexpensive accommodations (usually dorms) are available, we list them.

Prices have been dealt with in two ways. In most instances, a per-night price is given based on either double occupancy in the case of lodge rooms or two people using a one-bedroom condominium. (Studio condominiums will be slightly less, as will the per-person price in three- and four-bedroom condominiums.) In some instances, particularly when substantial savings can be effected, we quote a weekly per-person package rate (generally based on seven nights' lodging and six days of lift tickets). In some resorts, particularly in the Rockies, weekly packages are the primary method of renting. To convert nightly rates to packages, which are always quoted per-person, merely take one-half the nightly lodging rate, multiply it by seven, and add it to the price of the daily lift ticket multiplied by six.

Restaurants

There are a vast number of restaurants in ski country, and we have been to most of them. The decision on how to treat restaurants was difficult. To review them all in detail was obviously impossible for reasons of space. On the other hand, a mere listing seemed insufficient. We settled, instead, on discussing those restaurants we thought were the best in each area, as well as those which for various reasons (some having more to do with decor and ambience than cuisine) have become local favorites. We discuss the type of food available at these restaurants and in some cases make menu suggestions. We have attempted to cover restaurants at all price ranges, from elegant to fast-food. The reader should be aware, however, that the turnover in ski resort restaurants is phenomenal and should not be surprised if next year that fabulous little bistro we raved about has become a shoe repair shop.

Apres-ski and Night Life

In this section, we direct people to where the action is. The content of this "action" is fairly standard: one or more discoteques, some places with live entertainment (country-and-western was this year's theme), and a couple of quiet places to have a drink pretty much constitute ski resort night life. Nonetheless, the intensity of these activities varies tremendously from area to area. For example, though next-door neighbors, Aspen's night life is totally different than that of family-oriented, sedate Snowmass.

Children

In determining whether an area was suitable for children, we considered factors of convenience such as the distance of lodging from the slopes along with considerations of whether novice children would be able to ski with or even on the same mountain as their parents (at Sun Valley, Aspen, or Stowe this would be a problem). Also included are details on the existence, cost, and location of day-care and nursery facilities, as well as ski instruction.

Diversion

Here we listed what non–downhill skiing amusements were available. Common listings were cross-country skiing, skating, tennis, and helicopter skiing.

Costs

This section simply included our judgment as to the relative expense of the area, taking into consideration costs for lift tickets, restaurants, and lodging. 1978 prices have been used.

With some hesitation, we have decided to include a rating table in the back of the book in which we have ranked particular features of each resort using a scale of 5. The judgments are, of course, somewhat subjective, but the reasons for our rating will become clear after reading the chapter on the given area.

Having chosen eleven categories, we declined to total the ratings of these categories since totals are completely misleading. Several categories such as "entertainment" and "uncrowded and quiet" tend to offset each other. A high ranking for one usually corresponds with a low ranking for the other. Thus resorts that are very different would come out with similar totals.

If you wish to rate resorts using our rankings, you should decide which categories are important to you and then give more weight to these. Any scale will work, but we suggest a scale of 2, 1, and 0. If a category is important to you, multiply its rating by two. If a category is of some interest to you but is not important, multiply its rating by one. And if a category is of no importance whatsoever to you, do not add in its rating. Using this or any similar system, you can rank the areas.*

*For example, if you are an expert skier, do not care at all about the intermediate or novice slopes, are interested in night life but not strongly so, ski without your family, feel strongly that an area should not be crowded or hectic, and like to ski inexpensively, then multiply the expert trails factor, the quiet factor, and the inexpensive factor by two, and the entertainment factor by one, and ignore the other categories. This will give you a weighted scale by which you can rank the areas. If you take your family on some trips, change the weights given to the factors and recalculate.

SKIING THE BEST

1. Alpine Meadows

2. Bear Valley (Mt. Reba)

3. Heavenly Valley

4. June Mountain

5. Mammoth Mountain

6. Squaw Valley

7. Sugar Bowl

8. Mt. Bachelor

9. Crystal Mountain

10. Whistler Mountain

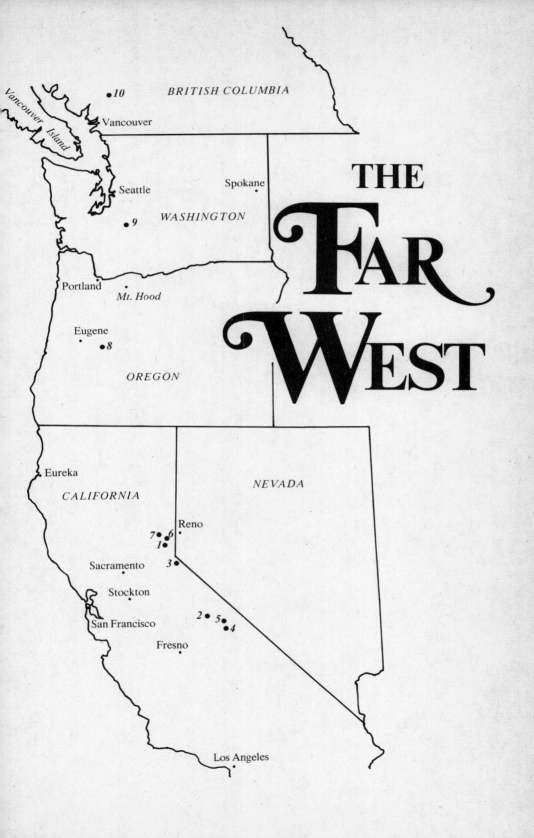

THE

FAR
WEST

BRITISH COLUMBIA

•10

Vancouver

Vancouver Island

Seattle

Spokane

WASHINGTON

•9

Portland

Mt. Hood

Eugene

•8

OREGON

Eureka

NEVADA

CALIFORNIA

Reno

7• •6
  •1

Sacramento

3•

Stockton

San Francisco

2• 5
    •4

Fresno

Los Angeles

1

Alpine Meadows

The relationship between Alpine Meadows and neighboring Squaw Valley is much like that between their southern counterparts, Mammoth and June. Developed as an alternative to the enormity of Squaw, Alpine has flourished as a pleasant family mountain. While often in the shadow of Squaw, the resort has forged its own identity and very real virtues. The mountain is prettier than Squaw, its runs dipping down frequently in and around the trees, and because of its more manageable size, it feels homier and better suited to the family (though families should remember that kids under twelve ski free at Squaw when accompanied by a skiing parent). Still, when planning a ski vacation, Alpine should really be considered an adjunct to Squaw, rather than an alternative, particularly from the point of view of good skiers. Accordingly, in discussing life at Alpine we refer to our chapter on Squaw Valley.

ACCESSIBILITY

Alpine is about a 3½-hour drive from San Francisco and approximately 50 miles from the Reno, Nevada, airport. Suggested routes for both auto and air are the same as for Squaw Valley (pp. 31–38).

THE SKIING

Alpine has only a 1,700-foot vertical, but the mountain is somewhat more interesting than other Western areas with comparable drops—Mt. Bachelor and Sugar Bowl, for example—primarily because of Alpine's nice balance between bowl and glade skiing.

Though Alpine advertises that the area has 25% novice terrain, this figure should not be relied upon. The beginner is more or less relegated to the bottom of the mountain on the Meadow chair and the Subway, Tiegel, and Lower Forty pomas. The advanced beginner has slightly more flexibility and should be able to handle the lower part of Weasel, an easy, open slope.

Intermediates have a nice bit of diversity here, more so than on many mountains. Alpine Bowl, from the top of the Summit or Alpine Bowl chairs, offers gentle terrain with some mild but challenging bumps on top. For the intermediate who wants an easy cruise, the whole backside of the mountain in the Sherwood area (off-limits unless the cover and conditions are good) provides a wide expanse of low-intermediate terrain through the open trees. The Roundhouse chair services many intermediate runs (there are very few cut trails at Alpine and runs tend to blend into one another as they drop through the trees), and among the popular trails are Rock Garden, Dance Floor, and Ladies Slalom. For the solid intermediate interested in bump skiing, Yellow Trail off the Yellow chair (marked expert but not) and Blue Trail off the Roundhouse chair are good choices.

For the most part, the expert at Alpine must be willing to give up the steeps in favor of some pretty skiing. All solid skiers should take a ride up the Summit chair, the top of which allows a spectacular view of about two-thirds of Lake Tahoe. From here, the drop down into Wolverine Bowl is a nice cruise into the Face, a nicely pitched bump run (7) which is a good bit like Cornice II at Squaw. Ducking down under the Alpine Bowl chair through some bumps on Terry's Return, you can pick up High Yellow, a pretty little run through some trees. Continuing away from the Alpine Bowl chair over toward the Sherwood area, you can reach the Palisades cliffs, off which are a couple of very narrow, fairly steep chutes (8). These chutes can't rival Jackson or Taos, but they're fun to ski and represent most of what there is of the steeps at Alpine. Also over in that direction we liked Our Father, which has a narrow top section winding down with good pitch (7.5) through a crevasse and then leveling off through some trees back down to the lift. The other recommended expert challenge at Alpine is the Scott Chute, the liftline of the Scott chair, which is narrow and relatively steep (8).

INTEGRATION OF THE SLOPES

Most of the lifts converge at or around the base lodge, and access from chair to chair is good. There is a cafeteria located upstairs at the base lodge and a snack bar on the mountain between the base of the Yellow and Scott chairs.

LIFE IN THE AREA

Because of the very limited accommodations and activities close to the mountain, most Alpine skiers utilize the facilities serving those who ski at Squaw.

ACCESSIBILITY TO THE SLOPES

A car is very helpful. Nearly all skiers stay some miles from the mountain, and while Alpine does run a ski shuttle throughout the Tahoe area, the system is not as well developed as those provided in many of the Rocky Mountain resorts.

ACCOMMODATIONS

The **Alpine Place Condominiums** are the only units directly at the mountain. Units range from 1- to 4-bedroom and are not very special ($45–90). Other accommodations along the 3-mile access road are the **Alpine Motor Inn** ($30) and **River Ranch** (p. 36). As is true for Squaw Valley, the preponderance of skiers stay in the Tahoe area.

For reservations, call 916–583–4232.

RESTAURANTS

See SQUAW VALLEY (p. 37).

APRÈS-SKI AND NIGHT LIFE

There is a bar at the base lodge but with no music or dancing; accordingly, it is not the center of much activity. For night life, see SQUAW VALLEY (pp. 37–38).

DIVERSION

The cross-country **Tour Center** is located in the base lodge. For other diversions, see SQUAW VALLEY (p. 38).

CHILDREN

The **Alpine Day School** operates daily from 8:30 to 4:30 and accepts children two to eight years old; the cost is $11 and includes lunch. The ski school accepts children from four years old.

COSTS

A lift ticket is $12. For costs generally around the Tahoe area, see SQUAW VALLEY (p. 38).

2

Bear Valley (Mt. Reba)

We know you've never heard of it, but it's really a pretty good mountain. Insular, rather inaccessible in relation to the other California ski resorts, and limited as to accommodations and amenities, Bear (often referred to as Mt. Reba) is generally not an area where skiers come to spend a week or more. Nonetheless, it's the only one of the newer California resorts (Northstar, Incline, Kirkwood) that offers interesting skiing for all levels.

ACCESSIBILITY

Bear Valley lies in the heart of California's historic gold country. During the summer, frogs still jump in nearby Calavaras, but Mt. Reba now totally dominates the winter scene. Los Angeles is approximately 8 hours away by car. The roads into Bear are all-weather and well maintained, but the last 70–80 miles is on two-lane roads; this is probably why the vast majority of San Francisco Bay Area skiers head for Squaw Valley and the Lake Tahoe area rather than Bear, though the distance is no shorter.

The nearest major jet-served airport is San Francisco, a 3½-hour drive away. More difficult to reach but slightly closer is the Stockton airport, 104 miles away and serviced by United and Pacific Southwest Airlines.

THE SKIING

The statistics for Mt. Reba are fairly standard for a California mid-sized area: seven chair lifts and a platter lift, a 2,100-foot vertical climb to a summit of 8,506 feet, 21 miles of skiable terrain, and an uphill capacity of 8,900 skiers per hour. On the other hand, in the quality of its skiing, particularly for advanced skiers, Bear outshines its comparably sized Sierra neighbors. In its first stage of development, Bear was primarily a mountain for advanced skiers with some beginner runs, good advanced skiing, and almost total neglect of the intermediate—a combination that traditionally proves financially ruinous. The recent construction of the Hibernia chair, however, and the development of the Bear West area expanded the ski area by 30% and increased intermediate terrain by 300%, resulting in a substantial balancing of the mountain's terrain.

From the Base Lodge, the Panda Platter and the Super Cub chair service novice runs. Runs off these lifts—Ego Alley, Rodeo, and Bunny Basin, for example—are typical novice trails, though somewhat short. (As to nomenclature, we feel the prevailing custom of assigning trail names based on degree of difficulty is unfair to the novice. Ski resorts would do untold psychological good if they would name a novice run something on the order of Suicide Chute, thus allowing the beginner to partake in the same after-ski hyperbole of his more advanced friends.) The beginner can find slightly more interesting and lengthy terrain off the Cub chair, which is 1,500 feet long and quite flat with a 200-foot vertical. Here the beginner can ski Cub Meadow, Cross Over, or Lodge Run.

Intermediate skiing is found off all the remaining five chairs; however, the major area for intermediates is the new Hibernation chair, which has nearly 1,000 feet of vertical and a respectable ratio of horizontal to vertical feet. The runs on this side of the mountain are carefully cut and well-groomed. Trails such as Satisfaction, Pacesetter, Bear Buggy, and Grouse Connection don't have great diversity in configuration or terrain, but they do provide relatively long, pleasant runs for the intermediate.

The slightly more advanced intermediate should go over to the Koala chair, where Sugar would be a good place for him to practice his bump skiing and Feather Duster is a good intermediate run with a couple of steep pitches.

A plus about the mountain is that an intermediate can ski the entire 2,100-foot vertical. We recommend taking Mokelumne West from the top of the Bear chair, traversing over past the Base Lodge, and continuing down on Snow Valley or the Goat trails (both delightful runs in a wide-open bowl) all the way to the base of the Kodiak or Grizzly chairs, which return to the Base Lodge area.

Depending on snow conditions, weather, and the type of skiing desired, the expert will choose to ski the trails off either the Grizzly, Kodiak, or Bear chairs. Given the size of the mountain, the diversity offered the expert skier is very high. Off to the right of the Bear chair, four cut trails (Yellow Submarine, Monty Wolf, National, and Mokelumne) descend a fairly steep common face divided by woods. National is a good expert bump run whose moguls tend to be rounded rather than tooth-loosening (7.75). Yellow Submarine is narrower, smooth, and fast (7.25). Some tree skiing can be had off that face by dipping down between Yellow Submarine and Monty Wolf. The common problem shared by the runs off the Bear chair is their length: they all are moderately short faces with substantial runoffs back to the base of the chair.

There are no less than seventeen runs designated as expert off the Grizzly chair, with such colorful names as Flying Serpent, Devil's Dwelling, and Parasite Pitch. It's a matter of little consequence, really, that you'll find none of these trails, since they blend indistinguishably and completely into one another. In any event, to talk about the Grizzly area is to talk not about runs but rather about the entire area taken as a whole. The area, from the Base Lodge to the bottom of the Grizzly chair, has terrific wide open bowl skiing. By altering your chosen route down the bowl, you can alter pitch and terrain nearly at will. The liftline of the chair is consistently steep (8), but to the right the terrain becomes very rolling as you coast over various knolls. The Grizzly area can also be powder paradise (though its low altitude often lends itself to wettish snow). When powder does hit, traverse over to the far right and ski the first-rate chutes down through the trees off the west ridge.

The expert will also want to ski the runs off the Kodiak chair, which, like those on Grizzly, drop over 1,000 vertical feet from the Base Lodge area. Freefall, the liftline of the Kodiak chair, is a long, consistently steep face (8.25) that offers good expert skiing in both packed and powder conditions. Traversing farther east from the top of the Kodiak chair, you'll find short steep chutes like Snoopy's Hangar, Hari-Kari, and other drops that are great in the powder.

The Grizzly and Kodiak chairs are excellent lifts. First, they service interesting and diverse terrain. Second, they're highly efficient chairs whose 2.5:1 ratios really make the most of your skiing. Finally, while lift lines are not really a problem at Bear (usually under 12 minutes even on weekends), they can be avoided almost completely by skiing these chairs.

Bear gets over 450 inches of snow annually—which, for the Sierras, is a ton of snow. (In fact, a few miles down the road is a marker commemorating the largest single 24-hour snowfall in the United States, over 70 inches.) And while Bear does get its share of "Sierra cement," the quality of the snow is still on a par with that of the other Sierra areas. Least dependable, however, because of relatively low altitude, is the snow off the Grizzly and Kodiak chairs. If you're planning a trip to Bear before the first of the year, it's highly advisable to call ahead and see whether these chairs are operating.

The fact that the snow is good in most California resorts is really secondary to the sun, which is glorious. Bear is clear and sunny approximately 65% of the season.

INTEGRATION OF THE SLOPES

All chairs other than the Hibernation chair and the top of the Kodiak and Grizzly chairs more or less converge at the Base Lodge, which houses all the facilities of the mountain including the only place to eat lunch.

LIFE IN THE AREA

What activities there are at Bear are carried on exclusively in Bear Valley Village, a self-contained complex 4 miles from Mt. Reba. The complex is less a village than a small group of restaurants and shops located in and immediately around the Bear Valley Lodge. Those expecting a village on the order of Sun Valley or Vail will be disappointed.

ACCESSIBILITY TO THE SLOPES

The Bear Valley Lodge is as close as you can stay to the mountain (4 miles away). Shuttle service is available between the Lodge and the mountain.

ACCOMMODATIONS

Accommodations are somewhat sparse. The attractive 55-room **Bear Valley Lodge** is designed in the manner of the new posh ski lodge. Its dark woods, plush lounges, and blazing stone fireplaces bring to mind the real beauties like the Keystone Lodge, Topnotch at Stowe, and Sunriver at Mt. Bachelor, yet the Lodge at Bear is actually a cut or so below. Nonetheless, it remains one of the nicer lodges in the Sierras. Rooms are a moderate $30 and lodge facilities include pool, sauna, and hot tubs. (Hot tubs, are Jacuzzis without circulating water and are popular in California, where swirling water is not considered mellow.)

The three sets of condominiums (**Bear Valley** and **Creekside I** and **II**), all rented through the Lodge, are fairly standard and range in size from studios to 4-bedroom units ($35–115). They are equipped with kitchens and fireplaces and share the pool, sauna, and hot tub facilities with the Lodge.

For skiers unable to book into the Lodge or those looking for homier accommodations, the **Red Dog Lodge** is a small lodge on the order of a pension, with small rooms and shared baths ($18). The Red Dog also has a sauna.

Skiers on a budget can find dorm space at both the Lodge ($7) and the Red Dog ($5). Bring your own sleeping bag.

For stays of 5 days or more, 10% can be subtracted from all prices. For reservations, call 209–753–2311.

RESTAURANTS

The choices are limited. The **Altitude** serves steak and seafood; the **Red Dog** has a broad selection of menu items, with an emphasis on Austrian preparations; the **Toll Station** is for family-style dining and serves burgers, pizza, and the like. Prices in all three restaurants are moderate.

APRÈS-SKI AND NIGHT LIFE

After skiing and before heading back to the Village, the first stop is usually the **Bear Paw Bar** at the Base Lodge, which on weekends has a band and dancing. Back at the Village, there is music and dancing (primarily on weekends) at the **Altitude** and **Red Dog.** Those who want to relax can sip quietly at the attractive **Monte Wolf Bar** in the Bear Valley Lodge.

At night, things remain the same: dancing at the Altitude or Red Dog, or drinking at the Monte Wolf or the **Toll Station.**

DIVERSION

Cross-country skiing is available in the Village. Equipment and instruction is at the **Bear Valley Nordic Ski School** in the Bear Valley sport shop.

CHILDREN

The compact nature of the area plus a substantial amount of novice skiing makes Bear a nice place for kids. The nursery at the mountain is open 9–4 P.M. and accepts children from two years ($8.50 with lunch included on weekends). The ski school will take children from four years old.

COSTS

Lodging, food, and lift tickets ($11) are all moderate at Bear. While this is generally true throughout the Sierras (Mammoth is an exception), the Bear Valley Lodge and its surroundings are attractive enough to represent quite a good value.

3

Heavenly Valley

Heavenly Valley, on the California-Nevada border at the south end of Lake Tahoe, is the largest ski area in the United States. It has 22 lifts spread out over 20 square miles of skiable terrain, views as spectacular as anywhere in North America, and a staggering 4,000-foot vertical drop. But, unfortunately, all of nature's largesse could not override the calamity which is South Lake Tahoe, with the result that Heavenly is the single least appealing and most unattractive area we have encountered.

The community of South Lake Tahoe, just below the base of the mountain, is a 3-mile stretch of casinos, motels, fast-food places, and gas stations—not exactly your basic Tyrolean village. And while the mountain has sensibly named trails like Canyon and Ponderosa, rather than Snake Eyes and Blackjack, the fact is that many if not most of the skiers come here as much for the gambling as for the skiing. For every guest with a healthy tan, there are ten whose pallor betrays a long night at the craps table. Actually, many vacationers may find the gamble-and-gambol opportunity very appealing; it's just important that they realize this is no Crested Butte.

ACCESSIBILITY

Heavenly is about 200 miles east of San Francisco on U.S. 50, a 3½-hour drive. Accessibility from all parts of the country is good. There are daily flights from the major cities in California and the Northwest by PSA, Air California, and Ponderosa Airlines into South Lake Tahoe airport, 15 miles from Heavenly. Bus service ($2) is available from the airport to lodging accommodations. From the East, United, Western, and Hughes Airwest fly into Reno, 55 miles away, where you connect with bus service ($6) for the ride into South Lake Tahoe.

For the day skier, Heavenly is about an hour's drive from Squaw Valley, Alpine Meadows, Kirkwood, and Northstar, the other major Tahoe areas.

THE SKIING

Skiing might not be the major attraction at Heavenly, but it could be. Heavenly is a good mountain and, next to Squaw Valley, the best in the Tahoe area. The skiing is divided between the California side of the mountain, rising directly above South Lake Tahoe, and the Nevada side, which can either be skied to from the top of the California side or reached by driving a few miles from town. Skiers are actually offered a two-for-one experience, since each face of the mountain is substantially different in terrain, snow conditions, and scenery.

The runs down the California side descend 3,600 feet and are arranged in three layers. From the base of that side, an aerial tram and two double chairs climb the initial 1,700 feet to the 8,300-foot "top of the tram" area. Liftlines and snow conditions permitting, the expert skier need go no farther, for most of the expert terrain on the California side starts here and goes to the base. East Bowl, under the tram, is a good, long expert bump run quite similar in pitch (8) to the East Face of KT at Squaw Valley. Gunbarrel, the liftline of the Gunbarrel chair, lays claim to being one of the 10 steepest runs in the world. It is indeed steep (9.25), though not frighteningly so, and drops consistently down the face of the mountain amid prodigious bumps much like Spiral Stairs or the famous plunge at Telluride. Pistol and West Bowl off the West Bowl chair are less demanding but solidly advanced runs.

The novice will want to ski on the second tier of the mountain at the top of the Waterfall or Powderbowl chairs. From that point, Maggie's and Mambo are both long runs ideal for the novice, who, if inclined, can then proceed all the way down the mountain on Roundabout. Almost hidden between these runs is Waterfall, one of the better bump runs on the mountain (8.25).

The third layer on the California side is the gateway to over 1,500 vertical feet of excellent intermediate skiing. Heavenly's setup of having at least two parallel chairs going to the top of each tier does much to alleviate lift lines— particularly on top, where the Sky and Ridge chairs are the most popular lifts on the mountain. From the top of these chairs, the view of Tahoe, one of the largest and most beautiful alpine lakes in the world, is unforgettable. The laid-back recreational skier will enjoy Betty's and Ridge Run off the Ridge chair, while the more aggressive intermediate will head over to Liz's or Canyon, both of which are nice, long cruises with good pitch and some varied terrain. Up top for the expert is Ellie's, a long run with two good faces (8) linked by some good rolling terrain.

When the snow falls, the best powder on the California side is down below on the steeps, particularly Gunbarrel and East Bowl. Runs off the top of the Powder Bowl chair are also popular. The best powder skiing, however, is probably down parts of South Fork Skiway off the top of the Skyline trail.

Crossing over into Nevada from the top of the Sky chair near Heavenly's 10,167-foot summit is like entering another world. The view changes from the peaks of the Sierras to the desolate Carson Valley and the Nevada Desert 5,000 feet below. The number of skiers thins dramatically, since the Nevada side is not nearly as skied as the California side even though it has nearly twice as much area. The expert will drop right into Milky Way Bowl, probably the best bowl on the mountain. From here, you can see all 4,000 feet of the mountain's vertical terrain. Intermediates can head into Nevada down Big Dipper to the base of the Dipper chair and then spend some time on that chair, which gives access to the favorite intermediate terrain in Nevada—Orion, Big Dipper Bowl, and Ponderosa. If there are any lift lines on the Nevada side, the Dipper chair is where they'll be. The crowning intermediate run at Heavenly, though, is Galaxy, beginning in the Milky Way Bowl and continuing nonstop for 7 extraordinary miles until it ends at the base of the Wells Fargo chair. The run is a wonderfully fun rolling trail unparalleled for the stronger intermediate.

Novices on the Nevada side will ski the long, wide runs off the Boulder chair. Snow conditions are generally better on this side, but it's not till the powder comes that the hordes really descend. The Nevada side has a tremendous number of powder areas, most of them in and around the trees, in contrast to the open bowls on the California side. The best powder skiers head for the trees around the West Perimeter and North Bowl skiways or the steep chutes off What the Hell. In packed or powder snow, the steep, bumpy terrain off the bottom of the Men's Downhill (8.5) is a challenge for experts.

The ski season at Heavenly extends 6 full months, till May 15. Heavenly boasts that it has sunshine on 90% of its ski days; we think this is a little high, but there's no question that from March through May spring skiing in California is as glorious as it gets anywhere in the world.

INTEGRATION OF THE SLOPES

The California-Nevada sides are well integrated, except for novice areas. To get to Nevada, go left on the Skyline trail from the top of the Sky chair. To get back to California, take either the California trail to the right of the Dipper chair or the Von Schmidt trail off of the East Peak chair. Most skiers tend to begin and end the day in California, since the base area on the Nevada side presently consists of a series of trailers, one cafeteria, and a snack bar at the base of the Boulder chair.

On the California side, there is a cafeteria at the Base Lodge and snack bars at the base of the Sky chair and at the top of the Waterfall chair. For a more elegant lunch, the Top of the Tram restaurant offers spectacular views.

Heavenly Valley North (Nevada side)   COURTESY HEAVENLY VALLEY SKI AREA

Heavenly Valley West (California side)   COURTESY HEAVENLY VALLEY SKI AREA

LIFE IN THE AREA

Life at Heavenly is dominated by the cluster of casinos in South Lake Tahoe with their restaurants, entertainment, and 24-hour action.

ACCESSIBILITY TO THE SLOPES

Most of the lodging at Heavenly is in motels or casino hotels down on Highway 50. Heavenly's base is about a mile east up steep Ski Run Boulevard. There is a city ski bus and an inexpensive taxi-limo service available from the various lodges to the Base Lodge.

ACCOMMODATIONS

There are nearly 200 motels in the area, many of which must be seen to be believed—plaster-and-neon horrors with a lucky buck under every pillow. Some nice lodging can be found, but nothing that really caters specifically to the skier.

Far and away the best accommodations are in the area's two casino hotels. **Harrah's** has been awarded the highest rating from every major travel guide, and it *is* the height of luxury; the rooms are lovely, and every conceivable activity is available 24 hours a day ($55). Less elegant, but also bustling with activity, is the **Sahara Tahoe Casino Hotel** ($38).

In the luxury motel category, the **Waystation** is an attractive place on Highway 50 with nightly entertainment ($40). Near the casino area is the **Forest Inn,** with sauna, Jacuzzi, and pool ($38).

The nicest condominiums are the **Lakeland Village** units down by the lake, where many of the apartments have spectacular views. Skiers, and particularly those with families, can escape the din and be close to the mountain by staying at one of the three condominium units at the California base. The **Heavenly Valley Townhouses, Concept Sierra Condominiums,** and **Sitzmark Condominiums** are all within walking distance of the lifts. The Townhouses are superior to the other two. Prices vary according to the size of unit.

For reservations, call 800–822–5951.

RESTAURANTS

The top restaurants are at the casinos. The **Summit** at Harrah's, the **House of Lords** at the Sahara Tahoe, and the **Sage Room** at Harvey's hotel-casino all aspire to gourmet cookery. The **Top of the Wheel** at Harvey's is California eclectic, combining Polynesian specialties and steak. Near the mountain, the **Christiana,** probably the best restaurant at Heavenly, has inventive cooking in a quiet atmosphere. The **Chart House** and the **Packing House** are two standard steak-and-salad restaurants, and the **Cantina Los Tres Hombres** has acceptable Mexican food. Twenty-four-hour coffee shops and fast-food joints of every description are as plentiful as locusts.

APRÈS-SKI AND NIGHT LIFE

The night life at Heavenly is big, loud, and nonstop. After skiing, the two bars in the California Base Lodge, the **Cork Room** and the **Red Chimney,** have dancing to live bands. On weekends, the bands come back at night, but by that time the real action has moved to the casinos. **Harrah's** presents superstars like Frank Sinatra, Sammy Davis, Jr., and Liza Minnelli. The other casinos also have continuous entertainment with both headliners and lounge shows. Those who would rather dance can also go to **Jason's Shingle,** the **Waystation,** and the **Packing House,** all of which have live music nightly.

DIVERSION

Night skiing is available 5–10 P.M. on the California side. Guided ski tours are offered on both the California and Nevada sides down some of Heavenly's best undeveloped terrain, taking in as much as 5,000 vertical feet of skiing. There is also some cross-country skiing.

CHILDREN

Heavenly is not a good place to take the kids. There are no nursery or day-care facilities at the mountain on either side. In town, the **Magic Hours** ($1 per hour) and the **Tiny Piney** ($2 per hour; $10 for 8 hours) accept children from two years old.

COSTS

Feeling lucky?

4

June Mountain

June Mountain is a friendly mountain—not "have a nice day" friendly, but friendly because it is an area run by genuinely pleasant people. Situated less than 15 miles from California's aptly named Mammoth Mountain, June clearly exists as an adjunct to its glittery neighbor. As a secondary mountain, however, it performs an important function: skiers who are spending a week at Mammoth can enjoy a day or two of respite from the crowds, without suffering too serious a drop in the quality of skiing.

ACCESSIBILITY

Located in the Sierras near the eastern border of Yosemite National Park, June is rather out of the way and thus generally skied in conjunction with a long stay at Mammoth. San Francisco and Los Angeles are each approximately 6 hours away by car, with the latter offering scheduled bus service. Do not be misled by a California road map. All the roads traversing Yosemite National Park, as well as those more northerly and appearing to render June accessible to various parts of the state, are closed all winter, and Highway 395 (a well-kept road) is the only method of access from both north and south.

The closest jet-served airport is Reno, Nevada, nearly 200 miles away. Sierra Pacific Airlines flies small planes from Los Angeles into the Mammoth–June Lake airport.

THE SKIING

"Not bad" is an appropriately noncommittal way to describe the skiing at June. Despite a 2,562-foot vertical and a 10,212-foot summit, enough serious flaws exist at the mountain to prevent its being considered along with the

Western giants. Nonetheless, these drawbacks are greatly mitigated by manageability and an overriding ambience.

Nothing except the ticket window is at the base of the mountain. From the base, Chair #1 travels the 1,045 vertical feet to the Grand Chalet Schweizerhof, the 19,000-square-foot structure that constitutes the hub of all activity on the mountain. Most of the skiing takes place above the Chalet either on Chair #2 or on the summit of the mountain, which is reached by Chairs #3 and #4.

The only trails designated as novice are Mambo and River Run off Chair #2. Each run is approximately ¾ mile long, has a vertical drop of 600 feet, and is well groomed. A third novice run, Silverado, is being cut off Chair #4 and will wind down for over a mile before running into the base of Chair #2.

There's a lot of intermediate skiing off both Chairs #3 and #4, with respective verticals of 1,006 and 850 feet. The runs here highlight one of June's flaws: its intermediate terrain tends to be a little too flat and has too many runoffs. This problem is evidenced by examining the ratios of Chairs #3 and #4, which are 5:1 and 7:1, respectively (3.5:1 is the standard Western ratio). Still, Schatzi and Sunrise provide some long, fun cruises off Chair #3. Bodie, Rosa Mae, and Lottie Johl, the intermediate runs off Chair #4, are somewhat more interesting, with slightly better pitch and more variation in terrain. Intermediates will find Lottie Johl a good run for practicing their bump skiing.

Advanced and expert skiers are provided for primarily by Chairs #1 and #3. From Chair #3, the advanced can ski down Davos Drop, a well-pitched, fairly narrow trail that goes off through the trees into lower Davos. Also feeding into Lower Davos is Powder Chute, which has a short face (7.5) and is nice to ski. While marked advanced, Matterhorn and Sunset, off Chair #3, are actually good high intermediate bump runs. This conservatism in the labeling of trails is frequent at June. The competent intermediate skier should not be deterred by anything off Chair #3, however marked. If at all possible, Chair #3 should be taken by every skier at June; even the advanced beginner can probably pick his way down Sunrise. The view from the summit of June Lake, Mono Lake, the Sierra Crest Range, and the surrounding high desert is nothing short of spectacular, with a distinctly surreal, mirage-like quality.

The only really advanced skiing is off Chair #1, on the area designated as the Face. While we suspect hyperbole in June's claim that the runs of the Face are among the 10 steepest in the United States (we hope someday to sponsor a competition among the 127 runs that lay the same claim), the runs do have good pitch and provide, especially in powder, some good advanced skiing. Carson is a nice, fast cruise, fairly steep and with no bumps. Gull Canyon (an 8.25 in difficulty, along with Carson) is another good advanced run. The expert bump skiing is on Slalom, which is reached through a good chute called the Face (8.5) that funnels into Slalom under the liftline.

Though the runs of the Face clearly provide the best skiing at June, for many skiers they are also the mountain's greatest impediment and inconvenience. There is really no way for the novice to ski to the base of the mountain, and for some reason many intermediate skiers choose not to take the one trail available to them. At the end of the day, scores of skiers take the ego-deflating ride down Chair #1 to the base. Fortunately, lift lines at June are not much of a problem; otherwise, the potential of a 40-minute line to go home would serve to dissuade just about anyone.

June usually gets plenty of snow, with an average annual snowpack of over 6 feet. Snow conditions at June are similar to those at most of the Sierra resorts, which is to say generally good. Storms tend to bring fairly wet snow, however, and the Alta type of white fluffy powder is seldom in evidence. Sunshine abounds. The thermometer is almost as likely to soar above 50° in January as it is in March.

INTEGRATION OF THE SLOPES

All trails at June ultimately end at the base of Chair #2 at the Chalet, the focal point of all activities including lunch, rendezvous, and après-ski. The Hutson Haus facility at the base of Chair #3 also has a cafeteria that provides lunch.

LIFE IN THE AREA

June Lake is a tiny town with a permanent population of only 450, but still it is fairly well geared up for the skier and can accommodate 1,200 visitors. When its own facilities are combined with those of Mammoth's, 15 miles away, a full range of activities is made available to the skier.

ACCESSIBILITY TO THE SLOPES

June Mountain is situated 1 mile west of June Lake Village, the site of most of the lodging. Other lodging is available a mile or two west of the mountain. There are no accommodations right at the mountain, and no shuttle bus service, so a car is useful.

ACCOMMODATIONS

None of the lodging at June is particularly inspiring, but nearby Mammoth offers the full panoply from elegance to dorm style. The best accommodations at June are in the village at the modern and reasonably attractive **Boulder Lodge.** The Lodge has motel units, 1-, 2-, and 3-bedroom suites overlooking June Lake with kitchens and fireplaces, 1- and 2-bedroom duplex housekeeping cabins, and separate 3- and 5-bedroom houses rustically set right on the lake. Prices are relatively modest, with a range of $25–115. The lodge also has an indoor heated pool, large Jacuzzi, and sauna.

A mile and a half from the village and ¾ mile west of the mountain, the **Four Seasons** has several 1- and 2-bedroom A-frame units, equipped with kitchens and fireplaces, set in the woods overlooking Carson Peak. The units are comfortable, and weekend rates require a $48 minimum for up to 4 persons, with $6 for each additional person. Midweek rates are approximately 30% less.

Near the Four Seasons is **June Lake Pines,** which has adequate housekeeping units in a pleasant wooded setting.

Several other motel and housekeeping accommodations exist both in the village or west of town toward Fernwood Creek. Those down toward Fernwood Creek are all quite rustic and might be nice for skiers in search of an unusually tranquil experience.

For reservations, call 714–648–7794.

RESTAURANTS

Restaurants are limited, but the **Carson Peak Inn,** with a diversified menu emphasizing beef and seafood, is the best place in town. The **Crazyhorse Saloon** has beer, wine, and Mexican food, and at the Sierra Inn burgers are available at the **Tiger Bar.** Also at the Sierra Inn is that California creation, a coffee shop. In the village, the Barvarian-oriented **Alpine** deli has some appetizing tidbits and will also prepare a box lunch for skiers to take on the mountain; at night, the deli serves pizza.

Most of the serious eating is done at Mammoth, an area with unusually good restaurants.

APRÈS-SKI AND NIGHT LIFE

Most all of the after-ski activity is at the **Chalet** on the mountain. Here, no matter what the level of revelry, not even the National Safety Council would object to "one for the road" since the long, cold chair ride back down to the parking lot is a guaranteed sobering experience.

At night, the center of activity shifts to the **Sierra Inn,** with its good atmosphere, fireplace, ski movies, and live entertainment. Downstairs at the Inn is the **Tiger Bar,** which schedules live entertainment and dancing. (The Tiger Bar, which has the third oldest liquor license in California, was popular during the 1920's for its fleet of rowboats providing livery service to and from the bawdy house that flourished directly across June Lake.)

DIVERSION

As of now, the main diversion at June is cross-country skiing, for which equipment and guides are available at **Tex's Sporting Goods** and **Ernie's Ski**

and Tackle. Improvements of the overall facilities at the mountain, however, are projected for the 1978–79 season. A new base lodge, complete with a sorely needed restaurant and bar, is planned at the parking lot level. From the new lodge, a chair lift will be built which will make night skiing available. Also planned at the base level is an ice-skating rink, to be open day and night.

CHILDREN

Because of its manageable size and clustering of relatively easy intermediate skiing, June is a good mountain for skiing children. The ski school also seems to take exceptionally good care of young skiers. Nevertheless, there is a serious problem for smaller children. Neither nurseries nor day-care facilities exist at the mountain or in town. Private baby-sitting arrangements can be made, but there is no central listing to facilitate that need.

COSTS

Prices at June are modest by any standard, but when compared to those at Mammoth they seem obscenely low.

5

Mammoth Mountain

If you're looking for an undistilled dose of California, this is the place. The hordes descend as a result of snow depth rather than surf height, and the Mercedes has replaced the Woody, but make no mistake— this is the Beach Blanket Bingo set grown up. The lift line is out of central casting; a Farrah-Fawcett look-alike contest could be held here on any weekend; and the men wear more gold than the Sierras have seen since Sutter's Mill.

But the mountain also attracts genuine ski enthusiasts in great numbers, and part of the impressive versatility of the area is that it is large, diverse, and developed enough to be all things to all people.

Though some attractive accommodations and good restaurants act as drawing cards, the central focus is the vast mountain. Twenty-two lifts, over 60 trails, and a 3,100-foot vertical drop combine to offer a mountain where it really is possible to ski for several days without being on the same run twice. And, for the intermediate, there is probably more terrain to ski at Mammoth than anywhere except Vail and Snowmass.

ACCESSIBILITY

The weekend commute between Los Angeles and Mammoth is the only one we know of more painful than the New York–Stowe trek. The 300-mile drive is a solid 7 hours, though in California that's like driving to work. For those already in the Sierras and wishing to include Mammoth in their itinerary, the drive is about 3 hours south on U.S. 395 from the Reno–Lake Tahoe area. Greyhound has scheduled bus service from Los Angeles and San Francisco.

The easiest, but expensive ($87 round trip) way to commute between L.A. and Mammoth is on Sierra Pacific Airlines, which has three flights daily. Sierra Pacific also has service from Hollywood and Burbank, the other two Los Angeles airports, as well as Fresno, Reno, and Las Vegas.

Improved air connections, and two years of decent snow when most of California was drought-dry, have broadened Mammoth's clientele, but despite its relative inaccessibility it is still very much dependent on the Southern California skier.

THE SKIING

Mammoth is primarily an intermediate's area, with vast amounts of cruising terrain. Topographically, the mountain breaks into two halves. The lower half is below the tree line and has innumerable carefully cut and groomed novice and intermediate trails. The top half, above the tree line, is a two-layered bowl, the lower of which opens up bowl skiing suitable for all intermediates, while the summit has a long ridge from which Mammoth's expert runs drop off into a huge bowl.

Lifts are everywhere, and conveniently there are three separate areas where tickets can be purchased and the trip up the mountain can commence: the Main Lodge, 4 miles up from town on Minaret Road; Warming Hut #2, about a mile from the village up Lake Mary Road; and at Chair #15, which descends into town at the west end of Meridian Road. Most skiers of intermediate ability and better opt at the beginning of the day either for Gondolas #1 and #2 at the lodge, which go up to the 11,053-foot summit, or for Chairs #1 and #2, which service all the lower-level intermediate terrain. On weekends, though, lift lines at the two-stage gondola and these chairs can swell to over an hour, so best to consider other starting points.

Novices have several alternatives. Starting from the Lodge, they can ski Chairs #6 and #11, remaining coddled on Jill's Run, Gus's Pasture, or, if they can bring themselves to tell their friends, Sesame Street. Looking for more vertical, they could venture up Chair #2 for St. Moritz and Mambo. To avoid the crowd at the Base Lodge, the beginner can ski Hansel or Gretel off Chair #7 at Warming Hut #2, or the much longer Sleepy Hollow or Christmas Tree over at Chair #15.

The novice benefits tremendously from the easy terrain spread out over the whole mountain. A third-day GLM* skier who has never skied before has more accessible terrain at Mammoth than anywhere we can think of. The route from Chairs #1 to #10 to #11 allows the novice to see and ski nearly one-third of this vast complex.

The intermediate can ski forever, though many of the runs have identical

---

*Graduated Length Method, in which the beginner starts on short skis and achieves a working skill in five days.

terrain. Chairs #2, #4, #8, #10, and #16 all open up relatively wide, gently pitched, heavily groomed recreational skiing—the Snowmass of the West. Bumps are summarily destroyed.

Mammoth has a couple of places no intermediate should miss. St. Anton is a 2-mile run from the top of #3 down to the Base Lodge. The ride up Gondola #2 to the summit is also a must for its spectacular view, with the jutting peaks of the Minarets overlooking the Owens Valley and desolate Mono and Crowley lakes presenting a spectacle of surreal beauty. On the backside of the mountain, Chair #14 is unique. On Red's Lake Run or Santiago, you can ski through the wilderness, and while riding up the chair appreciate a view different from that seen anywhere on the mountain. In the spring (which lasts nearly forever, since Mammoth's season is pre-Thanksgiving until well into June), Chair #14 gets the sun the entire day. Finally, the lower tier of the bowl on runs like China Bowl, Christmas Bowl, and Saddle Bowl is skiable by all intermediates, while Sanctuary, the liftline of Chair #5, is a good challenge for the more advanced intermediate.

For the expert, Mammoth is no Snowbird—or, sticking close to home, no Squaw Valley, either. There are a few steep faces and some very steep chutes that are seldom skied because they're too steep to hold snow, but for the most part real experts will find the tough stuff more or less a cruise. The expert will want to go up top right away, with a typical itinerary involving a couple of runs down the steep (7.5–8.5) walls on top of the cornice—Dave's Run (named after founder Dave McCoy, father of Olympic skiers Dennis and Penny), for example, and Climax, which is both steep and moguled—and the rest of the morning spent in the bumps off Chairs #3 and #5.

The best bump skiing on the mountain is on Climax, Cornice Bowl, and Center Bowl (#3 liftline); Stump Alley (#2 liftline); and Sliver and Sanctuary (#5 lift line). With the exception of Climax, most all the bump skiing is on intermediate terrain, a boon for both the upwardly mobile intermediate and the lazy expert.

Mammoth boasts that its 7,900-foot base elevation (the highest in California) guarantees it the best powder around. We've never been much impressed by California powder ("Sierra cement"), but when the dry stuff does fall there are plenty of places to ski it at Mammoth. The whole cornice area is good, as is all of Chair #9, which is well pitched at the top and has some nice tree dodging down below. The real place to go on powder days is a secret we're about to divulge: ski down Tarantula from the top of #5 or #9 and hike up to Lincoln Point, where Grizzly, Shaft, and Viva are three great powder runs generally skied only by locals.

INTEGRATION OF THE SLOPES

The lift system is complex but efficient, and no matter which starting point you choose, it's relatively easy to reconnoiter for lunch at the vast cafeteria in the Base Lodge or the one at Warming Hut #2, or, most centrally, at Mid-Chalet between Gondolas #1 and #2.

LIFE IN THE AREA

ACCESSIBILITY TO THE SLOPES

A car is of some importance at Mammoth. There are accommodations at the Main Lodge, and condominiums at the Warming Hut #2 area; however, much of the area's lodging, dining, and activity is in town, 4 miles from the Main Lodge. Shuttle buses run daily during skiing hours between the Main Lodge and Warming Hut #2 and from the major condominiums to and from the mountain. There is no bus service at night.

ACCOMMODATIONS

Mammoth has unusually nice accommodations for an area which could fairly be called a weekend resort. There are nice choices at each base area. The problem is cost. Lodging at Mammoth is the most expensive in California, though savings of up to 25% can be had at several places by booking midweek stays.

The most deluxe place to stay at the Main Lodge area is the **Mammoth Mountain Inn,** which has luxurious rooms, restaurants, a game room, saunas, and whirlpool ($45–$65). The crowd tends to be older and somewhat sedate. For the family, the **Mammoth Mountain Chalets** have several 2- and 3-bedroom A-frame units right at the mountain, with sundecks, fireplaces, and even a snow-cat to pick you up at the end of the day and take you to your doorstep ($80).

The nicest condominiums have developed around Warming Hut #2. The **1849 Condominiums** are among the best around, with 1- to 4-bedroom units available and saunas, Jacuzzi, and heated pool ($55). Equally plush, over at Warming Hut #2, are the **Snowbird Condominiums** ($50), which have a sauna and Jacuzzi. For a gaggle of facilities at #2, the **Mammoth Ski Racquet Club** has 13 saunas, Jacuzzi, two hot tubs, swimming pool, 4 tennis courts, and new racketball courts ($50).

At Chair #15 we recommend the **Summit,** with its big pool, 3 tennis courts, 5 Jacuzzi pools, and 3 saunas ($55).

Over toward and in town, the best bet for motel-type accommodations is the **Alpine Lodge** ($42). Slightly less expensive, though dependable, is the **Travelodge,** which has a regular pool, therapy pool, and sauna ($40). The **Sierra Inn** is a real bargain, with $34 providing access to its Jacuzzi, sauna, lounge, disco, and two restaurants. Another excellent value, slightly off the beaten track, is **Mammoth Creek,** which has been the winner of major architectural awards ($35).

For those on a tight budget, dorm space is available ($7–10 per person) at **Kitzbuhel Lodge, Mammoth Village,** and the **Pinecrest Lodge.**

For reservations, call 714–934–2528.

RESTAURANTS

In keeping with Mammoth's hallmark of being the mountain with more of everything, restaurant choices abound. The **Comstock II** is the fanciest place in town, with a gourmet menu, formal service, long-stemmed glassware, and a high rating by some major restaurant guides. The **Captain's Table** has the biggest selection of seafood we've seen in ski country, and **Moostachio Pete's** offers moderately priced Italian dishes. The **Rafters,** whose specialty is duck, is nevertheless one of the better steak-and-salad restaurants around. The **Mogul Steakhouse** is less expensive and allows you to cook your own steak. **Whiskey Creek** has a nice atmosphere and specializes in barbecued ribs, chicken, and prime ribs.

Since this is California, you can be sure that fast food is at its indigenous best. **Perry's** has fine Sicilian pizza, while **Hot To Go** has good take-out— particularly the chili.

The best inexpensive place to eat is **Berger's,** which offers huge sandwiches and burgers and a wonderful soup stew.

APRÈS-SKI AND NIGHT LIFE

The night life at Mammoth is slightly less frenetic than at many of its Western counterparts.

Those at the Main Lodge area go to either the **Yodler** or the **Mammoth Mountain Inn.** Over at Warming Hut #2, there is disco dancing at the **Austria Hof,** which continues after dark.

At night, establishments are about evenly split between places to dance and places to sip a quiet drink. **Andersen's Saloon** (of split pea fame), with live music and an emphasis on bluegrass, is the most popular dancing spot. **Mill City** also has dancing to live music and appeals to the younger crowd. The **Clocktower** has nightly dancing alternating between disco and live bands.

Whiskey Creek, Rafters, and **Moostachio Pete's** are all nice bars where you can sit down, listen to quiet entertainment, and have a sedate drink. For the opposite extreme, visit the **Mammoth Tavern,** the local haunt.

DIVERSION

Cross-country equipment, instruction, and tours are available at many of the ski shops in town. Check sport shops, too, about snowmobiling in the back country. You can skate on several natural lakes around town. Helicopter skiing will soon be offered through the **Sierra Guide Service.** Also, racing is a big deal at Mammoth. There is a racing department (headed by Dennis Agee, ex-coach of the U.S. women's ski team) which is totally separate from the ski school and provides the single best recreational racing program in the country. Finally, to soothe the aching muscles earned at the race clinic, try **Hot Creek,** a natural hot spring 10 minutes south of Mammoth.

CHILDREN

The vast, interlocking lift system makes Mammoth a good, though crowded, place to ski with children; nearby quiet June Mountain is probably better. The children's ski school takes six- to twelve-year-olds, and the special pre-ski school offers afternoon instruction to four- to six-year-olds.

The **Mammoth Day Care Nursery** is in two locations, at the Mammoth Mountain Inn and in the Village. The nursery is for age two on up, and the cost is $2 per hour with lunch available. Day care for infants can be arranged in private homes through the nursery.

COSTS

Costs at Mammoth are the highest in California but the bargain to look for at Mammoth is the midweek package rate. This is a poorly kept secret, since each weekday an astonishing average of 8,000 tickets are sold.

6

Squaw Valley

Squaw Valley is not usually on the standard list of great Western mountains, but it should be. Since 1960, when it was the site of the Winter Olympics, the mountain has been ardently developed to the point where now probably the largest, most intricate lift system in the world opens up all of Squaw's vast bowls and steep faces that converge into the Valley. To give a sense of size: Squaw's 25 lifts combine to provide an uphill capacity (26,500 per hour) fully 10% greater than that of Vail, the biggest mountain in the Rockies.

The regular influx of huge weekend crowds from the San Francisco area, the lack of sufficient accommodations in the Valley itself, and the greater ease with which Easterners can reach most Rocky Mountain resorts have all been factors in the slow development of Squaw into a major international ski resort. The restaurants, night life and lodging are all there, however, just less centralized than one might wish. And the skiing, at least for experts, is as concentrated as the other components of the area are diffuse: Squaw is the best-planned, most efficient mountain for experts we've ever seen—a rare example of the successful marriage between opportunity and implementation.

ACCESSIBILITY

Squaw is about 200 miles east of San Francisco near the north shore of Lake Tahoe. The drive is an easy 3½-hour trip on Interstate 80. Access from the East is through either San Francisco or Reno, about 40 miles away. All rental cars are available in Reno for the hour-long drive. Greyhound has bus service from Reno to Truckee, 10 miles from Squaw; taxi service is provided from there on into the Valley.

Cal-Air, a California commuter line, flies nine-seaters from San Francisco to Truckee several times daily.

THE SKIING

The runs at Squaw (it would be inappropriate to call them trails since virtually all the skiing is on open bowls, ridges, wide faces, and gulleys) are divided between those originating at or near the base of the mountain (designated as the Elevation 6,200 area) and those spreading out across the higher peaks from the top of the aerial tram and gondola area (Elevation 8,200). The total vertical is 2,700 feet.

At the start of the day, most skiers, and particularly novices and intermediates, head up to Elevation 8,200 by the 2,000-foot rise of either the gondola, tram, or Squaw Peak chair. The gondola, which drops skiers off at the Gold Coast area (a staging area for access to the other lifts), and the Squaw Peak chair, which climbs up the Valley a few hundred yards to the west, are both 18-minute rides, while the huge 125-passenger tram whisks skiers up the same distance in 8 minutes. A note of warning: On most weekends, getting to either the gondola or tram line at the appointed hour of opening may *still* result in a wait of up to 30 minutes. Best to be in line well before opening (8:30 A.M. on weekends). The Squaw Peak chair generally has a significantly shorter lift line, and an alternative for the better skier is to gain access to the upper lifts by taking the KT chair and skiing down its mildly advanced saddle to Cornice II, from which the rest of the mountain becomes accessible.

There are a variety of lifts for the novice at Elevation 8,200. From the High Camp area at the top of the tram, the Bailey's Beach, Links, and Belmont chairs all service open, flat snowfields which have become playgrounds for the beginner at Squaw. The East Broadway chair at the top of the gondola leads to the same reassuring terrain and also links up with the High Camp beginner lifts.

Intermediate skiers, according to their level of proficiency, go off to ski in and around three of Squaw's four great peaks. From the gondola, the Gold Coast, Mainline, and Emigrant lifts all scale parts of the face of 8,700-foot Emigrant Peak. The terrain on each is similar—open skiing, relatively flat with a few trees scattered about and an occasional bump. Emigrant is slightly more varied, with somewhat more pitch in the small bowl at its summit (6), but still presents nothing troublesome even for the most recreational of intermediates. The problem here, as with much of the intermediate terrain at Squaw, is that the runs are too short. All are well under a mile long and their vertical drops are proportionately modest, ranging 540–858 feet.

The most popular intermediate area at Squaw has always been the area off the backside of Emigrant Peak, nestled between Emigrant and 9,050-foot

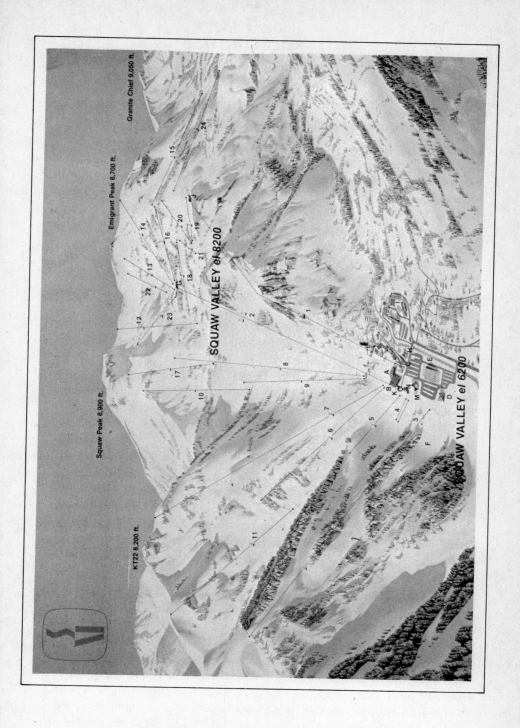

Squaw Valley   COURTESY SQUAW VALLEY SKI AREA

Granite Peak. Shirley Lake is the run intermediates head right for and talk about most—the Ruthie's Run of Squaw Valley. And as with Ruthie's, it's hard to understand all the hoopla. There are several different choices at the top—the shallow bowl to the left of the chair, the liftline, and the trail off to the right—but basically they're all the same, with a few minor bumps at the beginning, modest pitch (6.5), and converging finally in a wide flat area a few hundred yards from the top. The trail continues on, relatively flat, until it narrows for a short period and runs off into the lift line—the half-hour lift line. We'd call Shirley Lake a "ten turns and back into line" run, but its popularity remains overwhelming; recently, though, the Solitude chair was added to siphon off some of the pressure.

The main problem with the runs in the High Camp–Gold Coast area is that they have no vertical—750 feet is the maximum. That problem begins to subside as you move over to Squaw Peak. Siberia is the aptly named lift that takes you up 1,100 feet to the very top of the mountain between Squaw and Emigrant peaks. Here, even on nice days, the wind swirls and the snow blows. The view, if you have time to look around in your hurry to duck under the first ridge, is lovely. The run is marked intermediate, but if you take off into the huge bowl at the first opportunity instead of traversing to the left, as most skiers do, the pitch is fairly steep (8) and there can be some substantial bumps. The bowl, however, soon runs off into a flat second half back to the chair.

For experts over on Squaw Peak is the Headwall, whose highly efficient chair (2.8:1) zips up the steep 1,300-foot climb. From the top of the Headwall, either the face or the backside can be skied, both steep drops (8.5) with moderate bumps and not a tree in sight. If your choice is the backside, the Newport chair whisks you most of the way back up. Our favorite run on Squaw Peak is Cornice II, which has the same impressive 2.8:1 ratio for its 1,350-foot vertical. The run follows the same pattern, a moderate drop (7.75) into an open bowl spiced up by some good bumps on the way down to a flattish area. The terrain then becomes rolling, with several separate amusing little sections and mini faces as you work your way back to the chair.

What really makes Squaw a great mountain is the famous KT-22 and its neighbors—the expert runs at Elevation 6,200. KT, the fourth of Squaw's peaks, is impressive as well as handsome, with a magnificent view of Lake Tahoe from its summit. Composed basically of the Saddle, the East Face, and the West Face, it is an area solidly for experts. While the advanced-intermediate will handle the Saddle's bumpy cruise down to the gulley below, the two faces are more demanding. The East Face, site of the Olympic women's downhill, drops off steeply (8.5) into a huge bowl with plenty of lines to choose from. The next third of the 1,850-foot vertical run is somewhat less demanding, flattening out until it reaches the top of the Exhibition lift, then turning into a bump run that is not at all steep but knee-racking the whole way down to the base of the mountain. The West Face is one of the best runs anywhere. Dizzyingly steep (10) and fairly narrow, skiers who can keep their line here amid waist-deep moguls are pretty hot. There are no local stops on the West Face, so fall at your peril.

As if KT weren't enough, there are two other lifts at Elevation 6,200 where the skiing is as good or better. The long-awaited Olympic Lady lift now opens up the sensational terrain that used to be skiable only after a painful hike. Access to this lift is from the east face of KT or the top of the Exhibition chair. Once up top on Olympic Lady, there are at least three routes you can take, all of them steep (8.5), and whether you choose the wide bowl or the narrower gulley, there are substantial bumps to negotiate. About halfway down, the run funnels into a narrow trough full of challenging bumps. Under no circumstances should you traverse it: the bombers who are flying down the fall line will treat you like an errant tenpin.

And if that's not enough, there's Red Dog, the bump skier's dream. A 9-minute chair, the best on the mountain (2.75:1) with never a lift line, Red Dog offers 1,200 vertical feet of uninterrupted first-rate top-to-bottom bump skiing and is one of the few runs at Squaw without some sort of runoff or flat area.

The expert's bonus: On weekends, when lift lines can be 30 minutes at many places on the mountain, there will never be more than a 10-minute line at KT and next to none on Olympic Lady and Red Dog. We last skied Squaw on a Sunday in January when the temperature was in the 50's with not a cloud in sight. The 26,500 uphill capacity was being sorely tested all over the mountain, but we were never in a line that exceeded 5 minutes. Now, that's a well-planned mountain. An additional nice touch: Any lift ticket returned by noon will be accepted and credit given for the difference between the full and half-day ticket price.

INTEGRATION OF THE SLOPES

Both altitudes offer a full range of restaurants and services. The Gold Coast area has the Gold Coast restaurant and bar as well as the Taco Hut for Mexican food and the Bullwheel for delicatessen specialties. At High Camp, the restaurant and bar is new and attractive. These locations are accessible from most of the runs up at Elevation 8,200, and the confluence at 8,200 of runs for different ability groups makes it convenient for all skiers to meet up top for lunch.

Down at 6,200 there's a cafeteria at the Base Lodge and a large sundeck for those months of constant sunshine. Also in the base facility are several restaurants, but the best thing to do is grab a sandwich at the excellent deli here behind the gondola building.

LIFE IN THE AREA

There's plenty to do right in the Valley, but somehow Squaw's immediate environs have never exuded the feeling of being a full-service resort. The lack of accommodations in the Valley causes a spreading out to the Tahoe area as well as to neighboring Truckee.

ACCESSIBILITY TO THE SLOPES

All the accommodations in the Valley are within walking distance to the lifts. Most people stay outside the Valley, however, and for them a car is essential since scheduled public transportation is erratic.

ACCOMMODATIONS

The good news is that lodging around Squaw is relatively cheap. The bad news is that you get what you pay for.

The **Squaw Valley Lodge** is ideally situated right at the lifts but lacks the degree of taste or charm necessary to make it anything more than a functional place to stay. Nonetheless, it's a great bargain for its location. Deluxe rooms can be had for $22–25, and rooms with a share bath are as little as $16. A limited number of handsome duplex units are available with living room, loft, and kitchenette ($60).

The **Squaw Valley Inn** is just a short walk from the lifts and has a restaurant and bar on the premises. Its rooms are standard motel and cost approximately $35.

There are only about 30 condominium units available for rent in the Valley, and while most of the units are an easy walk to the lifts, they do not have the usual amenities like sauna, Jacuzzi, and pool. Condominiums can be booked through Squaw Valley Realty. Rates go from $40 on up, depending on size. There are substantial savings for midweek occupancy. A certain number of private homes in the Valley are also available for rental.

Since lodging in the Valley is limited, visitors head out 10 miles toward Tahoe City and beyond. **River Ranch,** a lodge with one of the most attractive bars in the area, is the only place before Tahoe City and is well situated on the Truckee River near the entrance to Alpine Meadows. Tahoe City, the focal point for much of the area's night life, is made up of a series of standard motels which are all adequate and essentially indistinguishable from one another. Prices are on the low side of moderate.

There are several very nice condominium developments with sauna, Jacuzzi, pool, and the like, located in or beyond Tahoe City. The best way to inquire and make reservations is by calling the free reservation service for the Tahoe City Area (916-583-2371). A couple of the developments to ask about are **Four Seasons, Chinquapin,** and the **Shores.**

For those really on a budget, Truckee has some dorm space available at the **Star, Alta,** and **Hilltop** for prices as low as $3–4 per person. For slightly more money, **Big Chief** has dorm space 2 miles from the Squaw Valley entrance.

For reservations, call 916–583–6966.

RESTAURANTS

The restaurants in the Valley don't offer particularly distinguished dining, but there are several good places to pick up a quick snack—most notably the deli in the base facility and **La Chamois** for pizza or sandwiches. For breakfast, the two favorites are the **Whale's Tail** downstairs at the base and **Big Chief** on the road just outside the entrance to Squaw.

Most of the major restaurants are toward the lake. **River Ranch,** at the entrance to Alpine Meadows, has good if uninspired food and an especially nice view of the Truckee River. **Victoria Station** in Tahoe City, about a 15-minute drive away, is the most popular steak-and-salad purveyor and is good of its kind. The **Hearthstone,** which used to be a steak house, now serves the other ski staple—Mexican food. (The concept clearly destined to make millions is to open a steak and Margarita bar restaurant.) **Bacchi's** in Lake Forest is a Tahoe landmark that serves family-style Italian meals. A few miles west of Tahoe City, in Homewood, is the **Swiss Lakewood Lodge,** with authentic Swiss dinners in a pleasant atmosphere. Finally, for breakfast in the Tahoe City area, **Congers** is far above average.

The last couple of years have seen changes in the trend of heading to the lake for dinner. The reason is the renaissance of Truckee, an old mining town and, until recently, pretty much an abandoned one. Attractive restaurants and bars have sprung up along Main Street in a conscious effort to revitalize the town. Aesthetically, the job has been a success, but reviews of the restaurants are mixed. **La Ville Maison** is French and the most ambitious. **Greg's Toll Station,** which specializes in crepes, and **OB's Board** are two other new entries.

APRÈS-SKI AND NIGHT LIFE

Following the pattern, the Valley is the center of after-ski activity and is fairly well abandoned at night.

Immediately after skiing, everyone converges on the two bars at the base facility. Bar One, upstairs, is the more favored; on weekends, when there's dancing to live music, the place is mobbed beyond belief. A late-afternoon beer and pizza at **La Chamois** is also popular.

At night, most people are attracted to the lake while locals tend to either stay in the valley or hit Truckee. In Tahoe City, the **Hearthstone** is the one and only disco. For disco music haters, it should be noted that California is one of the last holdouts and its discos do mix in some rock-and-roll.

Live music is usually reserved for weekends. Locals like the **Bear Pen** in the Valley, and an older crowd heads past Tahoe City to **Sunnyside Lodge.**

Two nice bars where you can simply sit and talk are **River Ranch** and **Victoria Station,** which has unbelievably comfortable couches and pillows to lie back on.

Truckee has some "kick-out" cowboy bars like the **Tourist Bar** and the **Pasttime Bar** and also some of the basic "Victorian chic" bars like the **Bar of America** (converted from a bank).

Those unlucky at love can try the casinos at the north shore of Tahoe, about a 40-minute drive from the mountain. If they're too short on glamour (the north Tahoe casinos have a distinct diner-like quality), the elegance and superstar entertainment of South Tahoe is only an additional 50 minutes. Reno is a drive of slightly over an hour.

DIVERSION

The **Nordic Ski Center** in the Valley programs the cross-country activities and can provide equipment and instruction. There's also ice skating indoors at the Olympic rink.

CHILDREN

Squaw Valley is quite a good place for kids. The diversity of terrain at Elevation 8,200 makes it likely that parents can ski off and still be within easy meeting distance. Even better is the fact that any child under twelve accompanied by a paying parent skis free, providing a very substantial potential savings.

Day-care services are available for two- to six-year-olds at the **Gingerbread House** right near the lodge. Ski lessons are available for children from three years old.

COSTS

As we've mentioned, lodging around Squaw is fairly inexpensive, with the possibility of even less cost if you take advantage of various midweek packages. Included in the packages is an interchangeable lift ticket good at Squaw, Heavenly Valley, Alpine Meadows, Kirkwood, Northstar, and Ski Incline.

7
Sugar Bowl

On reflection, it now seems highly inappropriate that Sugar Bowl's first investor, back in 1939, was Walt Disney. While Disney's characters have come to symbolize the culturally transcendent and classless quality of entertainment, Sugar Bowl has remained over the years very much cloistered and closed—a private club aspiring to be the Gstaad or Megeve of American skiing. Originally a place for San Francisco socialites to spend the holidays and entertain Eastern friends, Sugar Bowl has done little to shed that clubby image. Day skiers are actively discouraged, the lodge does virtually no advertising, dinner guests dress for meals, and children are tolerated (if their nannies are well-bred).

We include Sugar Bowl not only as a cultural anachronism but because it has some genuine skiing credentials, most notable of which is an astonishing annual snowfall of over 600 inches. One of the oldest resorts in all of the West, Sugar Bowl has developed into the fourth largest ski complex in California. It is also the home of the famous Silver Belt Race, which was held annually from 1939 to 1970 and has been won by the likes of Kidd, Werner, and Pravda. Finally, Sugar Bowl does have charm. The only ski area in the United States totally isolated from all automobile traffic, it succeeds in pampering its guests both on and off the slopes and providing them with a tranquil experience.

ACCESSIBILITY

Sugar Bowl is located just off Interstate 80, 190 miles east of San Francisco. Since no cars are allowed, skiers must park in the lot or on the highway, then ride the Magic Carpet gondola (California's first, built in 1953) into the ski area.

The closest jetport is Reno, Nevada, about 40 miles east.

THE SKIING

Sugar Bowl has historically enjoyed a reputation as being a mountain where serious skiers could find challenge. We don't know how this rumor started or how it has persisted so long. With one notable exception, Sugar Bowl is a mild mountain where the competent intermediate can easily ski any of the terrain.

The novice has a broad selection of wide, well-groomed trails both at the bottom of the mountain on Nob Hill (named after San Francisco's most fashionable address) on the lower part of Mt. Lincoln, or over on Christmas Tree Ridge. Jerome's Hill, Harriet's Hollow, and Sleigh Ride are long, smooth runs for the beginner. The advanced novice can ski all of Sugar Bowl's 1,500 vertical feet by riding the Lincoln #2 chair up to the 8,383-foot summit of Mt. Lincoln and skiing down to the base by way of California and then Henderson's Bowl. The only impediment to this top-to-bottom ski is the top traverse on Mogul Ridge, which is marked intermediate but which actually presents no problem to the confident novice.

More advanced skiers will ski nearly exclusively off the Lincoln #2 and Disney chairs. Schute I and Schute II, off the top of Lincoln, are marked expert but are mildly pitched runs down between the trees with bumps that intermediates can easily negotiate. Down toward the bottom of the Lincoln lift, however, Steilhang has one short face that has a steepish (7.5) drop.

Over on the Disney lift, the East Face is a mini bowl, very moderate in pitch and without bumps—a nice, fast cruise. On powder days (though Sugar Bowl is squarely in the "Sierra cement" belt), the East Face and Overland Trail, a good, long intermediate trail, have the best powder skiing. Most all the runs on Disney are bowl-like, with Market Street following the ridge down toward the lift and serving as the entrance for a series of trails that drop into the bowl. Of these drops, Donald Duck is the longest, while Eagle and Avalanche share the same pitch (6.5) and terrain (occasional mild bumps). The bottom of the Disney lift is a big, easy bowl and great fun for the intermediate.

The main and really the only reason for the expert to ski Sugar Bowl is Silver Belt. Winding under the Lincoln #2 chair down into and through a narrow gulley, Silver Belt is touted by Sugar Bowl as being the sixth steepest run in North America; it's not, but it does have several steep pitches (8–8.5). The narrowness of the gully and the winding of the trail through the trees make Silver Belt scenically lovely, and its consistent pitch, bumps, and shifting fall line make it demanding as a run for the weekend skier and nearly inconceivable as a downhill course.

Lift lines are no problem at Sugar Bowl, since the sale of lift tickets is limited on any day to 2,000. On busy weekends and holidays, the limit is usually reached before 11 A.M., so if you're staying elsewhere and planning to ski Sugar Bowl for the day, both the ticket limit and substantial parking problems dictate that you arrive early.

LIFE IN THE AREA

The strong focus at Sugar Bowl is on peace and quiet. There's little to do here, and driving elsewhere to find more activity requires a gondola ride to get back to your car. Those who wish to romp and stomp would do better at Squaw Valley 20 miles down the road, but if a good pipe smoke and a look at *Barron's* after dinner suits you, Sugar Bowl will do fine.

ACCOMMODATIONS

The only accommodations on the Sugar Bowl grounds are the **Lodge** and a few private homes rented through the Lodge. The Lodge is small, with only 29 rooms for up to 80 guests, and there is a firm policy against expansion. Great efforts are made by the Lodge to maintain an atmosphere of rustic European formality (coats and ties are requested for dinner). It has a cafeteria, bar, and formal dining room. The rooms are rustic, on the small side, and not very attractive (the old rooms at the Alta Lodge are a good comparison). Room rates range $35–50 per night. The Lodge is fully booked for the season as early as late fall, so plan ahead.

There are some other dorm- and motel-type accommodations near Sugar Bowl at the Donner Summit area; however, if you're going to do the Sugar Bowl experience, the Lodge is really a necessary ingredient.

The one exception we would make is the wonderful **Soda Springs Hotel** 2 miles west of Sugar Bowl. An Old West establishment founded in 1927, the Soda Springs Hotel is now completely furnished in antiques. In fact, the antique business is the real livelihood of the hotel. Literally everything there is for sale. If you like the Early American bed you just slept in or the English breakfast service, make an offer. Rooms here are also rustic but delightful, with lovely quilts on each bed. Rates are surprisingly low at $19–24, and dorms are $8 per person.

RESTAURANTS

Guests at the **Lodge** generally eat there. Nearly all midweek guests are on ski week packages that include dinner. The food is adequate though fairly expensive. The **Soda Springs Hotel** features an ambitious menu highlighted by homemade breads and desserts. In Truckee, the renovated mining town 11 miles away, several Contintental restaurants have recently opened; these are discussed in the chapter on SQUAW VALLEY (pp. 00–00).

APRÈS-SKI AND NIGHT LIFE

There are no after-ski activities at Sugar Bowl, and night life consists of a cognac and bed except for Tyrolean Night each Wednesday. This long-time Sugar Bowl custom includes a buffet followed by an Austrian show and dancing—and is exactly as corny as it sounds.

The **Soda Springs Hotel** has occasional weekend rock bands.

DIVERSION

Night skiing is scheduled Tuesdays and Saturdays on the novice slope.

CHILDREN

Children are discouraged. The ski school will not accept children under five, and there are no day-care or nursery facilities.

COSTS

The 5-day ski week is a Sugar Bowl tradition, and packages are available that provide for lodging, breakfast, dinner, lift tickets, and lessons. Ski week rates bring unusually high savings when compared to other areas and are booked months in advance.

8

Mt. Bachelor

As a mountain or as a ski resort, Bachelor does not meet the criteria we established for inclusion in this book. Outside of Bend, in central Oregon, Bachelor is not among the ski areas within short driving distance of a metropolitan area; its vertical drop is less than 1,500 feet, and its skiing is fairly ordinary. We include it nonetheless, primarily because of a couple of very appealing and gracious places to stay in the vicinity—particularly the extraordinary Sunriver, which ranks as one of our favorite lodges in North America.

ACCESSIBILITY

Bachelor is about a 3½-hour drive from Portland and a 3½-day trip from anywhere else. Actually, it's not quite *that* bad. The drive from Seattle is only 335 miles and not too much farther than that from northern California. Because of the proximity of so much skiing in the Northwest, however, Bend is not a weekend area except for Portlanders.

Alternate transportation from Portland includes Hughes Air West to the Redmond Airport 15 miles from Bend. A limousine meets each flight and will take you to your lodge. To go by bus, take the airport limousine to the Trailway Depot in downtown Portland, where there are five departures daily to Bend ($9).

THE SKIING

Bachelor is a place where the recreational skiing family can ski together. For novices, it has a lot of advantages. Six of its seven chair lifts have terrain suitable for the beginner. Also, Bachelor offers the novice the rare opportunity of skiing an entire mountain top to bottom. Skyliner, from the top of the Black chair, is a long, wide, gentle run which will take the novice from the peak of the mountain down to the Base Lodge. From the northeast face of the mountain, Chipper, off the Blue chair, is another long, pleasant novice run. Novices who don't yet feel ready for the assault on the summit can stick closer to home on the Orange triple chair or the Yellow chair, both of which venture only slightly up the mountain.

Intermediate skiing at Bachelor is fairly standard, with carefully cut, heavily groomed trails. Intermediates should be unperturbed by the trails marked expert. With the exception of some of the terrain on the Outback lift, there's nothing at Bachelor that a solid intermediate can't handle. In this view, Bachelor becomes a super mountain for the aggressive intermediate.

Experts won't find much to impress their friends back home with—at least on the cut trails at Bachelor. Liftline Black (not much pitch but some decent bumps) and Canyon off the Black lift, and Thunderbird, Grotto, and Tippytoe off the Red lift, are the best bet for the advanced skier but will not provide a significant challenge for the expert. An exception is some of the terrain on the Outback lift. For the expert, this lift is what Bachelor will be all about. Open only in good snow, and skied primarily in powder, the Outback is a whole face of the mountain left as unpacked trails, bowls, and meadows. Save for Ed's Garden, the one packed intermediate run on the Outback, the snow-cats are forbidden and powder is left to be powder and crud to be crud. Having hit a good powder day, we spent the day in the Outback; the terrain is not steep, but there's enough diversity to make it quite interesting. Traversing across the Outback to find new faces, it's possible to ski from trees to meadows to bowls before finally heading back toward the lift.

The Outback was a big improvement for Bachelor, and another is planned for the 1980-81 season: a new lift is to be built going up to the glacier above the northeast face. This lift would greatly increase the vertical of the mountain, add to Bachelor's extraordinary season (November 15–June 15), and potentially provide year-round skiing.

INTEGRATION OF THE SLOPES

Bachelor is well planned. Skiers of all levels can reach the base of all lifts and thus meet up with friends anywhere on the mountain. At the attractive Base Lodge is a restaurant and deck, as well as George's Soup Kettle at the top of the Orange chair and the Blue Lodge at the base of the Blue chair, where breakfast and lunch are served Thursdays through Mondays. For skiing purposes, the base of all chairs is easily accessible from the top of the short Yellow lift.

LIFE IN THE AREA

All after-ski activity takes place in Bend, some 22 miles from the mountain. Bend is a combination truck stop and Main Street, U.S.A. Downtown Bend looks somehow Midwestern, but when you reach the outskirts and the junction of Highway 97, the illusion is dispelled. Here the hallmarks of the New West, neon and fast food, are king. If there's a fast-food franchise that hasn't found its way to Bend, we have yet to hear of it.

ACCESSIBILITY TO THE SLOPES

The 22-mile drive to the mountain from Bend, where virtually all the lodging is located, is obviously less than convenient. The closest accommodation, the Inn of the Seventh Mountain, is still 15 miles away. Buses do run regularly between the mountain and the lodges in and around Bend ($3).

ACCOMMODATIONS

Bachelor-Bend actually has several nice places to stay. The two nicest are the **Inn of the Seventh Mountain,** which is lovely, and **Sunriver,** which is spectacular.

The Inn of the Seventh Mountain, 7 miles west of Bend, is a beautifully designed cluster of lodge and condominium units structured so that each of the 300 rooms overlooks adjacent mountains and lava beds. Accommodations vary in size from standard lodge rooms ($32) to studios with kitchen facilities ($40) to 3-bedroom units. A full range of resort facilities are available, including swimming pool, ice-skating rink, saunas, and Jacuzzis. There's a plush bar featuring live entertainment and Josiah's, an attractive restaurant.

Ranked outstanding by AAA, and with a four-star rating by the Mobil Travel Guide, Sunriver is really a self-contained resort community of over 5,500 acres located 15 miles south of Bend. The size of the resort and the tasteful grouping of living units gives a great feeling of spaciousness which is well suited to its magnificent setting in the high desert. There's a tremendous amount to do at Sunriver; in fact, it's like summer camp. Besides the usual saunas, Jacuzzis, and skating, a daily activity calendar posted in the lobby goes the whole spectrum from gymnastics to bridge to photography to Chinese cooking classes. The 20 miles of terrain which become bike paths in the summer are used for some excellent cross-country skiing routes. The architecture at Sunriver is worth the walk around the grounds; the Great Hall, an incredibly impressive structure of log and stone, is particularly noteworthy. Sunriver's bar and restaurant (which has the best food in the area) are both elegant and attractive. A shopping mall on the grounds has a nice variety of shops and eateries. Prices range from $42 for a standard lodge room to $55 and up for condominium accommodations with kitchen facilities. Tremendous savings can be had, however, by taking the 5-day package, which will save you up to 30%. Unfortunately, Sunriver is 39 miles from Mt. Bachelor, though free bus service operates regularly through the day.

Other good accommodations in the Bend area include the **River House Motor Inn,** a first-rate luxury motel with restaurant, pool, sauna, and Jacuzzi ($18), and the **Bend Riverside,** another motel with pool, tennis courts, sauna, and Jacuzzi ($18). For an atmosphere slightly closer to that of a traditional ski lodge, the **Entrada Lodge** on the road to the mountain has a family-style breakfast, after-ski refreshments, game room, pool, and sauna ($20).

Dorm space is available at the **Bunkhouse,** and more tacky motels than exist anywhere east of Las Vegas can be found on Route 97.

For reservations, call 800–547–0916 (in-state, 223–7355).

RESTAURANTS

Certainly the best food in the area (and the most expensive) is at the dining room at **Sunriver.** Here the setting is gracious, the service good, and the menu Continental. The dining room at the **River House** is more than adequate and not as expensive as at Sunriver. **Cyrano's** is the local French restaurant and a longtime favorite. **Le Bistro** is also quite nice. **Josiah's** at the Inn of the Seventh Mountain is a most attractive dining room, though the quality of food is debatable. **Original Joe's** is the place to go for a late-night snack and serves reasonably priced Italian meals. The **Black Forest** is German and also moderately priced.

To describe only the sit-down restaurants is not to do Bend justice. What Paris is to *haute cuisine,* Bend is to junk food. When Michelin expands its vistas to fast food, Bend will be the first to be awarded three neon rosettes.

APRĘS-SKI AND NIGHT LIFE

After skiing, people gather, primarily by default, at the Base Lodge bar, which has recorded music. At night, things move down to town. The bar at the **Inn of the Seventh Mountain** has live music and dancing. The bar at the **River House** looks out over the Deshutes River and attracts a slightly older, more sedate crowd. The **Cinders** is the local disco, though not likely to be mistaken for Studio 54. The young set goes to **Bogey's** for beer and dancing, and if Jimmy Buffet, the Amazing Rhythm Aces, and an occasional fight are more to your taste, try the **Woolen Mill.**

DIVERSIONS

Most diversions are part of the activities at the various lodges and, where they exist, have been described above.

CHILDREN

There's a nursery at the mountain, but it operates only Fridays through Sundays, on holidays, and during Oregon school vacations. The cost is $8 per day for children under two and $7 per day for older children, with an hourly rate of $1.25 for a minimum of 2 hours. Rates do not include lunch.

The nursery will provide ski instruction at $18 per day or $15 if the child has his own equipment. Check with the various lodges concerning independent child-care arrangements.

A number of factors combine to make Bachelor a good area for children. The skiing is relatively easy; the lift system is well integrated and it is easy for families to meet up at various spots; and certain lodges (**Sunriver, Inn of the Seventh Mountain**) plan activities for children. The only problem to keep in mind is the 15- to 40-mile trek between mountain and lodge.

COSTS

Bachelor is not expensive. Lift tickets are only $8, and children under twelve ski for $4. Moreover, many lodge facilities offer substantial rate reductions for stays of 5 days or more.

9

Crystal Mountain

It's a bitter pill for the Eastern skier to swallow that the Northwest has nearly 30 ski areas within 90 minutes of the major metropolitan areas. While most of these are "day" areas from which skiers usually return home after a day or night of skiing, a few are beginning to make a serious bid for resort status. Crystal Mountain, with its great accessibility, long season, and truly excellent terrain is certainly the most likely candidate. In fact, major status would probably have been attained long ago were it not for the captive Seattle-Tacoma area audience who already more than fill up the lift lines. It is with some reticence, then, that we offer our opinion that Crystal is simply too good a mountain to be left to the locals.

ACCESSIBILITY

Crystal is located in Washington's cascade range in the Mt. Baker–Snoqualmie National Forest on the northeast boundary of Mt. Ranier National Park. The drive from Seattle (76 miles) or Tacoma (64 miles) takes approximately 1½ hours.

The Seattle-Tacoma International Airport is serviced by United, Western, Pan American, Northwest Orient, Continental, Eastern, Braniff, SAS, Alaska, and Air Canada, making it one of the most accessible airports in the United States. There is also an airport for private planes at Enumclaw, 39 miles from the mountain.

Crystal is usually reached by private or rental car through Enumclaw on U.S. Highway 410. Bus service from Seattle is also available daily with a connection in Enumclaw.

THE SKIING

The factors that combine to make Crystal such a good mountain are its size, the diversity of its terrain, and its balance of novice, intermediate, and expert runs. Crystal is vast (over 4,500 acres of skiable terrain). The terrain itself is widely varied, including long, well-groomed rolling slopes, open bowls, narrow chutes, ferocious bumps, and even some Eastern-type trail skiing through the trees off the backside of the mountain. The trails are well connected by five double chair lifts (a sixth triple chair lift services a separate face of the mountain but has not been operational during the last few years) and eleven rope tows and one T-bar at the bottom of the mountain primarily for the beginner. This lift complex gives Crystal an uphill capacity of 7,000 skiers per hour.

Despite the alarming number of rope tows, the beginning skier is not relegated to this atavistic method of uphill transportation. In fact, beginners and low intermediates have their own chair lift in Chair #4, which has two primary runs down its 1,000-foot vertical face. Quicksilver, over a mile long, is an unusually good beginner's run. Boon Doggle, an easy intermediate run, is nearly as long and can be readily skied by the intrepid beginner. Skid Road, which traverses Chairs #1, 4, and 5, is another mile-long beginner's run, valuable because it opens up Chair #1 to the beginner and thus reduces lift lines. Chair #6, when operational, has Blue Bell and Ted's run, which provide even more terrain for the novice.

Crystal has good intermediate skiing—a fact, we think, having much to do with the planners' determination to leave the mountain alone and not "cut" trails solely with the intermediate in mind. The immaculately cut intermediate mountain is neither very interesting nor conducive to improving one's skiing. Snowmass is a classic example; not so, Crystal. The intermediate runs provide enough terrain changes to prevent tedium and to improve skiing. Chair #5, with a vertical drop of 1,773 feet, is the center of much of the intermediate skiing. Downhill Race Course is a good, standard intermediate run—long, wide, and groomed. Of the same ilk is Mr. Magoo, which parallels Race Course off Chair #5. Rolling Knolls, also off Chair #5, is a nice little path through the trees that has manageable bumps for the intermediate.

From the bottom of the mountain, intermediates can also use the Chair #1 and #2 combination and ski Crystal's full 2,430 feet of lift-served vertical by taking Powder Bowl into Gandy's Run, or, from the top of Chair #2, they can get a taste of bowl skiing by turning right and going down Green Valley, a pleasant, mild bowl terminating at the bottom of Chair #3. Then it's up

Chair #3 and down Snorting Elk, one of the most popular intermediate runs on the mountain. The view from the top of Chair #2 makes it an absolute must for both the intermediate and advanced skier. Staring you in the face, 14 miles away (though it looks like a snowball's throw), is majestic Mt. Ranier, 14,410 feet high. Incredibly, also visible from the top of Chair #2 on a clear day are Mt. Adams (85 miles), Mt. Hood in Oregon (110 miles), Mt. St. Helen's (63 miles), Glacier Peak (85 miles), and Mt. Baker (125 miles).

The expert skier can have a field day at Crystal. For starters, try the K2 Face off Chair #5. It's very narrow, very steep (9), and, though not often skied because of generally mediocre snow conditions on the face, is an absolute must for those considering themselves hot. One note of warning: There are no local stops on this run; a fall will put you conveniently and speedily at the bottom of the chair. If the Face is too intimidating, try Frisco—a nice, fairly steep chute off to the left of K2.

Chair #2 provides a series of expert choices. Sunnyside, the #2 liftline, is a long, wide-open, very steep (8.5) trail with enormous bumps. Its pitch and bump structure are comparable to those at the National at Stowe or Prima at Vail, and that's saying something for a mountain that three-quarters of the skiers in the United States have never heard of. Off to the other side of Chair, #2 you can ski down Iceberg Ridge to Exterminator (8.75). Upper Exterminator lays claim to being the third steepest run in North America. (Frankly, 80% of the ski resorts in the United States have a run about which they make the same claim, and we've never adequately understood the calculus requisite for refutation. Suffice it to say that Exterminator is very steep and should be skied by all experts looking for challenge.) A little more manageable, off Chair #2, is Lucky Shot, which is rated as intermediate but has both substantial pitch and bumps and would be rated by most areas as expert. Nearby is Iceberg Gulch, a good bump run that narrows down substantially toward the bottom.

Off Chair #3, experts who have skied the bowl in Green Valley can ride out and ski Grubsteak Face, the liftline of #3, a wide-open, steep run. Much of the expert terrain at Crystal is saved from awesomeness solely because it is wide, allowing great margins of error even for the expert. True fall line skiers, however, may allow themselves the luxury of the open slopes.

Our favorite skiing at Crystal is really off the backside of the mountain, where the vertical extends to over 3,000 feet and the runs are long with much shifting of terrain. Spook Hill is a particular delight. Starting from the top of Chair #2 and taking a long traverse, you ski down a steep bowl in and out of bumps and gulleys and finally into some lovely, quiet Eastern tree and trail skiing. A seldom skied area of the mountain, it holds its snow excellently and exists as a real secret haven on powder days. A shuttle bus takes you from the bottom of the run back to the main lifts a mile or two away. Also on the backside of the mountain, runs like Northway and Gun Tower offer much the same kind of skiing, as well as a couple of spectacular bowls for powder days.

Remember that the Northwest is wet. It rains at Crystal more often than at its competitors in Utah and in the Rockies, and along with the rain come the foul conditions of ice and crust; however, snow conditions here are as good or better than almost anyplace in the Northwest and are really not that fickle. Crystal does get a lot of snow, and as a result the season is exceptionally long, from November through mid-May, with weekend skiing often extending all the way into July.

A word about lift lines: They can be long at Crystal, bordering on horrendous. This fact is mainly accounted for by a rite indigenous to the Northwest known as "Ski School." These are schools that have no ski area affiliation but rather are run by schools, churches, civic associations, and ski shops. The interest in and popularity of these schools is overwhelming, and the result is that each Saturday morning at Crystal, commencing with the resumption of school in January, there will appear in the parking lot 100—yes, 100—buses full of children from toddler age on up. Results on the lift line are predictable, but have you ever tried to get out of a parking lot behind 100 buses?

INTEGRATION OF THE SLOPES

All the trails at Crystal except those on the backside of the mountain converge at the base of the resort, at which point all lifts are accessible by either a walk of a few yards or transfer rope tows. Food is available at the cafeteria in the day lodge at the base of the mountain or at the Summit House located at the top of Chair #2. The problem with the Summit House (which also serves wine and beer) is that it's virtually inaccessible to novice and low intermediate skiers, who can find no easy way down the mountain from that location.

LIFE IN THE AREA

Life in the area is adequate. No more, no less. The skier looking for elegance, glamour, and cuisine can find many better choices, though Crystal does cover all the basic needs.

ACCESSIBILITY TO THE SLOPES

The lodges and all other facilities at Crystal are clustered right at the base of the mountain and are within easy walking distance of the lifts. A car is definitely unnecessary.

ACCOMMODATIONS

Crystal has three lodges and two condominium complexes. The **Alpine Inn** is the most charming, with the look of a European hostel. It houses in its basement the most popular and lively après-ski bar and has its own restaurant. Packages including lodging, breakfast, and dinner are available for 3 or 5 nights. The 36 rooms, however, are extremely small and sparsely appointed, and many either share a shower or have none. Rates are reasonable, with a room with a private shower running approximately $22 (slightly less during midweek).

The **Crystal Inn** is the largest lodging facility. It has a bar and a restaurant, and its standard motel-type rooms each have a private bath. A double room is approximately $26, with packages available at a slightly lower price.

The **Crystal House** is another motel-type accommodation, comprising 24 rooms with private bath and shower. Rates are about the same as those at the Crystal Inn. For somewhat more money, the **Silver Skis** condominiums are recommended. These are plain and simple, and do not compare in any way with the plush condominiums of Aspen, Vail, or Sun Valley. Nevertheless, each apartment has a kitchen, 1 or 2 bedrooms, and a private bath. There's also a heated swimming pool. Rates are quite low: a 1-bedroom apartment with fireplace that can sleep up to 8 people costs $36 per night for two, plus $5 for each additional person. Modest savings can be obtained through midweek and 5-night packages.

Slightly less expensive and slightly less nice are the **Crystal Chalets,** 36 apartments each with kitchen facilities and private bath. Many of the units have fireplaces.

At the bottom of the hill, 6½ miles from the mountain, lodging is also available at **Silver Springs.** Other than the accommodations directly at the mountain, Silver Springs is the only place to stay between Crystal and Enumclaw. Besides its few rooms, Silver Springs also has a restaurant and disco.

For reservations, call 206–663–2265.

RESTAURANTS

There are only two restaurants at the mountain: the dining room at the **Alpine Inn** and the restaurant in the **Crystal Inn.** The Crystal Inn is basically a steak-and-salad bar restaurant, with veal, seafood, and chicken dishes offering some variety. The Alpine Inn has a more Bavarian flavor in a more intimate, attractive setting. The food at both restaurants is adequate. Down the hill, at **Silver Springs,** is the area's only other restaurant, offering standard American fare in an atmosphere much like that of a Southern California coffee shop.

APRÈS-SKI AND NIGHT LIFE

After skiing, everyone goes to the **Snorting Elk Cellar** at the Alpine Inn. This is a charming cellar that transports you rather authentically to Munich. The Cellar serves lunch until 2 or 3 P.M. and then pizza, chili, and sandwiches on into the late evening, when it continues to be one of the two places to go at night. Its competitor for the sparse night life crowd is the **Rathskellar,** located in the Crystal Inn. This long and rambling bar includes a disco and a substantial dance floor. The only other place for nighttime activity is the bar and disco 6½ miles down the hill at **Crystal Springs.**

The relative dispatch with which we deal here with Crystal accommodations, restaurants, and night life underscores the fact that, for better or for worse, despite all its great skiing, Crystal really has not yet been developed. While we would not necessarily recommend it for those wanting to spend their two-week vacation at a ski resort, the quality of the skiing makes it an important mountain to try even for a few days.

DIVERSION

The main diversion at Crystal is night skiing. Chair #4 operates till 10 P.M. nightly except Monday.

CHILDREN

The physical compactness of Crystal, in both its lift structure and its facilities, makes it a good mountain for children. The confluence of chairs at the base of the mountain facilitates meeting up with children, and the variety of different runs off each chair allows parents who might not ski with their children to at least ride the chair with them.

COSTS

Prices at Crystal are standard for the Northwest, which is to say lower than the rest of the Western U.S. On the other hand, with the exception of Mt. Bachelor, none of the resorts in the region offers a significant variety of accommodations, food, or services.

10

Whistler Mountain

Whistler is an extraordinary place to ski, particularly if you have a spirit of adventure. Virtually unskied by Americans because of the number and proximity of day areas in the northwestern part of the United States, Whistler is primarily the stomping ground for skiers from Vancouver and the rest of British Columbia. Though many of the over one million Vancouverites make the 80-mile trip to Whistler with some regularity, the area remains sparsely developed, having almost none of the accouterments normally associated with a major ski area. As a skiing experience, however, Whistler offers so much that we think a certain lack of amenities is a small price to pay. To tick off the statistics on Whistler is to understand immediately what this mountain has to offer. A vertical drop of 4,280 feet (the longest in North America); over 450 inches of annual snowfall (as much as Alta or Snowbird); an intermediate run over 7 miles long and the equivalent of any of its kind in Europe; over 10 square miles of skiable terrain; and a season that extends from mid-November through May. So what if there's no grocery store.

ACCESSIBILITY

Whistler is 80 miles north of Vancouver, about a 2-hour drive that should definitely be made during the day. The first half of the drive is one of the most beautiful we've ever seen, combining mountain and coastal beauty in a way unparalleled in our ski trips. The bad news is that about 15 miles of the drive is harrowing beyond belief. A super-narrow two-lane road, hairpin turns, steep drops from cliffs, and no guardrails make this stretch of the road suitable for a Hitchcock car chase. In inclement weather, snow, or ice, the drive would seem unthinkable, yet steely-nerved Vancouverites assure us that it's not all that difficult. From Seattle, Washington, the drive takes approximately 5½ hours, following the same route.

The British Columbia railroad passenger train leaves North Vancouver daily at 8 A.M. and departs from Whistler daily at 6:45 P.M. The trip takes about 2¾ hours and is magnificent. S.M.T. Coach Lines also provides daily bus service from various locations in Vancouver.

THE SKIING

Whistler is a tough mountain. It is by no means a place for the novice. The trail map, which codes over 40% of the terrain as beginner, is very misleading by American standards. Most of the green runs are at least low intermediate, and some are even more difficult. There is an absence of the wide, flat, immaculately groomed trails that have become associated in American skiing with novice runs. Throughout, we have decried the homogeneous quality of intermediate terrain at such slopes as Keystone and Snowmass. This is not a problem at Whistler. There is diversity of both terrain and pitch. Each of its nine lifts services good, interesting, and in some cases exciting intermediate terrain.

Every morning, all skiers climb the initial 2,100 vertical feet of the mountain on either the Olive chair or the gondola. The average daytime temperature is 20°, and Whistler can be a cold and windy mountain. The hearty can take advantage of this by avoiding the half-hour queues on the gondola and riding the Olive chair, where on cold weekend mornings in January or February there are not likely to be lift lines. From mid-Whistler, access to the rest of the mountain is through the Red chair, which rises another 1,750 vertical feet. A good diversion for the intermediate before going up top is to ski Downhill, the liftline of the Orange chair. A quite good intermediate run, Downhill is steep at the beginning (7), relatively narrow, and then pitched again, dropping nearly 1,300 feet to mid-Whistler. Once up top, the skier has access to the two Green chairs, two T-bars, and the Blue chair. The Green chairs service four good lower intermediate runs: Ego Bowl, Jolly Green Giant, Whiskey Jack, and Green Acres—the hardest of the four. The Green chairs serve the flattest terrain at Whistler, with ratios approximating 4.4:1.

Whistler affords the advanced intermediate a rare opportunity. From the top of the T-bars at the 6,420-foot summit, the whole mountain opens up and the advanced intermediate can begin a 4,200-foot descent uninterrupted by lifts, catwalks, or traverses. The best route is to take Ridge Run down into Franz's Run, which then travels the entire length of the mountain. Moderately pitched (6.5), with well-spaced and rounded bumps, Franz's goes down and down and down. Scenically lovely, it very much recalls the Alps, where you ski in canyons closely surrounded by jutting peaks on all sides. Franz's is

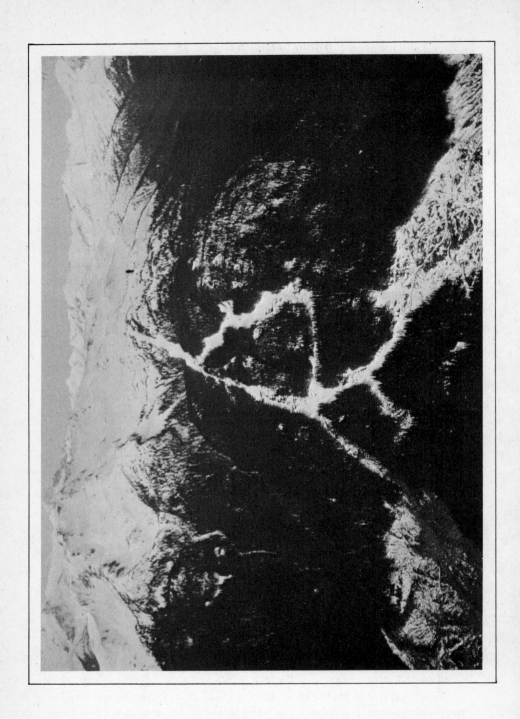

Whistler Mountain   PHOTO BY CHRIS SPEEDIE

simply one of the best advanced intermediate runs there is. And, as if Franz's were not enough, the less advanced intermediate can ski Olympic, a run nearly 7 miles long, which makes the famous Big Burn at Snowmass look like the neighborhood rope tow. Wide, undemanding, and endless, Olympic wanders down the north side of the mountain before ending 2 miles from the gondola. Buses wait at the end of the run to take skiers back to the lifts.

For the expert, Whistler has just as much to offer. Some will choose to ski much of the day on the gondola, which has a good pitch but long lift lines. Whistler's low base altitude (2,140'), though, can make skiing the lower lifts problematic in the early winter. Off the Orange chair, but unmarked on the trail map, is a very good steep bump run called Goats Gully. This semi-chute, along with Chunky's Choice over on the Blue chair, is one of the two major bump runs at Whistler. Chunky's (9.25) is the equivalent of any of the great Western bump runs (Limelight at Sun Valley, Prima at Vale, or Snakedance at Taos). Much of the best expert terrain on the mountain is over at the Blue chair, with Dad's Run and G.S. both challenging alternatives to the rigors of Chunky's.

When the lift lines get long, and they do on weekends, the T-bars provide some excellent and time-saving alternatives to the chairs. Taking the T-bars into the back bowl area, you can either do some bowl skiing in Harmony Bowl or opt for a good steep bump run (8) right off the T-bar. Lines on the T-bar are generally short, and the runs are varied enough to interest skiers for a good part of the day.

On powder days, go up the T-bar and ski in either direction along the ridge to Boomer or Whistler bowls. For the energetic, there are some great hikes to extraordinary Alta-like powder faces. Also, you can climb past the T-bar and traverse out of bounds to either West Bowl or Far West Bowl.

If you're skiing Whistler for the first time, no matter what your level, be sure to take the free guided tour to familiarize yourself with the mountain. There are two tours on weekdays, the first leaving at 9:30 A.M. from the gondola, and the second at 1:15 P.M. from the top of the Red chair. Weekend tours are available on request.

INTEGRATION OF THE SLOPES

The Roundhouse at the top of the Red chair is the confluence of all the summit chairs and T-bars, and its cafeteria provides an easily accessible meeting place for people skiing anywhere on the mountain.

LIFE IN THE AREA

There are towns that are primitive and charming, and there are towns that are primitive and inconvenient. Whistler is decidedly the latter. There is no market, no drugstore, no hospital, and virtually no shops. Just a damn good mountain.

ASSESSIBILITY TO THE SLOPES

A car is essential at Whistler. Certain accommodations are more or less within walking distance from the lifts, but the bulk of the lodges, condominiums, restaurants, and bars are spread out over a 4- or 5-mile area along Highway 99.

ACCOMMODATIONS

Accommodations at Whistler range from adequate to Spartan. The nicest are in the **Whistler Inn,** about ¼ mile from the lifts. Half the rooms here are standard motel rooms ($33), and the rest are studio units complete with full kitchen and fireplace ($45). The rooms are modern, and facilities include dining room, sauna, and Jacuzzi. Weekly and midweek rates are available.

Also within walking distance of the lifts is the small **Cheakamus Inn,** which has dining room, sauna, and lounge ($32). The **Christiana Inn,** about a mile from the lifts, has recently been renovated and features a cocktail lounge, dining room, cabaret, and sauna ($25). The **White Gold Inn** is the largest lodging facility in the valley and is located 3½ miles north of the gondola; it has a dining room, pub, and sauna, and offers free transportation to and from the lifts ($23). With the exception of certain of the units at the Whistler Inn, most of the lodge rooms at Whistler are strictly standard motel and quite undistinguished.

One possible alternative to lodge accommodations is a condominium unit. The **Tamarask,** 1 mile south of the lifts, is Whistler's largest (140 units) condominium development and provides a good value; each unit has a sunken living room, fireplace, indoor barbecue, and private sauna ($35–43). For families needing larger accommodations, the **Alpenforst,** about 4 miles from the lifts, has 2- and 3-bedroom units from $53 to $80 per night.

For reservations, call 604–932–5756.

RESTAURANTS

Excellent cuisine, like luxury of accommodation, is not a reason to come to Whistler. The best restaurant, with a highly ambitious French menu and relatively high prices, is **JB's** at the Whistler Inn. Also French and well thought of is **La Vallée Blanche.** Canada is not immune from the steak–and–salad bar epidemic, and Whistler's entry is the **Keg;** the most popular restaurant at the mountain, the Keg does not take reservations and long waits are thus the rule. Other uninspired menus are offered at **L'apres,** at the Base Lodge, as well as in the dining rooms at the **Christiana, White Gold,** and **Highland** inns.

If you're staying at a condominium unit, grocery shopping is available on a limited basis at the Gulf station in town or at the deli located next to the Huskie station. The Canadians apparently believe in combining the more inflationary aspects of their economy.

APRÈS-SKI AND NIGHT LIFE

All of the action immediately following the close of the lifts (3 P.M. till February; 3:30 P.M. thereafter) takes place at the bar at **L'apres.** At night, the energetic go either to the **Keg,** which has a disco and is populated by a youngish crowd, or to the **Christiana,** which has dancing to live country-and-western music. For a quieter time, the bar at the **Whistler Inn** has live entertainment and is a nice place to go for a drink. There is usually also some sort of live entertainment at the **Cheakamus Inn** and at the **Pub** in the White Gold Inn.

DIVERSION

Whistler has a number of outdoor winter diversions. There is a variety of cross-country terrain spreading out over frozen lakes, logging roads, trails, forests, and alpine land. Equipment can be rented at the ski shops in town. There is also snowshoeing along cross-country trails. Curling, a newly popular sport in Canada, is played regularly on the lakes surrounding Whistler, and ice skating is also available on these lakes with rentals found at the **Magasin De Ski.** For fishermen, the ice fishing on Whistler's lake is good and the supply of trout abundant.

For the powder skier, **Whistler Heli Ski, Ltd.,** offers helicopter skiing throughout the many glaciers surrounding Whistler. There are runs from 2,000 to 5,500 vertical feet on glaciers and through glades. The cost is approximately $100 for 4 runs of about 15,000 vertical feet, with a charge thereafter of $5.00 per thousand vertical feet.

CHILDREN

Whistler is a terrible place for children. Stringent British Columbia regulations concerning the licensing of day-care facilities effectively preclude day care at Whistler. There is no nursery or any organized day-care facility in the area. Some makeshift baby-sitting can be found at private homes in the area, but no centralized system exists to ensure the availability of this service.

Also, since most of the terrain at Whistler suitable for the lesser skier is located at the top of the mountain, children must ride to the summit; this could be a cold, unpleasant experience for them.

COSTS

The $8 lift ticket at Whistler (children ski for $4) is one of the great bargains around. Whistler offers no packages that combine lodging, lifts, and instruction; however, various midweek and 7-day discounts are available at most lodges. For Americans, costs will vary with currency fluctuations.

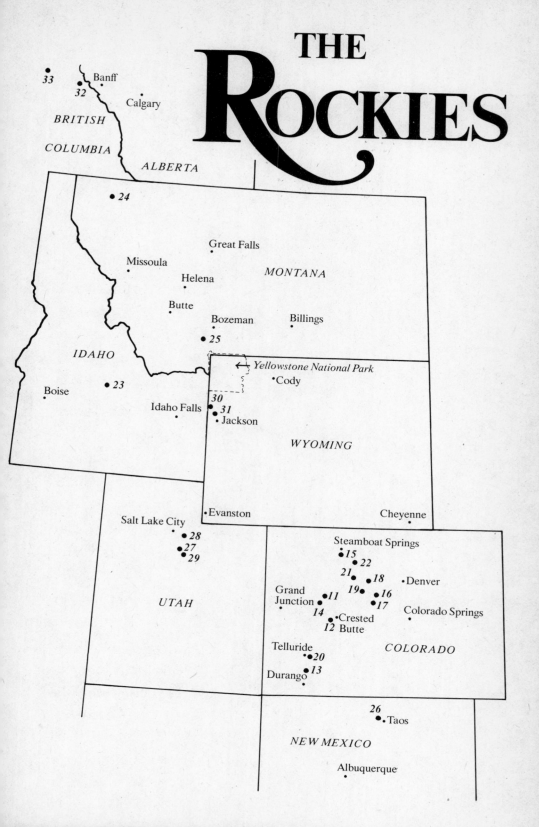

THE ROCKIES

11

Aspen

Conventional wisdom has labeled Aspen the resort with incomparable skiing, the swingingest night life, the best restaurants, and the most glamorous people. The emerging view of the ski counter-culture holds that Aspen is a somewhat overrated mountain located in a substantially overrated town populated by vastly overrated people. Which is correct? Both.

Knocking Aspen is not hard. Its principal mountain (interchangeably called Ajax or Aspen Mountain) is not that interesting, prices for nearly everything are prohibitively high, and the natives—Aspen's fabled beautiful people—tend to be either slavish est devotees or trust funders who've traded Porsche for jeep and have come to seek the mellow life.

Yet Aspen nearly lives up to its hype. Four major mountains within a 10-mile area provide skiing for all abilities. There are more than 80 restaurants of every conceivable persuasion. And the bars and discos are far and away the most elegant of any resort.

In the final analysis, skiing is really a supplement to Aspen, a fringe benefit. Aspen's main export is glamour. The perception that Aspen is a decadent Disneyland for the rich may be somewhat exaggerated, but it is an image the town fastidiously perpetuates. This year's best-selling T-shirt emblazoned Aspen's three staples: Cocaine . . . Cash . . . Caviar.

ACCESSIBILITY

By winter routings, Aspen is 210 miles west of Denver and 130 miles east of Grand Junction. The drive (all major car rentals are available from both airports) is about 4 hours from Denver and 2¾ hours from Grand Junction. Continental Trailways has scheduled bus service from Denver several times daily, from Grand Junction on Fridays and Saturdays, and to Grand Junction on Saturdays and Sundays.

The more popular route from Denver is by air, and connections are excellent: both Aspen Airways and Rocky Mountain Airways have many flights per day (approximately $32). (Flying time is only about 35 minutes, but the queasy should be warned that flights can often be rather dramatic.) From Grand Junction, which is served from the west by United and Frontier, it was necessary, until recently, to depend on car rentals or the chartered limousine service provided by Aspen Reservations, Inc. Now Bonanza Airlines is flying 26-passenger DC3's from Grand Junction into Aspen ($28). From the Aspen airport, cabs and buses are available for the short drive into town or out to Snowmass.

THE SKIING

The Aspen mountains are the underachievers of skiing. Though statistically imposing (four mountains in a 10-mile area, three of these with a vertical drop of over 3,000 feet), they are simply not as interesting as they should be with those qualifications. The culprit is not terrain; there's plenty of good stuff at both Ajax and Aspen Highlands. The flaw is in the planning, which is close to abysmal at both mountains.

Of the four mountains, we treat three here. Ajax (Aspen Mountain), which rises directly from town; Aspen Highlands, with its 3,800-foot vertical, one of the longest in North America; and Buttermilk, the family mountain. Snowmass, the largest of the four, is really an independent area with its own village, and we treat it separately in another chapter.

Ajax. Seven lifts service its 600 acres of trails. If it had nine, or even eight, it could be a terrific mountain. Yet it is problems of planning and integration, rather than capacity that plague its lift system. Ajax is trough-shaped, and some of its best skiing is found on the upper walls of Bell Mountain, which empty out into the gulch below. The problem, simply, is that there are no chairs back up these faces. One is forced to ski down in the relatively flat gulley nearly to the base, then take a thirteen-minute chair ride back up.

The mountain is basically divided into three sections. Bell Mountain climbs up on the east, and its face, saddles, and ridges account for much of Ajax's expert terrain. Paralleling the Bell lift, Chairs #1A and #8 climb the west face, which has steep chutes at the bottom and long cruises higher up. The top of Ajax, from which one can head for either Bell or #1A, is a large area devoted to the intermediate, with a substantial network of groomed trails.

The expert will want to divide his time between the Bell runs, the chutes off #1A, and International–Silver Queen, the formidable run heading down the west face of the mountain.

Ajax Mountain at Aspen; Little Nell and Bell Mountain on left, Ruthie's on extreme right   COURTESY ASPEN SKIING CORPORATION

The Ridge of Bell (the liftline of Chair #5) is a challenger. Not very steep at the beginning (7), its constant bumps are a warning of what is to come. After this warm-up directly under the chair, the Ridge becomes one of the West's more taxing bump runs, with a long, steep face (9) pocked with ski pole–height moguls. By the time you empty out into Spar Gulch for a short respite, your legs may welcome the 13-minute ride back up. Staying on Bell, there are various alternatives. Several good runs drop off the backside of the mountain to the left of the chair. Our favorite is Christmas Tree, a beautiful run that drops off steeply at first (8.75) amid large moguls, then narrows as it passes through a natural slalom of trees. Christmas Tree empties out into Copper Bowl, a wide intermediate trail with moderate bumps that heads back to the lift. When skiing down from the top of Bell, a nice alternative to Copper, which is often mobbed toward the end of the day, involves cutting over to Gentleman's Ridge on the eastern boundary of the mountain. This ridge is a fairly flat traverse off which is a series of good drops along the lower face of Bell. Glades #1, #2, and #3 are short, fairly steep (8.25) drops through the trees and into the bottom of Copper Bowl; following the ridge down farther, the skier reaches Jackpot, a steep drop into Spar Gulch with some good bumps.

To gain access from Bell to the top of Ajax or to the runs on the west face, choose the runs to the right of the chair down the face of Bell. Intermediates should take Deer Park, a little cruise from the top of Bell over to Chair #3 going up top or to #6, which opens up the rest of the mountain. Experts get to the same place on Sunset, a wide bump run (7.75). Unfortunately, the steepest (9) and best runs down the face drop down through countless trees *below* both Chairs #3 and #6, and you have to ski all the way down the mountain on fairly uninteresting terrain. A chair going up the face of Bell is desperately needed.

The tremendously efficient 4-minute Chair #6 gives access to two major runs. The first is flat (6) at the top, dropping off slightly into a long runoff, followed by another fairly flat mogul field (7), some decent bumps, and finally a runoff to the base of Chair #8, where you can sit for 11 minutes and then do it again. Boring, you say. We think so, too—but this is the famous Ruthie's Run, which for some reason that totally eludes us is one of the most famous runs in all of the West. Ski it so you too can be mystified when someone back home asks in awe, "Did you ski Ruthie's?"

The other run off #6 is one of the best on the mountain. International–Silver Queen runs down to the base by way of a series of several heavily moguled faces of increasing steepness until at last, when you think you've had enough, the aptly named Elevator Shaft, (9.5) rounds into view.

After a run down Silver Queen, and especially if lines are painful up top, good skiers may want to stay on #1A, which is only 7 minutes long and never has a lift line. Off #1A, stay in the fall line of steep Corkscrew (8.25) or even try to find the fall line of adjacent Corkscrew Gulley.

Going back up #1A and #8 to the top of Ruthie's, Red's Run and Little Percy are two short bump runs with nice pitch (8).

Intermediates (there is *no* novice terrain on Ajax) will want to go up top where the sun is hot, the view terrific, and the runs groomed. The usual route is to take the #3 chair up, but lift lines are often horrendous and few have yet seemed to realize that skiing down to #6 and taking #6 and #2 is much faster. Trails at the top spew out in all directions and are standard intermediate. For the nicest view take Buckhorn, which is to the far left as you start down the hill. Facing down, the runs to the left tend to be wider and bowl-like, while off to the right on Silver Dip and Silver Bell the intermediate will find more trees. For advanced skiers the runs up top offer a great cruise, where you can really let go and move out. The only thing to consider is the line on #3 and the 10-minute ride back up.

Northstar, which can be handled by advanced intermediates, is a favorite run at the end of the day. It starts at the very top of the mountain and heads down pleasantly until it meets up with Gentleman's Ridge, at which point intermediates may bail out into Copper while experts can head for the Glades or Jackpot. Taking this route enables the skier to make the last run of the day one that covers the entire mountain top to bottom.

There are two restaurants on Ajax. The Sun Deck at the top of the mountain and Gretl's, down from the top of Chair #8. Gretl's is the best on-mountain restaurant there is, and no afternoon's skiing is the same without a piece of Gretl's strudel.

Aspen Highlands. Located 3 miles outside Aspen, the Highlands has become increasingly popular, particularly with novice and intermediate skiers. As one would expect of a mountain with a 3,800-foot vertical, there is also some steep, exciting expert terrain. Regrettably, the steeps are usually either very short or impossible to get back to. As a result, experts usually stay over on Ajax, no paradigm of planning itself.

Four consecutive chairs climb from the base to the 11,800-foot summit. Most of the intermediate and advanced skiing is done up top, which unfortunately means a 35–50-minute chair ride in the morning.

Novices are given an unusual opportunity at the Highlands. By riding the first three chairs up, you can ski to the base, 2½ miles and 2,900 vertical feet below, on wide, gentle, perfectly groomed slopes. From the top of #3, take Meadows into Andrew's and then cut into Exhibition, which will join with Park Avenue to the base.

Intermediates primarily stay up top and ski off either #3 or #4. A ride to the top on #4 is a must, as the view of Pyramid Peak, Maroon Bells, and the surrounding valley is unsurpassed anywhere in Aspen. Up top on #4, Loges and Kandahar are nice intermediate cruises with a few bumps to keep you honest. If you don't mind being watched, Floradora, the liftline of #3, is a great moderately pitched (7) intermediate bump run where the Friday hot dog contest is held. If you're not up to showing off, Heatherbedlam and Gunbarrel flank Floradora on either side and have approximately the same terrain. On days when the liftlines are a problem or the ride up top seems too time-consuming, Golden Horn off the Golden Horn poma (A high-speed, automatic poma is as much a challenge as the hill) is a good wide-open intermediate run.

The Highlands is frustrating for the good skier. Alps, off #3, is a steep face (8.5) with big bumps, but the drop is only for about 100 yards before it joins a low-intermediate runoff back to the chair. The same is true with the Wall, said to be the steepest slope in Aspen (9.5). The Wall goes nearly straight down and has sizable bumps, but again, ten turns and then you're off into a boring runoff.

Down on the lower chairs, Moment of Truth off #2 is the best bump run at the Highlands and, when coupled with Lower Stein, which bumps on down to the base lodge, provides a good alternative for the expert who doesn't want to go all the way up top.

The newly opened Steeplechase area has sensational terrain, but access is a catastrophe. Off to the left of #4, Steeplechase has four or five faces which may be the best skiing in Aspen. Fairly long, steep (8.5–9.5), and relentlessly moguled, these are runs which the expert would be happy to ski all day. Unfortunately, the faces end in a nearly 2-mile-long cat track which goes all the way to the bottom of #3, thus requiring another two chairs to get back up. Intermediates who maintain that they can "get down anything" should think twice before attacking Steeplechase—not so much because of the runs, but because of the absolutely terrifying cat track, which is steep, about 2 feet wide, winding, and bumpy. If your control is not perfect here, you're likely to have a close encounter with a tree.

The Highlands has restaurants at the Base Lodge and at the base of #3. Free bus service between Aspen and the Highlands runs every 15 minutes during the morning and every half-hour for the rest of the day.

Buttermilk. This is a family area geared to novice and low-intermediate skiers. It is a good-size mountain, with seven lifts, an uphill capacity which nearly matches Ajax, and a 2,000-foot vertical. The lifts at the base and over at West Buttermilk service primarily novice runs. The more difficult runs are over at the #5 Tiehack lift. Much of this terrain is marked expert, but most intermediates will have no trouble here.

With its lower elevation and mild slopes, Buttermilk is a possible first-day acclimator for flatlanders not accustomed to high-altitude skiing.

Buttermilk is 3 miles from town, toward Snowmass. Free bus service between Aspen and Buttermilk runs every 15 minutes.

LIFE IN THE AREA

Aspen was once a quaint little mining town. No longer. It is not the place to go if you want to get away from it all; more likely, you'll need a vacation *afterwards*. It's where the action is, and where the singles are, but it's not everybody's cup of tea.

ACCESSIBILITY TO THE SLOPES

Most all the lodging in town is within walking distance of the lifts on Ajax, though the walk may extend to 10 or 15 minutes. A car is a convenience in Aspen, primarily for access to the other mountains, but it is by no means a necessity since frequent bus service is available at nearly all hours. There are, however, no parking lots around Ajax, and parking in town is a disaster. Coming from Snowmass, it's a good idea to ride the bus or add the price of a parking ticket to the day.

ACCOMMODATIONS

Accommodations are not what Aspen's elegant image would lead one to expect. In fact, lodge accommodations are very ordinary, and condominiums are not, on the average, as nice as those at resorts like Vail or Keystone. With well over 1,000 lodging facilities, however, it is no hardship to find a satisfactory place to stay. Booking early is crucial for the more desirable locations, which are gauged by facilities and proximity to the lifts; a year in advance is not too soon. Prices are high. Packages tend to book Saturday to Saturday, and lodging commencing midweek can be difficult to find—especially in the spring.

Of the standard motel-type lodges, the better ones are: **Molly Gibson Lodge,** on Main Street about 5 blocks from the lifts, with pool ($44–56); **Limelite Lodge,** a couple of blocks from lift #1A, with two pools, Jacuzzi, and large lounge ($34–52); **Fireside Lodge,** with pool and including full breakfast ($40–58); and **Gasthof Eberli,** intimate and less expensive, including full breakfast ($30–38).

At the base of the lifts is Aspen's largest lodge, the **Continental Inn,** with bar, restaurant, and indoor and outdoor pool ($36–56). Another large and fully equipped lodge, popular with ski clubs and groups, is the **Aspen Inn,** 2 blocks from the base of #1A ($36–56).

Our absolute favorite, and a marvelous way to economize, is the **Hotel Jerome** on Main Street, an old Western hotel and the only place in Aspen with real character. To be sure, the rooms are far from elegant, and the sounds of the bar and disco below tend to waft up until the wee hours. Nevertheless, the

Jerome is great fun. Rooms are spacious, and some have sitting rooms furnished in antiques from Aspen's mining days. At $22–42, the Jerome is a steal.

For those really on a tight budget, several lodges have dorm space. The **Little Red Ski Haus** is a restored Victorian which includes a full breakfast and has a homey lounge ($11.50 per person). The **Copper Horse** on Main Street is also a Victorian house. ($9–15 per person).

Many of the beds in Aspen are in condominium units. The nicest—and most expensive—condominiums are at the **Gant,** the **Aspen Alps,** and the **Clarendon** (all $100 and up), near the Little Nell lift and with complete facilities including pools and Jacuzzis. The best condominium value is at the **Aspen Square;** while not as luxurious as those above, unlike the Gant and the Alps they have several studio ($50–65) and 1-bedroom units ($65–84) available. Book far in advance for Aspen Square. Though not terribly distinguished, condominiums that can be skied to are **Fasching House** ($56–72) and **Fifth Avenue,** which has only 2- and 3-bedroom units available ($85–135).

Testing what the marketplace will bear, the **Aspen Club** condominiums, a mile up Independence Pass, are not well located, but they do have private saunas and you can rent the smaller units for a mere $275 per night.

RESTAURANTS

The dining possibilities in Aspen are extraordinary. The choice includes not one but several restaurants in each of the following categories: French, German, Italian, Swiss, American, Chinese, Austrian, Middle Eastern, Mexican, and Alaskan. And each night the famous **Copper Kettle** serves a dinner from a different country.

The Aspen restaurants are ambitious and expensive, and several are quite good. For skiers from many parts of the country, Aspen may offer culinary experiences unavailable at home. Visitors from San Francisco, New York, Montreal, and other cities with distinguished restaurants might stick to the basics in Aspen, since for the $25–30 per person check prevailing in Aspen's better restaurants they're likely to find better food at home.

There are several steak–and–salad bar restaurants. The best of these, though its menu extends to other areas, is **Galena Street East; the Chart House** and **Steak Pit** are also favorites, and **Jake's** offers a good no-frills steak at a low price. Traditionally Aspen's best restaurant (though it has just changed hands) the **Golden Horn** features Austrian cuisine; the venison is a must. In the Continental Inn, **Don Giovanni's** has northern Italian food, while in the Hotel Jerome, **Sayat Nova** has two sittings for Middle Eastern delicacies. In the Aspen Inn, the costly **Arya** alternates six international cuisines served in plush private dining rooms. Also plush, private, and expensive is the **Parlour Car,** a Victorian railroad car which has two sittings nightly for elegant cuisine. **Arthur's** is a nearly first-rate Szechwan restaurant, though its prices are too high and its portions too small. **Maurice's** is traditional French and reasonably good. The **Crystal Palace** requires reservations well in advance for dinner amid its Victorian memorabilia; dinner includes a nightly cabaret performed by waiters and waitresses. The **Golden Barrel, Captain's Anchorage,** and **Shannon's Galley** all specialize in seafood. Reservations must be made three months in advance for the Alaskan–organic food experience at **Toklat** in the valley at Ashcroft.

Not everyplace costs a fortune. **La Cocina** and **Toro's** are Mexican, moderate, and good. The **Shaft** serves ribs, fried chicken, and other Western specialities, and the line starts getting huge by 6 P.M. **Little Annie's** is the local hangout but has good, cheap burgers and the like. The **Mother Lode** offers moderately priced Italian food. The **Souper** has good soups, breads, and stews. Late at night, when everything else is closed, **Country Road** has burgers and inexpensive snacks.

Oddly enough, some of Aspen's best and most reasonably priced fare comes from its fast-food places. The crepes at **Poppycock** are unrivaled, and the fresh fruit smoothies are spectacular. The **Sub Shoppe** has good though expensive sandwiches made with homemade breads. **Pacos Tacos,** across from the Little Nell lift, is the place for a genuinely good fast-food enchilada or quesedilla. **Chip Chip Hooray** has the best cookies in the world.

For lunch, try **Ute City Bank;** located in a restored turn-of-the-century bank, it advertises Continental dining but lunch is better and much cheaper. For breakfast or brunch, the **Hotel Jerome** is delightful. Plant-filled **Andre's** is another favorite.

For reservations, call 303–925–4000.

APRÈS-SKI AND NIGHT LIFE

Aspen is a single's bar on skis. If you can't find your true love here, however ephemeral, you might as well stick to the local rope tow.

The fertility rites begin immediately after skiing, when *everybody* goes to **Little Nell's.** Bogner suits mingle with French jeans, and plans are hatched for the evening. In the hours between Little Nell's and dinner, lest anyone waste time, mating continues in pools and Jacuzzis.

At night, the town moves into high gear. There are five discos, countless bars, and much live entertainment. *The* disco in all of ski country is the **Paragon.** Its bar is made up of Victorian sitting rooms with red velvet couches and antique mirrors, and the disco itself is all hanging plants, wicker furniture, and stained glass. It is the focal point of Aspen night life and deserves to be, except for its arrogant policy of charging a door fee to obvious or suspected tourists while letting locals in free.

Rebecca's at the Aspen Inn has an ornate Victorian decor and is also very popular. The **Center** at Little Nell's has a disco as well. **Danny's,** another disco, has seen better days, and the **Rock N Horse** under the Jerome plays rock-and-roll instead of disco music to a mostly local following.

There are several nice places for a more sedate evening. The bar at the **Jerome** is an Aspen landmark, though it might get a little noisy at times. The **Tippler** at the Copper Kettle is an attractive, quiet bar frequented by an older crowd. The nicest place for a drink, though, has yet to be discovered: **Casey's,** the former home and studio of artist Tom Benton, has been turned into a beautifully decorated three-level bar; leather chairs and couches, fireplaces, sitting rooms and a natural wood environment combine to make Casey's the most tasteful structure in Aspen. For a rowdy time, Aspen's two quasi-cowboy bars are **Little Annie's** and the **Pub** (where a pickup with a dog in the back seems obligatory).

Live entertainment abounds. **Jake's, Andre's,** and the **Red Onion** usually have local Colorado bands. The **Cabaret** often books headliners, generally of the country-and-western persuasion, and **Hurry Sundown,** at the Holiday Inn near the airport, also books big-name talent.

Aspen is the birthplace of the T-shirt contest, and these are a frequent addition to scheduled entertainment.

DIVERSION

Aspen has all the standard diversions and then some. Cross-country skiing is available at various places but is unparalleled at Ashcroft. Snowshoeing is also available. Winter camping trips and ice fishing can be arranged through **Aspen Reservations, Inc. Colorado First Tracks** offers helicopter skiing ($119 for five runs of between 2,000 and 4,000 vertical feet). And only in Aspen could you arrange a 2-day dog sled trip. Those with energy left over for more athletics can play tennis at the **Aspen Racquet Club** near the airport and squash or racketball at the **Aspen Athletic Club** in town. Finally, shopping in Aspen is unsurpassed, with many boutiques and specialty shops.

CHILDREN

We have mixed feelings about the situation for children in Aspen. The town is overwhelming; there are waits for everything, including potentially long ones for dinner; and Ajax is not a good mountain for children unless their skiing is quite proficient. On the other hand, Aspen Highlands is a good family mountain, and Snowmass and Buttermilk are particularly family-oriented. For instruction, **Snow Puppies** at the Highlands does an extraordinary job with children two to six years old, and the program developed there by Kristin Lawrence and Bill Reynolds is one of the best in the nation. Buttermilk also has instruction for young children. There are several nursery and day-care facilities in town but none at the slopes on either Ajax or the Highlands.

COSTS

Along with Vail, Aspen is the most expensive ski resort in North America. Its cost-of-living index is second only to that of Anchorage, Alaska. At least in terms of activity, however, you get a lot for your money.

12

Crested Butte

Success has been a struggle for Crested Butte. While most of the Colorado resorts need worry only about whether the snow falls, Crested has had to survive a national political scandal, bitter divisiveness between the ski corporation and the town, severe problems of accessibility, *and* the drought of 1977. Yet, while many of its problems stubbornly persist, when we were there this last snow-filled spring the booked restaurants, half-hour lift lines, and no-vacancy signs seemed to indicate that Crested had overcome.

A substantial reason for Crested's resilience is the unspoiled charm of the town. Along with Telluride, Crested remains one of the few mining town–turned–ski areas that have managed to keep their heritage nearly intact. Crested's heritage extends from 1870, when Crested was the hub of Colorado's gold and silver mining, till the 1950's, when Crested's last working coal mine was closed. Delightfully, Crested still looks authentic, helped by the fact that most of the condominiums and other trappings of modernity are housed at the mountain 3 miles away.

The nagging threat to Crested's success remains the size of its mountain, which, while not insubstantial, is limiting. The expert skier will find enough to keep him amused for a day or two, but longer periods will be stifling. The intermediate, too, has less to choose from here than at most other "family" areas. The urgency to expand was the focus of national attention when Development Corporation head Howard "Bo" Callaway was forced to step down as President Ford's campaign manager as a result of his alleged improper pressuring of Forest Service officials to obtain approvals for development. The scandal has subsided, but plans for expansion remain cloudy.

ACCESSIBILITY

Accessibility to what is Colorado's most remote major area has been greatly improved in 1978, but Crested remains a stone's throw from nowhere. Crested is 230 miles from Denver and 160 miles from Grand Junction. Thus the most convenient access is by air to Gunnison, a jetport 28 miles south of town. Gunnison is presently served from Denver by Frontier and Aspen Airways, which is operating that route under temporary authority. Frontier also flies into Gunnison from Grand Junction. Crested Butte Air Service schedules two flights daily on small planes from Denver directly into the Crested Butte airfield. Crested Butte Stage Lines meets each scheduled flight for the ride up to the mountain, which takes 45 minutes and costs $3. For the skier who wants to drop over from Aspen for the day, the Air Service makes the 16-minute hop a couple of times daily.

Bus service and car rentals are available from both Denver and Grand Junction, and driving time is approximately 5 and 3½ hours, respectively.

THE SKIING

Crested's mountain statistics are relatively mild for Colorado: a vertical drop of 2,100 ft; 6 chair lifts; a T-bar; an uphill capacity of 7,300 skiers per hour; 350 acres of skiable terrain. Mild also fairly describes the preponderance of the skiing, which is nearly 80% novice and intermediate.

The beginner is well pampered at Crested. The Keystone chair, a long chair with a 951-foot vertical, opens up miles and miles of novice terrain, with Houston (not inappropriately named since the demography of Crested's skiers is heavily Southern and Southwestern) being the longest and most popular of the trails. Novices also ski the T-bar at the bottom of the mountain, which ought to be skied once by everyone because of the spectacular view from its summit of the entire valley.

Intermediates will likely spend most of their time on the north side of the mountain, skiing either the East River or Paradise chairs. Lamentably, initial access to these chairs is only from the top of the Silver Queen chair, the enclosed bubble chair that climbs the entire 2,100 vertical feet from the Base Lodge, so early-morning lift lines to the top of the mountain can be a problem.

Canaan and Ruby Chief are long intermediate trails that run the full length of the mile-long Paradise chair. Over on the East River chair, Black Eagle, Red Lady, and Treasury are wide, groomed, moderately pitched trails that are easy cruises for the laid-back recreational skier. From the top of the Paradise chair, traverse over to Paradise Bowl—a strictly intermediate wide-

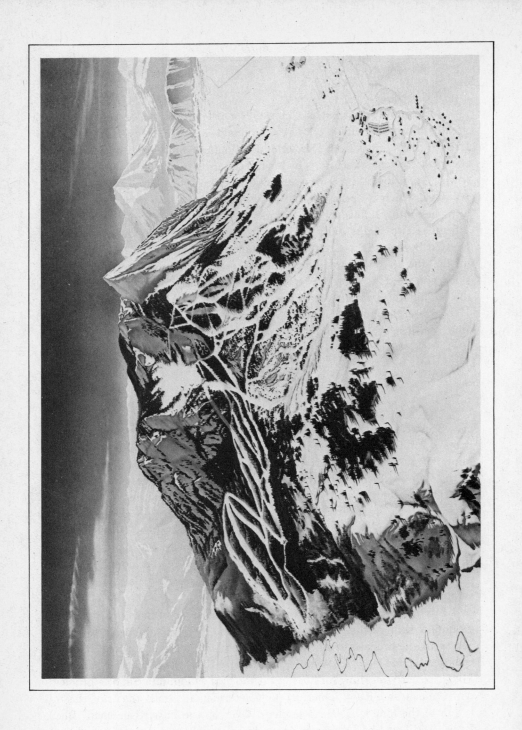

Crested Butte   COURTESY CRESTED BUTTE

open bowl that runs into the narrower tree-lined trails leading back down to Paradise or East River.

Crested's expert runs, at least those marked on the trail map, are likely to be slightly too tame for the really hot skier. The corollary to this, however, is that these runs provide an excellent testing ground where the advanced intermediate can work on mogul technique and get out of the flats without being terrorized. None of the marked expert trails efficiently served by the Twister chair are terribly steep and their bumps are generally manageable. Keystone, Jokerville, and Twister are all similar runs, moderately pitched at the top (7) and flattening out into runoffs toward the bottom of the chair. All have good bumps, which the maintenance crews generally leave alone. The two other marked expert trails are Resurrection, the liftline of the East River chair, which is a nice sustained bump run, and International, the liftline of the Silver Queen chair.

At Crested, experts need to seek out the unskied trails and the unmarked steeps. First is the seldom-skied North Face. From the top of the Paradise Chair, take the combination traverse, hike, and climb (10–20 minutes) northward across Paradise Bowl and on into the north face. Then pick your line. The face is long and steep (8.5)—and in the powder, when most people trek on over, steep and deep.

Even steeper is the terrain over in the Horseshoe area. From the top of the Paradise chair, start traversing to the right on the cat track, looking down to your right till you see a cliff (10) with lots of tight trees plunked fearfully close to the fall line. Then go for it. This unnamed face is genuinely an expert's expert run, as steep as any you'll find. If you're still feeling adventurous, try Banana Peel and Banana Slot, the very steep chutes that are unmarked and out of bounds but that can be hiked to by going southward from the Silver Queen chair.

The bottom line is that Crested needs to expand in order to come into its own as a major mountain. Intermediates need more trails and more diverse terrain; experts need lifts to service some excellent terrain that already exists.

LIFE IN THE AREA

The "area" really consists of the wonderful town of Crested Butte, 3 miles from the base of the mountain, and Mt. Crested Butte, the newly incorporated village at the mountain itself. Unfortunately, the ability of these two self-contained communities to coexist is uncertain. The fact that 80–90% of the area's accommodations are now at the mountain, combined with the fact that transportation between the two areas is erratic, has resulted in a substantial erosion of the town's economy.

ACCESSIBILITY TO THE SLOPES

Virtually all the accommodations on the mountain are within skiing or short walking distance of the lifts. For those with cars who wish to stay in town, parking on the mountain is adequate. Buses run between the mountain and the town every half-hour 8–10 A.M. and 3–11 P.M. and hourly from 10 A.M. to 3 P.M. ($.25). Skiers accustomed to late nights of socializing should take note of this schedule so as to avoid a 3-mile jog back to the mountain.

ACCOMMODATIONS

Accommodations are primarily on the mountain and most are condominiums. Some, particularly the larger condominium units, are excellent values.

The nicest units are at the **Snowcrest,** within walking distance of the lifts and with 37 2-bedroom, 2-bath apartments, some of which have lofts. All units have kitchens with dishwashers and fireplaces. Guests also have free access to the Crested Butte Health Club's whirlpools, saunas, and massage and exercise rooms. Regular-season rates range from $65 for double occupancy to only $75 when occupied by 6 people. All rates at Crested rise about 20% during the Christmas period.

Also nice are the **Village Center** condominiums, owned and managed by the Ski Corp. Units are 1- to 3-bedroom and range from $47 to $105; guests also have access to the health club.

The **Chateaux Condominiums** (2- to 4-bedroom, $67–105) have a recreation building with saunas, pool, bar, kitchen, and meeting rooms. You can ski to the lifts and home again from the **Columbine** (1- to 3-bedroom, $50–95).

If you choose to stay in a lodge, the best at the mountain is the **Ski Crest,** with 58 rooms, a heated pool, sauna, game room, and restaurant and bar ($30).

Accommodations in town are mostly lodges. The **Ore Bucket Lodge** caters to families and has a cozy lobby with a big fireplace ($50). The **Crested Butte Motor Inn** is just that—a perfectly adequate standard motel ($32).

There are a couple of quaint places to stay in town. The **Elk Mt. Lodge** used to be a rooming house for miners; accommodations here range from dorms to kitchenette units, and prices are the most reasonable in town. The **Forest Queen Hotel** is one of the original buildings in Crested, dating back to 1880; the atmosphere is rustic, and accommodations range from bunks to rooms with private baths.

RESTAURANTS

Given the size of the town, there are some unusually pleasant and attractive restaurants in Crested, the best of which are in town rather than at the mountain. Consistently acclaimed as superior to the rest is **Soupçon,** a tiny room seating no more than 25–30 people and featuring some interestingly prepared gourmet items (duck) and especially fresh seafood (salmon Florentine). Prices are surprisingly moderate. Beware: you should book *at least* a week in advance.

Beautifully decorated and set in a greenhouse environment is **Penelope's,** also with a gourmet menu including a good beef Wellington; on weekends, excellent breakfasts are featured.

French, and highly rated, is **La Bosquet.**

For a wide variety of steaks in an elegant Victorian setting, try **Slogar's.** **Sancho's** is a good Mexican restaurant in a terrific building right out of Viva Villa; the real action, though, is at the bar, where owner Peter Spelke makes the single best Margarita in the Rockies.

For less elegant fare, the **Wooden Nickel** has good cheap burgers and salads; **Chili's** has what you'd expect; and **Lawrence of Oregano** is the local pizza purveyor.

Up on the mountain, the **Artichoke** is an attractively decorated steak-and-salad place. Austrian specialities are available at the **Alpenhof,** and those wanting to stay at the mountain can also dine at the **Crested Butte Lodge** or the **Red Lady.**

APRÈS-SKI AND NIGHT LIFE

After-ski activity centers around what it should in an old Western mining town: drinkin'. So put away your Aspen disco duds.

After the lifts close, those who stay up on the mountain go over to the **Red Lady,** a cavernous unattractive bar above the Base Lodge that has live music (usually country-and-western) and dancing. More serenity, but no music, can be found over at the **Artichoke.** Locals will eschew the mountain and head down to **Sancho's,** the **Wooden Nickel,** or the **Grubstake.**

At night, the scene is about the same. The **Alpenhof** on the mountain has a disco; the Red Lady continues; the **Ski Crest** has occasional music and is otherwise a quiet place to go for a late drink. In town, **CBS** is the only disco, and a tacky little number it is.

A great place for the adventurous in town any time up to 4 A.M. is the **Sunshine Paradise Bathhouse.** It has saunas, Jacuzzis, and ice plunges, and is a very mellow place—often chemically induced. Don't go if you're modest; do go if you're loaded.

DIVERSIONS

Crested has lots to do. Cross-country skiing is excellent, with many maintained trails in close proximity to the lifts and over 100 miles of nonmaintained trails in beautiful parts of the valley. Outdoor ice skating is over near the lifts and rentals are available.

For powder hounds, **Colorado First Tracks** will take you by helicopter to anywhere in the valley. This costs an expensive $119 per day per person.

Nighttime sleigh rides pulled by snow-cat (a one-horse open snow-cat?) up to the Twister warming hut are available, with a hot catered dinner of barbecue ribs served by candlelight on the mountain.

The **Crested Butte Health Club** is open to the public at nominal charges depending on the activity.

CHILDREN

A nursery is available at the mountain for toilet-trained children ages three to seven. The cost, which includes lunch, is $10 for the first child and $7 for each sibling. For skiing children three to five the **Little People Ski School** includes all-day instruction in its nursery program. The total cost (with lunch) is $18.

In town is **The Place,** an amusement center for older children with TV, pool, football, and teen dances on weekends. The hours are 9 A.M. to 10 P.M. and midnight on weekends.

COSTS

Prices at Crested are equivalent to most of the other Colorado resorts excluding Aspen and Vail, which are in an expense category of their own.

13
Purgatory

Purgatory, by the standards of this book, is a small ski center with a limited vertical drop, limited terrain, and limited accommodations at the mountain. The area is predominantly a day ski center for people from Durango, 25 miles away, though it does attract vacationing skiers from New Mexico and Arizona, and does have unpretentious condominiums at the mountain. The resort has no night life of its own. Entertainment is found in the wide-open Western town of Durango, which is lively, freewheeling, and informal.

ACCESSIBILITY

The area is 40 minutes north of the Durango airport, which has direct flights from Denver or Albuquerque. If you're staying at Purgatory or at Tamarron, 8 miles south, you should arrange with the resort to be met at the airport.

For those wishing to drive, Purgatory is 5 hours northwest of Albuquerque, New Mexico, and 9 hours from Phoenix, Arizona.

THE SKIING

Purgatory is predominantly an intermediate-novice mountain, combining mostly mellow skiing with pleasant, warm weather and reliable snow conditions. The Spud Mountain lift, the major lift on the mountain, has a 1,500-foot vertical over 6,200 feet long. The terrain on the top half of this lift is open and gentle. The bottom half is like a rollercoaster, with short (100–400′), steep, moguled drops (short 8's) followed by flat transition areas. Three trails in the bottom half of this lift area—Hades, Pandemonium, and Catharsis—all have short bump drops. On none of them is there a continuing expert challenge. The balance of the mountain is an expansive novice and intermediate area, serviced by three chair lifts spread out across the mountain. All three have similar length/vertical ratios of about 5 to 1. One, the Grizzly Peak chair, is located well away from the other chairs and has several long, gentle intermediate runs. Two of the trails marked expert—Snag and Dead-Spike—are in fact long, challenging intermediate trails. The middle of the mountain between the Spud and Grizzly chairs, served by the two other chairs, has novice slopes. The runs down from the top of the Spud chair, all the way to the bottom of Grizzly, are entertaining for novices. There are lots of turnoffs, crossovers, and route choices. Novices and intermediates can also stay up top and ski the Engineer Mountain chair. The easygoing skier should feel at home at Purgatory.

Purgatory can have lift lines on weekends, though except on rare occasions these should not be more than 15 minutes long. There are no lines during the week. For the size of the mountain, the lifts are long and travel between them is easy.

LIFE IN THE AREA

There is really very little to do at Purgatory after the lifts close. For entertainment and good restaurants, you must travel to Durango or to Tamarron. The ski area does have two day lodges, some condominiums, a lodge, and a restaurant, but these facilities provide only the mere basics.

ACCOMMODATIONS

At the mountain are several adequate, clean, pleasant-looking but not elegant condominiums. They all offer kitchens and fireplaces, but only the **Angel Haus** has television in the room and a sauna. (1-bedroom for 4 persons, 7 nights, 6 days, with lifts: $124 per person). The **Brimstone** and **East Rim** are quite simple. The East Rim has only studio condominiums (2 persons, 7 nights, 6 days, with lifts: $189 per person). The Brimstone has large 2-bedroom units. Also at Purgatory, a few hundred feet from the lifts, is the **Lodge,** a simple hotel that runs the only bar and restaurant at Purgatory ($27.50 per room; children under 12 free).

Eight miles south of Purgatory is the impressive resort of Tamarron. Built on 600 acres in the middle of nowhere, Tamarron is an imposing hotel-condominium complex with game rooms for all ages, a huge indoor-outdoor swimming pool, sauna, Jacuzzi, several bars and restaurants, 4 indoor tennis courts, horses, and golf. Many of the public rooms at Tamarron are elegant; others are less tasteful. Shuttle service is provided every 30 minutes to Purgatory. Rates start at $56 per room.

Durango has innumerable hotels and motels. In town is the old, elegant

Victorian **Strater Hotel,** with lounge, restaurant, and entertainment. North of town is the **Ramada Inn,** offering an indoor pool, shops, entertainment, and shuttle service to Purgatory (7 nights, 6 days, double occupancy with lift tickets: $145 per person). There is general bus service from Durango to Purgatory, and the Durango hotels and motels offer a lift ticket–room package.

Reservations can be made at Purgatory or Durango through a toll-free number, 800-525-5427.

RESTAURANTS

Up at the mountain, there's really not much to choose from. The **Elk Restaurant** at the Lodge serves a good standard American meal. The **Columbine,** about a mile south of the mountain, has acceptable food if you can tolerate the restaurant's deteriorated appearance. Tamarron has unexceptional food. In Durango, there are several good steak and fish places, but we would recommend three: **Sweeney's,** near the Ramada, which is perhaps the best; the **Ore House,** and the **Palace.**

APRÈS-SKI AND NIGHT LIFE

Since Purgatory is primarily a day resort, the mountain stops when the lifts close. For entertainment, most people rely on Durango. Depending on the schedule for the week, there's rock or country-and-western music in town at the **Cellar** or **Francisco's.** Durango can be lively, but it may take a little searching to find the right spot.

DIVERSION

The major activity center is Tamarron, where you can enjoy cross-country skiing, tennis, swimming, platform tennis, and, in the spring, horseback riding. At the mountain, there's cross-country skiing but little other activity.

CHILDREN

Purgatory has a nursery on the slopes ($1.25 per hour) for children six months to eight years old. For children three to five, the ski school has introductory lessons. There are no special activities for children after skiing at Purgatory. None of the condominiums or the Lodge at the mountain has a game room or pool. The mountain, however, is a good one for kids to learn on, as there are many easy slopes and the tough slopes are short.

COSTS

Purgatory is relatively inexpensive. Lift tickets are $10 per day; ski lessons are $7. Tamarron offers 6-day, 7-night packages, without meals, that range from $100 per person double occupancy to $190. There are very inexpensive accommodations in Durango.

14

Snowmass

For the intermediate skier, Snowmass is Camelot. Trail after trail of mild slopes, some up to 3½ miles long, descend 3,500 vertical feet from the 11,750-foot summit. Incipient moguls are mowed down ruthlessly in nightly search-and-destroy missions, with the result that virtually all of the mountain's 1,400 acres of trails are immaculately groomed.

Aspen is 10 miles away, but if you wish it can be 1,000. Unlike the Highlands, Snowmass is not an adjunct of Aspen but rather a wholly separate and independent resort with a full range of facilities and activities. Distinctly absent is the frenetic quality of Aspen, and the resort, long termed "Slowmass" by its detractors, appeals to families and older skiers as opposed to singles. For those wishing to mix their experiences, Sodom is only a 20-minute drive away.

ACCESSIBILITY

Directions and routings are the same as for Aspen (pp. 65–66). Bus or cab service is constantly available at the Aspen airport for the 10-minute ride up the hill to Snowmass. In addition, some lodges and condominiums provide pickup service.

THE SKIING

Buttermilk is better for novices. Ajax and the Highlands are better for experts. But nowhere is better for the recreational intermediate. Of its 11 chair lifts (Snowmass has an impressive uphill capacity of 12,550 skiers per hour), 8 give access to nearly exclusively intermediate terrain.

Snowmass is divided into five areas: Alpine Springs (Chair #9); Elk

Camp, one of the two summit peaks (#10); Big Burn, the other peak (#4); Sam's Knob (#3); and the neighboring Campground, the major area for advanced skiing (#5).

The mountain is adequate though not ideal for the novice, who is relegated to the bottom half of the mountain and misses the opportunity available at Buttermilk and Highlands to ski top to bottom. From the top of Sam's Knob, though, the combination of Sunnyside, Lunchline and Dawdler is a long, uninterrupted series of trails easily negotiated by the beginner. More novice terrain is found off Chair #7 as well as #1 and #6, the two beginner chairs at the base of the mountain. Other novice terrain is limited; taken together, beginner's runs account for less than 15% of the terrain at Snowmass.

At Elk Camp, Chair #10 climbs 1,500 feet to five or six classic, groomed intermediate runs like Grey Wolf and Sandy Park, which are well over a mile long. Adjacent, at Alpine Springs, are over 200 acres of intermediate trails, slightly narrower than Elk Camp but still long and ideal for a carefree cruise. Nonetheless, these areas are foreplay. The main event for intermediates at Snowmass is the Big Burn—the biggest, widest, most talked-about intermediate run anywhere. The Burn (also known as the Big Liftline) is 1½ miles long, has a vertical drop of nearly 2,000 feet, and is an unbelievable half-mile wide. It is the cruise of all cruises. Dallas Freeway is the main way down, but that tells you more about the demographics of Snowmass than anything else. All the routes down are the same—wide-open ego boosters that make the most ordinary skier feel ready for the World Cup. An added plus is the spectacular view from the top of the Burn into and beyond the valley below. On powder days, even the experts will brave the formidable lift lines on the Burn for the first-rate tree skiing on the edges of the trails.

All this perfect intermediate terrain at Snowmass brings into focus the potential major fault of the area: it can be boring. With the exception of the Burn, which is unique, all the intermediate trails off all the lifts are substantially identical, and, while we suspect the concensus would be against us, we can't help but feel that this lack of diversity in intermediate terrain and pitch is a real deficiency.

Snowmass is not favored by the experts except on powder days, when they head for the Burn and the Campground lift. The vast amount of terrain at Snowmass guarantees that the powder will stay around longer than on steeper Ajax, where the powder hounds line up at dawn knowing the mountain will be skied out by midafternoon.

The bulk of the advanced runs are at Campground. A long (16-minute) chair with a 1,400-foot vertical opens up six advanced runs which are generally left ungroomed. The best of these is Powderhorn, the major bump run at Snowmass. A moderate top section has some mild bumps that grow as you descend to two steepish faces (8) toward the bottom, where the bumps have been allowed to build to a few feet. The run is a good one for the expert to practice on, but it certainly does not offer the challenge of the Steeplechase at the Highlands or the Ridge of Bell at Ajax. The other runs off the Campground lift are similar to each other in having moderate bumps and only moderate pitch (7.5) till they end with a steeper face at the bottom. In general, they are no harder than Ruthie's at Ajax, and the solid intermediate who is comfortable with minor bumps should have no problem.

Other advanced terrain is found off the Couloir chair (#9), which is the alternate route to the Burn. Runs like Glissade, Garret Gulch, and Free Fall are nice runs, not terribly difficult, occasionally groomed, and reminiscent of Northstar at Ajax. Also, the confident intermediate should be undeterred by the terrain marked expert at Sam's Knob (#3), where Fast Draw and Promenade are never very steep (7) and have only occasional bumps.

A cause for some rejoicing among experts is the new lift promised for the 1978-79 season. The lift will extend a mile above the Alpine chair and will open up new terrain almost equivalent in area to the whole of Ajax. Of this terrain 25% will be above the tree line for bowl skiing, and of the 10 projected runs, 8 are designated expert.

There are four restaurants on the mountain: the Rack, a short-order restaurant between Chairs #7 and #10; Sam's Knob at the top of #2; Uhrl Hof at the bottom of Big Burn; and High Alpine at the top of #8. For more diversity, it's easy to ski down and lunch in the Mall.

LIFE IN THE AREA

With its population concentrated in a relatively small area, Snowmass is busy though quiet. The focal point of the village and the center of activity is the Mall, with a wide variety of shops, bars, and restaurants. Lodging is primarily in condominium units near the Mall and a short distance down the valley. Designed in 1967, the village is largely functional and aesthetically falls about midway between the grace of Keystone and the confusion of Vail.

With the exception of two glaring deficiencies, Snowmass exists independently from Aspen. It has no supermarket or drugstore, however, so condominium dwellers must travel to Aspen every time they need to shop. There are plans to build these facilities in Snowmass itself, and hopefully they'll be ready for the 1978-79 season.

ACCESSIBILITY TO THE SLOPES

Convenience is one of the area's selling points. From most condominium units, you can ski directly either to the lifts right at the Mall or to #6 slightly beyond. Virtually all other units are only a short walk to the lifts. A car is unnecessary, though if you plan to partake of Aspen night life, be advised that the last bus leaves Aspen for Snowmass at about midnight. Taxis are available all night at moderate cost for the ride back. Skiers with cars can avoid morning lift lines by parking in the Campground lot and riding #5 up.

ACCOMMODATIONS

Virtually all accommodations at Snowmass are well located, and the variation at competing lodges and condominiums as to both accouterments and price is minimal. All units either have pools on the premises or have access to nearby pools.

One of the more attractive lodges is the **Stonebridge Inn,** which houses a bar and restaurant with nightly entertainment as well as pool and sauna ($46–64). The largest lodge at Snowmass is the **Wildwood Inn** ($38–50) located just above the Mall; the Inn offers modern hotel accommodations with pool, sauna, and the well-thought-of **Wineskin** restaurant. Similar to the Wildwood are the **El Dorado** and the **Silver Tree** lodges, both modern with restaurant, pool, and sauna on the premises ($40–48). Slightly less expensive are the **Inns at Snowmass** and the European-style **Mountain Chalet,** which serves a family dinner to guests on Sunday nights.

Among the nicer condominiums is the **Stonebridge,** where studios rent from $50 to $70, 1-bedroom units from $70 to $90, and 2-bedroom units from $80 to $125; units with up to 4 bedrooms are available. The **Top of the Village** condominiums are somewhat of a walk to the Mall but are elegantly furnished with beautiful views of the mountain; the units are 2- to 4-bedroom, and prices are about the same as at Stonebridge. You can ski to your door at the **Interlude,** a nice condominium that has 1-bedroom units with dens as well as 2- and 3-bedroom units; prices are comparable to those discussed above. The largest complex (studio, 2- and 3-bedroom units available) is the well-located **Crestwood,** which has a staff of 80 plus 24-hour service. Located down by Chair #6 are the **Seasons Four** and the **Snowmass Mt. Condos;** both have free shuttle service to the Mall.

For reservations, call 303–925–4000.

RESTAURANTS

Parked at the door of Aspen, the restaurant capital of the ski world, Snowmass can nevertheless compete in variety of attractive restaurants. No longer is it necessary to make the trek into Aspen for a good meal, though the best eating remains there.

The top restaurant at Snowmass is the **Peppermill,** cozy and French with a menu offering Provençal casseroles and other traditional dishes as well as an assortment of steaks. Also favored is the **Wineskin,** which serves an ambitious beef Wellington and a veal Cordon Bleu. While these Continental restaurants are by no means cheap, they're more moderate than their opulent Aspen neighbors. For steak and seafood, the **Refectory** offers a good surf-and-turf menu and is mobbed nightly. The **Tower's** emphasis is also on steak and prime ribs, and its bartenders perform nightly magic shows that have become wildly popular. **Hussong's Cantina** despite its name, specializes in seafood, with dishes foreign to the Easterner like abalone and mahi-mahi. **La Pinata** serves quite good Mexican food in a pleasant setting at the Inns at Snowmass.

The proximity of the Mall to the lifts means that Snowmass restaurants do a healthy lunch business. For burgers cooked outdoors, or soup, chili, or bratwurst, try **Casa Che** in the El Dorado Inn. Another favorite for lunch is the **Stew Pot,** with its homemade soups, stews, sandwiches, and salads. The **Village Deli** has hot and cold sandwiches, soups, and chili.

APRÈS-SKI AND NIGHT LIFE

The goings-on at Snowmass are substantially quieter than in Aspen, where every night bristles with Saturday night fever. In fact, a conscious and commendable effort has been made by local proprietors not to allow Snowmass to become disco heaven. At Snowmass, live entertainment is more popular.

When the lifts close, most skiers head right to the **Timber Mill** for drinks and live entertainment in an atmosphere that combines saloon and cafeteria. If you're not up to romping and stomping that early in the day, try the **Tower** or the **Refectory** for quiet predinner socializing.

At night, entertainment is about evenly divided between dancing to local rock or country groups and listening to a quiet guitar or piano. **Husong's** presents both local and imported rockers, and the **Wineskin** gets down with country-and-western. **Casa Che** also brings in groups to entertain. The **Peppermill** is the most popular place for a quiet nightcap. There is no disco.

DIVERSION

Aspen is the champion in this category (p. 74), but Snowmass has a range of activities available right at the village. Free ice skating is available from 8 A.M. to 8 P.M. right below the Mall. There is indoor tennis just down the hill at the **Snowmass Country Club.** Call **Snowmass Recreation** to arrange for paddle tennis, cross-country skiing and overnight tours, and a nighttime sleigh ride with dinner and entertainment.

The Anderson Ranch, a fine arts center only a 10-minute walk from the village, offers beginning, intermediate and advanced work in ceramics and wood.

CHILDREN

Snowmass is a fine place for kids. Its size is manageable, and since no cars are allowed in the Mall area, young children can be left to wander. If the children are slightly better than novice skiers, the mountain is planned so that families can ski nearly the whole mountain together.

Kinderheim, the nursery at Snowmass, is known for the high quality of its program. It offers ski instruction and outdoor-oriented day care for children three to six years old at a cost of $15 per day. Advance reservations are required.

COSTS

The brochure says that at Snowmass one pays for quality. Freely translated, that means everything at Snowmass is expensive as hell. Best to resign oneself to the fact that Snowmass is a luxury resort where the price of lodging is particularly high. Given the generally stratospheric prices in Aspen, the advice we're about to give seems hardly credible. But, if you want to ski Snowmass and still operate on some sort of a budget, we advise you to stay in Aspen at one of the economy lodges.

15

Steamboat Springs

Imagine a family dinner where Aspen is the pretty daughter home from finishing school; Sun Valley, her regal parents; and Telluride, the talented but very quiet brother. Steamboat would join the group as the second cousin from out of town, whom everybody likes but no one pays much attention to.

Steamboat is not often mentioned in the same breath with the "biggies." Statistically, this is hard to understand. Steamboat has over 600 acres of skiable terrain on a mountain with a 3600-foot vertical drop (the second longest in Colorado). Fifty-three trails and 15 lifts allow for substantial diversity. There are a number of attractive places to stay and a series of more than adequate restaurants both at the mountain and in town. In fact, everything at Steamboat is pretty good. It is a mountain whose report card is littered with Bs and B-pluses. It is not a mountain of superlatives. In the off-season, when your friends are discussing their fabulous meal in Aspen, their spectacular day in the back bowls at Vail, or their terrifying attempt at Corbet's, you may feel slightly defensive about talking about the "nice time" you had at Steamboat—yet that would indeed characterize your experience. We should point out, however, that Steamboat is wildly popular in certain regions of the country, most notably Texas and the Southwest (Steamboat is owned by LTV, the Dallas conglomerate).

ACCESSIBILITY

Steamboat is slightly off the beaten track, 157 miles northwest of Denver. Rocky Mountain Airways offers commuter service from Denver to Steamboat airport 6 miles from the lift. For those coming from the west, Frontier Airlines has flights from Grand Junction into the Yampa Valley airport, 23 miles from the lifts. Frontier also flies into Yampa Valley from Denver. Continental

Trailways has express bus service daily to Steamboat, from both the Denver airport and the Denver bus terminal. The cost is $11.83, and a shuttle bus is available in Steamboat to take Continental passengers to their respective lodges.

By car, the drive is approximately 3½ hours from Denver and 4 hours from Grand Junction. Budget and Dollar rent-a-cars can be dropped in Steamboat.

THE SKIING

There's plenty of good skiing at Steamboat, particularly for the intermediate, but again, there's not much of the exciting skiing that characterizes the really great mountains of the West.

Before describing all that's good about Steamboat skiing, we should point out its three primary deficiencies, two of which are fairly minor. First, while there are indisputably some good advanced runs, nothing at Steamboat really challenges the true expert. The mountain is basically for intermediates. This fact appears to be a function of policy rather than geography, for Steamboat, as a concession to either its clientele or its insurance company, has established a "mowing cycle" wherein all trails are groomed each 13 days. Accordingly, the bumps that would convert some of Steamboat's good advanced trails into real toughies are never allowed to build up. While this is probably not the proper forum for our crusade to leave some terrain on each mountain permanently ungroomed, we would think that Steamboat is certainly an expansive enough mountain to do so.

The second problem is that Steamboat unfortunately does not make use of its 3,600-foot vertical. Most all the skiing on the mountain is "lift skiing," wherein the skier is limited to the vertical of the various chairs. And while the chairs have very respectable verticals (the Priest Creek chair has nearly 2,000 feet), it's impossible to ski the mountain top to bottom without being interrupted by several catwalks, runoffs, and traverses.

The third problem is more serious. A substantial portion of the mountain faces south, which is decidedly the least desirable direction for mountains to face. As a result, snow conditions at Steamboat tend to be less good than most places in Colorado. Ice is somewhat more plentiful in the winter, while slush and hardpack come earlier in the spring. There is no comparison between conditions at Steamboat and Eastern conditions, however; we just mean to point out that the snow at Steamboat is less perfect than in most of the Rockies.

Enough negatives. Steamboat lovers read on. The skiing at Steamboat (the mountain is really called Mt. Werner, named after Steamboat resident and

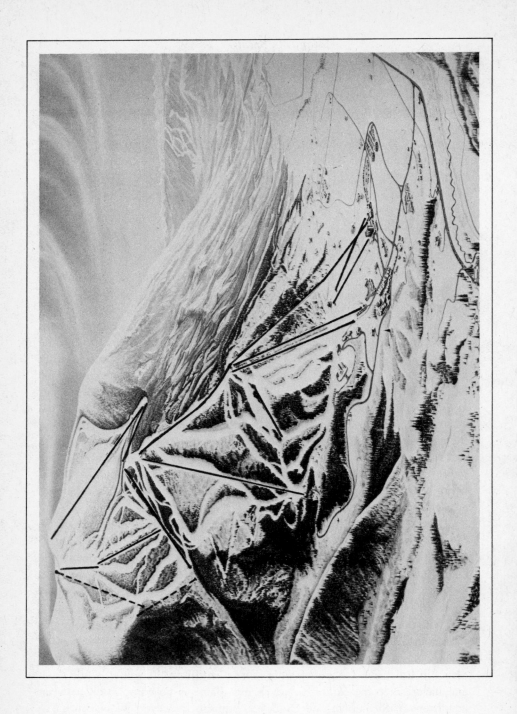

Steamboat   COURTESY OF STEAMBOAT SKI AREA

Olympic skier Buddy Werner, who died in a European avalanche) takes place in four separate and distinct areas: the terrain from the top of the Gondola to the base, Thunderhead Peak, Storm Peak, and Sunshine Peak. And, despite the fact that these areas really are separate parts of the mountain, lift accessibility from one to the other is excellent.

In the morning, virtually everybody takes the gondola, which rises 2,200 feet to Thunderhead Peak—the hub of activity on the mountain and the gateway to the other areas and chairs. Most skiers will then go up top, but there are several good runs right off the gondola. Heavenly Daze, the gondola liftline, is a wide-open intermediate cruise and one of the most popular runs on the mountain. Experts can take the steep and sometimes bumpy (depending what day of the cycle you hit) Vertigo back down to the gondola or, to avoid lift lines, back to the base of the Thunderhead chair, which takes you right back up to the top of the gondola. From the Thunderhead chair, the expert can ski Concentration or Oops, two short runs but steeper than most on the mountain (8.25). The intermediate can wind down to the base of the Thunderhead chair on Vagabond, another intermediate favorite. The novice, too, can ski the Thunderhead chair by going down Why Not, which winds around forever in and out of the trees before ending up at the base of the chair. The other major alternative for the beginner is to avoid the gondola and stay below, utilizing the Christie I and II chairs. Several of the runs off these chairs, like Bashor and Yoo Hoo, are quite good for beginners, but since they constitute the main thoroughfare home at the end of the day, beginners should accustom themselves to be used as human slalom gates for the speedy and reckless.

The rest of the mountain opens up from Thunderhead Peak. Going off to the left, two different sets of chairs take the skier to Storm Peak at the 10,500-foot summit of Mt. Werner. Storm Peak has a truly excellent concentration of intermediate runs. Off to the left is Big Meadows, a tree-studded challenge to the intermediate. Adjacent to that run is Buddy's Run, the most popular intermediate run on the mountain, long, wide open, and great fun. The advanced intermediate seeking to practice his bump skiing will definitely want to take the Summit poma and ski Storm Peak—an excellent wide-open, bowl-like, mini-bump run. For experts over on the Storm Peak side of the mountain, there are several decent runs served by the highly efficient Four Points chair (2.8:1). Off Four Points, Tornado is a good, moderately pitched bump run (7.25), long and consistent. Hurricane is steeper than Tornado though not as long, while Twister is longer than Tornado but not quite as steep. All these runs have one characteristic in common that is probably Steamboat's best quality—consistency. Steamboat's runs tend not to have long, flat stretches or runoffs but rather to go at a consistent pitch from top to bottom. This is particularly true over at the Sunshine Peak area. Our two favorite runs are on Sunshine Peak, served by the Priest Creek chair. High Noon is a magnificent intermediate run. Continuing for 2½ miles along the upper ridge of Sunshine Peak, High Noon has a spectacular view of the surrounding mountains and Yampa Valley below. The run is really a must for skiers of all levels. Also off Priest Creek is Shadows, one of our favorite runs in the West. Shadows is a moderately pitched (7.5) expert trail, very long and dropping magnificently down the 1,930-foot vertical of the Priest Creek chair through grove after grove of lovely Aspen trees. From the time you take your first turn till the time you get back into the lift line, the skiing on Shadows is continuous with never a letup. At times, the trees spread out so that you're almost in a bowl, closing so quickly at the next stop that you can use the Aspens for gates. Down through the bumps and into glade after glade, Shadows is one of the best runs we've encountered for consistent, unrelenting skiing. For more, if slightly less intense, tree skiing, stay to the right of the Priest Creek chair and ski Twilight, another pretty trip through the aspens. Finally, for the hard-core bump skier, there's the Burgess Creek liftline.

LIFE IN THE AREA

Life at Steamboat is physically split between the mountain and the town of Steamboat Springs 3 miles away. Over the years, Steamboat, like areas such as Crested Butte, has developed an independent, wholly self-contained village at the mountain. Steamboat Springs continues to exist as a typical Main Street Western town. Some of the nightspots and a few of the good restaurants have remained in town; however, since most of the accommodations in town are standard motel, Steamboat Springs is unable to compete with the facilities at the mountain and has become something of a dowdy annex to Mt. Werner. The corollary, though, is good for the skier. The nicely designed village has everything anyone would need and is very conveniently laid out.

ACCESSIBILITY TO THE SLOPES

Most of the lodges and condominiums at the mountain are within walking distance of the lifts. For those who stay in town, transportation is provided by a free bus service running every 30 minutes from the west end of town directly to the gondola.

ACCOMMODATIONS

Most of the accommodations at the mountain are condominiums. The **West** and the **Rockies,** both owned and managed by LTV, are two favored units, occupancy in either of which entitles the guest to use all facilities at the

Steamboat Village Inn, including pool and sauna ($60). **Storm Meadows** is the largest complex, having over 300 units. The stay at Storm Meadows includes membership at the Storm Meadows Athletic Club, which has a pool, sauna, Jacuzzi, exercise room, and racketball courts ($60–90). Ten other condominium complexes are situated at the mountain. Most of these are a very short walk to the lifts, and there are some from which you can ski directly.

For those preferring lodge accommodations at the mountain, the **Thunderhead Inn** is the luxury hotel; the Inn, from which you can ski to the lifts, has several restaurants, an attractive lounge, sauna, and heated pool ($45). Very nice too is the **Steamboat Village Inn,** which also has restaurants, lounges, shops, a pool, and sauna ($50). A charming and less frenetic lodge located right at the base of the mountain and one that has a devoted clientele is the **Ptarmigan,** which has a large, lovely living room with a big fireplace and wonderful view, as well as a pool and sauna ($45).

For one willing to forgo the convenience of being right at the mountain and having more luxuriously appointed rooms, a lot of money can be saved by staying in town. The perfectly adequate **Ramada Inn** and **Holiday Inn,** both of which have sauna and pool along with free transportation to the mountain, average $10–15 a night less than the lodges at the mountain. The **Nordic House,** which also has sauna and pool, is even less expensive.

For reservations, call 303–879–0740.

RESTAURANTS

Steamboat has a good variety of restaurants as to both type of cuisine and price. Everyone's favorite is the lovely **Brandywine,** located in town; antique brass bedstands serve as seating in this elegant, Victorian restaurant that creates gourmet preparations with an emphasis on beef and seafood. The **Stubbel Goos Castle** is at the mountain and specializes in English food, particularly wild game and seafood; bowls of complimentary fresh shrimp are served to guests in a quiet and quaint atmosphere. The food here usually gets high marks but the service has been known to be seriously deficient. The **Butcher Shop,** at the mountain, is the favorite steak-and-salad joint, while nearby **Dos Amigos** is a better-than-average Mexican restaurant. **Cantina,** the Mexican restaurant in town, is a local favorite. For rustic, Western atmosphere, try the **Pine Grove Ranch,** where barbecued ribs and prime ribs are the specialties. The Pine Grove is located in a renovated barn with decor featuring antique farm implements complete with a potbellied stove. For even more variety, try Swedish specialties at the **Scandinavian Lodge** or Chinese food at the **Cove.** The two main lodges at the mountain have their own restaurants. The **Robber's Roost** is at the Steamboat Village Inn and has a varied menu in an attractive setting. Dining is also available at the **Thunderhead Inn.** Brandywine's main competition for potential gourmet status is the **Gallery** at the

Storm Meadows Athletic Club, high on a hill overlooking the village and Yampa Valley. A favorite place for breakfast is the **Cameo** in town.

APRÈS-SKI AND NIGHT LIFE

Steamboat is full of life. After skiing, the crowds gather near the gondola at the **Afterglo Pub,** which, by the way, has the best burgers at Steamboat. The local males observe the traditional Colorado fertility rite by perching on the porch of the Afterglo waiting for the rancher's daughter to wander by. Hordes also flock to the **Hole In The Wall** and to the **Sundance Room,** both in the Steamboat Village Inn, where there is afternoon dancing and occasional live entertainment. The post-Afterglo locals will ultimately find their way to the **Tugboat Saloon** in Skitime Square, which is the local and ski patrol watering hole. (Trivia mavins will take note of the fact that the wood of the bar at the Tugboat comes directly from the bar where Butch Cassidy used to hang out.) **Cassidy's** is another popular afternoon bar where ski movies, including videos taken on the mountain that day, are shown. Bars in town that fill up after skiing are the **Cameo** and **El Rancho.**

People looking for the usual ski resort night life stay at the mountain, while those wanting a more down-home experience visit town. At the mountain, the **Sundance Room** has the biggest dance floor and often attracts big-name entertainers. The **Hole In The Wall** has dancing each night. Dancing to live music can also be found at **Diamond Liz's Saloon,** an elegantly decorated and attractive bar, as well as at the **Tugboat,** where the emphasis is on bluegrass. **Cassidy's,** right across from the Afterglo, is the other mountain disco. A lovely place for a quiet drink, either afternoon or evening, is the **Conservatory** at the Thunderhead Inn, a nice space with floor-to-ceiling plants, a huge fireplace, and quiet entertainment.

In town, the **Shortbranch Saloon** combines its long, well-attended bar with the only disco. If you're looking for the real thing in country-and-western music and dancing, and if you're ready for some serious drinking, head on over to the **Cove,** the **Hatch,** or the **Pioneer.** No Gucci shoes, please.

DIVERSION

Howelsen Hill, located near town, is the center for most of the area's diversion. Night skiing is available here several times a week. There is also an ice-skating rink, as well as a recently completed ski jump complex that is suitable for international competition. A full-service cross-country skiing center operates out of the clubhouse at the **Steamboat Village Country Club,** with instruction available from the **Steamboat Ski School.**

CHILDREN

The mountain is cut so that skiers of different abilities can ski off the same chairs, particularly Thunderhead and Christin I and II. The versatility of the lift system makes Steamboat a fine place to ski with children, especially those who are near-intermediate skiers. The nursery at the gondola terminal accepts children six months to seven years old and is open daily from 8:30 A.M. to 4:30 P.M. The cost is $6.50 per day and $4.50 for each sibling. Lunch is not included but may be purchased for $1.50 per day. Steamboat takes special interest in its children's ski school, and instruction is available for children from three years old.

COSTS

Steamboat's prices are standardly expensive for the West—somewhat less than Aspen and Vail but at least as much as everywhere else. Of interest is Steamboat's snow insurance policy, which, though vaguely stated and subjective, is an idea more areas should consider:

"If snow conditions as reported by the Steamboat ski area are less than fair (marginal or poor) three days prior to arrival, participating lodges in Steamboat will grant a full refund less a handling charge of $5.00 per person, per package, should a guest desire cancellation of reservations."

Snow conditions are determined by action of a committee made up of the president of the ski area, the ski school director, the ski patrol director, and the vice president of marketing. What ever happened to consumer representation?

THE SUMMIT AREAS

A-BASIN, BRECKENRIDGE, COPPER MOUNTAIN, AND KEYSTONE

While none of the four mountains designated as the Summit areas could by itself be considered a major mountain, the combination of the four coupled with their near-ideal location results in some impressive statistics. The four areas together total 38 lifts, 180 miles of trails and bowls, a lift capacity of 48,850 skiers per hour, and 8,703 vertical feet of skiing. Moreover, each area has something distinct to offer. A-Basin has an impressive expanse of wide-open bowl skiing above the timber line; Breckenridge maintains much of the charm of its nineteenth-century mining town origins; Copper Mountain is an extremely well-planned and attractive ski area; Keystone has an elegance of accommodations that we feel is nearly unparalleled. As we shall discuss, each of these mountains has major flaws to stand alongside its accomplishments. Nevertheless, the fact that the four areas can be skied on a single package ticket, are linked to each other by a free efficient shuttle bus service, are all within 80 miles of Denver, and do not require travel over mountain passes to be reached makes them definitely worth visiting.

16

A-Basin

Of the four Summit areas, A-Basin (formerly Arapaho Basin) is the only one that remains a day area. There are no accommodations at the mountain, though Keystone and Dillon are not far away; nor are there any of the other accouterments now associated with what were once called ski resorts but which now, in the parlance of the package tour operator, are referred to as "destination areas."

A-Basin's lack of development turns out to be a blessing in disguise. The armies of weekend skiers from the Denver area tend either to stop five miles down the road at Keystone or to venture down the highway one more exit to popular Breckenridge. Together with the mountain's other assets, namely, the highest altitude in Colorado (12,500 feet), one of the longest seasons in the country (early November through early June), unusually good snow, and suprisingly good and diverse skiing, the minimal lift lines make A-Basin a particularly attractive place to ski for a couple of days while recuperating from the crowds elsewhere on the Summit.

ACCESSIBILITY

A-Basin is only 66 miles from Denver, and driving time is under 1½ hours. As a secondary mountain, A-Basin is also well located, only 10 minutes from Keystone and 30–40 minutes from Breckenridge. The Ski-the-Summit bus shuttle links the four areas and facilitates easy access to and from the mountain.

THE SKIING

A-Basin is divided into halves. The bottom half has gentle novice runs through the trees on its north face and challenging expert terrain of substantial steepness on its south face. The top half is a gigantic powder bowl, wholly above the tree line, where the intermediate can ski forever in any direction and the expert can shoot over to the powder walls off the ridge to the south.

The mountain's deficiencies affect primarily the novice. Runs like Chisolm Trail, Meadow Trail, and Wrangler aren't bad, but they're right next to each other and confine the beginner to that one corner of the mountain. Also, they all initiate off the lower chairs, which account for only about half of A-Basin's scant 1,700-foot vertical.

Intermediates will delight in staying on top and skiing off Chairs #3 or #4. Unlike some of the huge bowls at Vail or Sun Valley, there's no part of the A-Basin bowl that cannot be easily negotiated by the intermediate. While the trail map designates some six or seven intermediate trails in the bowl area, we defy you to find them. Don't even look for trails. Just go up top, point your skis in any direction, and come down. The bowl is really a pleasure.

Experts are by no means as neglected as they are at most of the Summit areas. (Breckenridge has some good expert terrain, but its disastrous lift system renders the steep slopes nearly inaccessible.) Off the lower lifts, there are a series of good, unremitting bump runs that afford real workouts. Exhibition, the liftline of the lower chair, is a good show-off run if your mogul technique is up to it. The runs get steeper over to the south, with Lovers Leap's steep (8.75), moguled face providing the toughest challenge on the mountain.

Up top, experts have several alternatives. In the powder, they'll want to ski over to the south ridge and come down several short but very steep faces. The more energetic will head north, where various hiking possibilities allow the powder phenoms to make new tracks way up on the cornice. In packed snow, the whole bowl can be a blazing, fast cruise. The top lifts also give access to two other good expert trails: Gun Barrel and the steep (8.25) and infrequently skied Palivacinni.

The mountain is small and can be skied completely in a day. A visit to the Summit areas should definitely include A-Basin in conjunction with its more opulent, if not more skiable, neighbors.

LIFE IN THE AREA

There is none. A-Basin has only the bare minimums: a cafeteria (though one Sunday morning there was no coffee), a ski shop, a nursery, and two bars at the Base Lodge for après-ski. Do not come to A-Basin to romp, stomp, party, or carouse. Come and ski for the day and then stay somewhere else.

17

Breckenridge

Breckenridge has been unusually successful at treading the fine line between preservation and expansion, with the result that it is simultaneously the most developed and most charming of the Summit areas. Its history goes back to 1850, when, as a booming gold town, $300 million was taken out of the ground within four years. The discovery of a huge silver lode followed in 1878, and Breckenridge again displayed the trappings of Western prosperity. The old mining town still stands, and Main Street is much like the unspoiled streets of Crested Butte and Telluride; nevertheless, the expanse of skiing (750 acres) offered on Breckenridge's twin peaks, as well as the proximity of Denver, has resulted in substantial development.

Would that the mountain were as well planned as the town. There is good skiing for all levels of skiers at Breckenridge but getting to it, particularly the expert trails, can be a frustrating and time-consuming undertaking. Yet most people forgive this, and Breckenridge, because of a combination of desirable factors including extraordinarily economical prices, consistently ranks as one of the three or four most popular areas in America's number one ski state.

ACCESSIBILITY

Breckenridge is 86 miles west of Denver and, like the other Summit areas, is best reached from that city by car or bus. Driving time is 1¾ hours. All car rentals are available at the Denver airport, and Continental Trailways has service to Frisco, 10 miles away. Shuttle buses run from Frisco to Breckenridge during daylight hours, and at other times pickup is available from the Breckenridge Taxi Company. Shuttle buses run morning and evening, linking Breckenridge with the other Summit areas.

THE SKIING

If the airline ads have convinced you that "getting there is half the fun," or if you feel exhilarated by long peaceful rides up mountain peaks, Breckenridge will be something of a mecca. On the other hand, those who prefer to ski will be frustrated by this extremely ill-planned area (though fairness compels us to point out that Telluride wins the catastrophic planning award hands down, while lift-deficient Aspen Mountain at least rivals Breckenridge). Frustration is born only of possibilities, however, and the fact is that Breckenridge does have a substantial amount of good skiing, if only one could get to it (or, more appropriately, back to it) more easily.

The skiing is done on Peaks 8 and 9, Breckenridge's two separate but overlapping mountains. Peak 9 begins its 1,830-foot rise from right behind the Four Seasons complex, the modern focal point of town. Peak 9 is primarily for the novice and intermediate, though there are a couple of quite good expert trails toward its west face. Peak 8 is the larger peak, situated about a mile west of town and rising 2,213 feet to its 11,843-foot summit. Peak 8 is about evenly divided among novice, intermediate, and expert terrain.

Over on Peak 9, the beginner will want to ski primarily on Chairs A1 and A2, which combine to offer six different novice runs including the bottom half of the 2.6-mile-long Lehman trail—the longest, most popular run on the mountain. Breckenridge's problems of lift effectiveness, however, become apparent even on these two novice chairs, since they require a total of 16 minutes to climb 920 vertical feet.

Intermediates have some nice, long, well-cut trails like Columbia and Spur off of Chairs C and D, but again, the lifts are a problem. Each is a 12-minute chair, and the D chair has only a 940-foot vertical for its 6,163-foot distance (6.5:1) while the ratio for the C chair is also flat (4.75:1).

Not even the expert can prevail over the layout. For instance, Devil's Crotch is an excellent steep, narrow run through a tree-filled gulley, but getting back up to ski it again involves 24 minutes' worth of chairs and skiing novice to low intermediate runs between chairs.

Things are much the same over on Peak 8. Nice skiing, bad planning.

Beginners have substantial choices toward the bottom of the mountain. They can either practice on the super-gentle runs off the two lower T-bars or go up Chair #5 or Poma #1, devoted solely to novice terrain.

Intermediates wanting to stay over on Peak 8 should be undeterred by the trail map indicating a preponderance of expert terrain. Chair #2 is really a good advanced-intermediate chair. Besides Springmeier and Crescendo, two

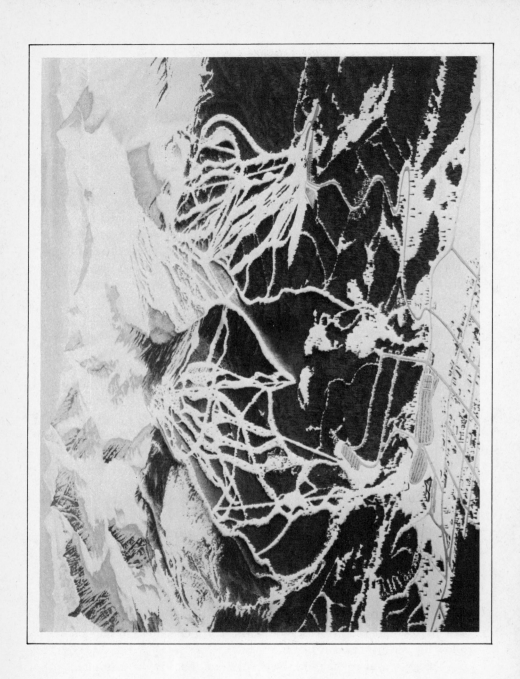

Breckenridge   COURTESY BRECKENRIDGE SKI AREA

classically cut, groomed intermediate trails off Chair #2, there is Spruce and Callie's Alley, both of which are marked expert but are in fact nice, moderately pitched runs only slightly steeper than most intermediate trails yet with more interesting terrain—exactly the kind of run that upwardly mobile intermediates should spend time on. Also off that chair is Glades, a lovely intermediate wind through the trees.

Experts on Peak 8 get to take lots of chairs—and pomas—and traverses. Things start out well enough. From the top of Chair #2, you take Poma #2 to the summit. From there, several choices can be made. Horseshoe and Contest Bowls are a traverse away and are particularly nice in the powder. Again, these bowls, while marked expert, can be easily negotiated by the intermediate. Our favorite route down, though, is Psychopath, a narrow, pretty gulley emptying out at the bottom of Chair #3. Going off to the left and over the ridge from Poma #2 are several short medium-advanced runs like Amen, Hombre, and Solitude that also filter down to #3. By far the best run off the poma is Tiger; one of the three genuinely challenging runs at Breckenridge, it has impressive pitch (8.75) and two different sharp drops along its route.

Be sure to enjoy the skiing on the expert runs off the poma, because getting back to them is an unremitting pain. The layout of the mountain forces you to ski down to Chair #3, take that up and ski a nothing run down to Chair #2, take that back up, and *then* get on the poma again. Catastrophic. We're told a new chair is planned for the 1978-9 season that would obviate much of the problem. Planned chairs don't always get built, but we certainly hope this one does.

Along with Devil's Crotch and Tiger, the other real challenger is Mach I at the base of Chair #3. Said, with only some hyperbole, to be the steepest slope in Colorado, Mach I is impressive. It is short, very steep (9.5), and significantly moguled, which makes skiing fluidly through its fall line a real challenge.

INTEGRATION OF THE SLOPES

Though Peaks 8 and 9 are separate mountains, each having a full complement of base facilities, it's relatively easy to ski from one peak to the other; the routes are well marked on the trail map. Peak 9 has a restaurant on the mountain on top of Chair C, and there are several picnic areas at convenient meeting places on both peaks.

LIFE IN THE AREA

ACCESSIBILITY TO THE SLOPES

The Peak 9 lifts are within easy walking distance of the many condominiums and lodges located near the Four Seasons complex. Peak 8 is reached by taking a car or the shuttle 1¼ miles up Ski Hill Road. Parking is ample, but be advised that the traffic coming down the hill at the end of the day can be bad and cause delays getting home.

ACCOMMODATIONS

There are about 3,000 beds in the Breckenridge area, at least 2,500 of which are in condominiums. In the lodge category, only a minute from Peak 9 but strictly standard motel, is the **Breckenridge Inn** ($32). **Tannenbaum by the River,** right in town, also has lodge rooms which it says are done in rustic elegance ($30). For skiers with a car who want just a room, the most attractive lodge is the **Shangri-La Inn** on the Blue River about 6 miles from town; the rooms are standard, but the setting and drive to the mountain is lovely, and the Inn has its own restaurant and bar ($30). The **Ramada Inn** in Silverthorne is only a 10-minute drive from Breckenridge, Copper, or Keystone, and bus service for all three mountains stops here; good facilities are available, including sauna, Jacuzzi, and pool ($30–50).

For the young and the budget-minded, dorms are available at **Crofutt's Nap-Sack** ($9.50 per person), to which you can ski home via Four O'clock Run, and at the **Fireside Inn,** a restored Victorian house with a warm, pleasant atmosphere ($9.50 per person).

Many of the major condominium developments are built behind the **Four Seasons** complex at Peak 9. Attractive, well-located units can be rented at the **Columbine,** which has access to a nearby pool and Jacuzzi ($45). Another luxury condominium, **Trail's End,** has private decks in all units ($50). For large families or groups, the **Tamarisk** has nice 2- to 4-bedroom units ($75–115). Only a couple of miles out of town is the **Ski and Racquet Club,** with pool, Jacuzzi, and sauna; each unit also has a private deck ($45).

At Peak 8, the closest accommodations are the **Ski Watch,** to which you can ski home and which has a recreation room, lounge, and sauna ($75–115 for 2- to 4-bedroom units), and the **Gold Camp** condominiums 500 yards from the lifts ($50).

Prices for condominium units are very low—nearly half what Aspen and Vail charge and even as much as 20% lower than comparable units at other Summit areas like Copper. Right now, lodging at Breckenridge presents a terrific value. We've been informed, however, of the intention of many condominiums to raise prices about 20% for the 1978–79 season.

For reservations, call 303–453–2918.

RESTAURANTS

Breckenridge has a wide variety of restaurants, but no one is likely to suggest that Michelin pay a visit. The **Miner's Camp** at the Four Seasons is the local steak emporium and is the most popular spot in town. The **St. Bernard** sticks with hearty and simple Italian food and is good of its kind. The **Greenhouse** on Main Street serves up its brand of gourmet food by candlelight. A pleasant surprise for us was **Mi Casa**—an exquisitely decorated Mexican restaurant, complete with hand-painted tiles throughout, that was vastly superior to the Mexican restaurants ubiquitous at ski areas—but its prices might shock skiers who think they're going out for a budget Mexican meal.

For burgers, omelets, sandwiches, and salads, we recommend **Angel's Rest.** The **Claim Jumper,** with its homemade sweet rolls, is the town favorite for breakfast.

APRÈS-SKI AND NIGHT LIFE

When the lifts close, the hard-core après-skiers begin a pilgrimage down Ski Hill Road. The first stop is the **Berginhof,** the bar at Peak 8. As traffic thins, people go down the hill to the **Depot** or **H. P. Cassidy's,** two college pub–type bars that show ski movies. The most popular bar is **Your Place Or Mine,** which combines a nice atmosphere with hearty drinks and occasional entertainment; the highlight of "happy hour" at Your Place is a ritual called the Upside-Down Margarita, wherein apparent volunteers subject themselves to lying prostrate on the bar and having the ingredients of that drink poured in great quantities down their throat. And you thought ski resorts weren't kinky.

At night, people head back to Cassidy's and the Depot both of which have dancing. Locals will drink and dance at **Shamus O'Toole's** across from Angel's Rest, and the younger crowd will disco at **Miner's Camp.** The **Whale's Tail** and the **Briar Rose** are for quiet drinking. One of Breckenridge's most attractive restored Victorian houses has the unlikely name of **Andrea's Pleasure Palace;** this restaurant-bar is meant to recall the local gold rush bordello, and though the interior is a little heavy on the flocked wallpaper, Andrea's is still a lovely building and particularly pleasant for a late-night drink upstairs at the piano bar.

DIVERSIONS

Cross-country skiing is available, and equipment can be purchased or rented at most of the ski shops. There is also ice skating on a natural pond near the Four Seasons.

CHILDREN

Both Peaks 8 and 9 have nurseries for all ages from 8:30 to 4:30 P.M. ($7; $5 for each sibling). Rates, however, do *not* include lunch, and the nurseries request that parents come down off the mountain to tend to their children's meal. The nursery ski school will teach children ages three to six ($7 morning and afternoon lessons); no equipment is provided.

COSTS

At least at present, Breckenridge remains a great bargain. Its lodging is modestly priced; its lift tickets are a steal ($8 weekdays; $11 weekends); and children under twelve ski for only $4.

18

Copper Mountain

Several factors, most notably geological good fortune and careful planning, have combined to make Copper in many ways the perfect mini-resort. Its location is superb (less than 2 hours from Denver and well under an hour from Vail, Breckenridge, Keystone, and A-Basin); its mountain is well balanced between levels of difficulty and its natural contours segregate skiers by ability to different faces of the mountain; and its village is compact and convenient. Aesthetic appeal, however, is Copper's real triumph. Its 40 miles of trails are masked so that from the base it looks like a picture-book ski mountain, with steep moguled runs alternating with gentle runs winding through enormous stands of spruce. Down in the village, planners have observed the kind of taste and decorum that should be more widely in evidence. Condominiums are nestled in trees directly adjacent to lifts, and many are built with their exposures reflecting the natural copper tones that pervade the village and the surrounding red hills. Buildings are well spaced, and a rare feeling of tranquillity exists. The master plan for the entire village provides for only 280 acres, two-thirds of which will consist of parks, trails, and woods. All this surrounded by 1,000,000 acres of national forest.

ACCESSIBILITY

Copper is at the foot of Vail Pass on Interstate 70, only 75 miles from the Denver airport. The drive is an easy one, with no mountain passes to cross. All major car rentals are available in Denver; however, only Dollar and High Country cars can be dropped at the mountain. Trans Rent-A-Car has a special Summit area rate.

Continental Trailways provides bus service from both the airport and downtown Denver. Shuttle service is also available between Copper and the other Summit areas.

THE SKIING

Nothing very special here: no terrifying steeps, no wide-open bowls to cruise, no 10-mile run for the intermediate. Yet we thoroughly enjoy the skiing. Copper is a relaxing mountain, a pretty mountain, and its runs, while not spectacular, are quite good and seldom boring.

What is unusual, though, is that each level of skier virtually has his own mountain to ski, with one or more of Copper's eight chairs to take him up the 2,450 feet to the 12,050-foot summit. The natural contours of the mountain have resulted in terrain that gradually increases in steepness from west to east.

Beginners can ski Chairs G, H, or I, all of which are nearly a mile long. Gentle runs like Loverly and Loverly Lane wind down through the trees to the Base Lodge. Unlike many ski areas, Copper allows the novice to ski the entire mountain from top to bottom. From the top of Chair I, the combination of Copper-Tone to High Point to Care Free allows the novice more uninterrupted skiing than is found in many places.

The intermediate has a significant number of choices since 60% of the terrain is designated intermediate. Many of the more popular intermediate runs, especially in inclement weather, are off Chair F, the 6,000-foot covered chair (the only other in the state is at Crested Butte) that travels from the Base Lodge about two-thirds of the way up the mountain. Choices there range from a show-off run down the liftline Main-Vein to the wide Bouncer or the narrow, tree-lined Bitter Sweet. Moving eastward to avoid crowds (despite an uphill capacity of 9,200 skiers per hour, the area's popularity and its proximity to Denver can make lift lines horrendous, particularly on the weekends), the intermediate can ski the Chairs I or J, reached from the top of H. There, trails like Copperfield and American Flyer broaden out among the trees at the top and make for some pleasant skiing.

The intermediate seeking somewhat more pitch and some manageable bump skiing might wander over to short Chair E and ski C.O.D., while more crowd dodging is possible by going all the way to the top and skiing the intermediate runs off Chair B-1.

The expert will not be particularly challenged at Copper, but there are a series of good advanced runs. All the advanced skiing is off Chairs B, B-1, and E. Brennan's Grin and High Pitch off Chair E are two relatively good bump runs with moderate pitch (7), and Hallelujah is off to the right in a kind of mini-bowl. Off B-1 (all Copper's lifts sound like vitamins), Oh No is the steepest run, though still nothing that a solid intermediate couldn't handle. Another alternative is for the advanced skier to go up top and ski Chair B, with its well-pitched bump runs like Treble Cleff and Rosi's Run. The longest, sustained advanced skiing is to take Drainpipe from the top of B-1 down into Two Much, a long, narrowing trail alternating between mogul fields and runoffs that finally funnels out into the far western end of the village. Substantial snowmaking, and 250 inches of snow annually, generally ensure skiing from Thanksgiving through the end of April. Considerable package savings are available in April.

INTEGRATION OF THE SLOPES

Despite the fact that families or friends of different abilities may be skiing different parts of the mountain, the two main meeting and eating places, the Base Lodge and Solitude Station, near the top of Chair E, are both accessible from almost any point.

LIFE IN THE AREA

ACCESSIBILITY TO THE SLOPES

All of Copper's condominiums and lodge rooms are within walking distance of all lifts. Free shuttle buses run regularly from one end of the village to the other, but even that distance is less than half a mile.

ACCOMMODATIONS

Most of Copper's lodging is in condominiums, and prices are standard in each of its 14 separate units. Prices are somewhat below those of the major areas but are still not insubstantial. Studio units run about $48, while 1- and 2-bedroom units will cost approximately $66 and $96, respectively. Units are available with 4 bedrooms and a loft that can accommodate up to 12 people ($196).

The nicest and most attractive of the condominiums is the **Anaconda**, which houses its units in wood frame buildings with cedar siding. In addition to the standard accouterments (all condos at Copper have kitchens, fireplaces, and television), the Anaconda has a sauna and Jacuzzi. Located behind the Anaconda, also in the east section of the village, is the **Snowflake**—another luxury place that adds a sauna to its other facilities.

Two condominiums offering heated pools and saunas are **Copper Valley** and **Timber Creek**. Copper Valley also offers standard inn-type rooms ($32). Other inn rooms are available in the village at **Copper Junction, Copper Mountain Inn,** and **Wheeler House.** Timber Creek's units are nestled right at the base of the mountain and have a pleasant, rustic atmosphere.

For reservations, call 303–668–6477.

RESTAURANTS

There are no restaurants at Copper to rave about, but given the size of the area there is a good variety in both style and price. Besides, for those seeking gourmet treats, Vail is a scant 18 miles away.

Farley's is everyone's favorite, serving steak and prime ribs. **Companero's** is the required Mexican restaurant, while **Tuso's** is the newest (and prettiest) restaurant in the village, featuring Italian foods and with a huge, attractive bar that makes the wait for dinner less painful. The **Copper Still** has a charming atmosphere with a German flavor and specializes in homemade soups.

For less intense appetites, **Zambini's** has deli sandwiches and homemade pizza in the evenings. The **Trail's End** has soups and chili. Finally, for junk food, there's an **Arby's.**

APRÈS-SKI AND NIGHT LIFE

All life centers in the village. After skiing, the crowds are split fairly evenly among the restaurants. **Companero's** has a small disco and video replays of some of the day's skiing. The **Midnight Sun,** the village's main disco, also has dancing. **Farley's** is the other après-ski favorite.

At night, people dance at the Midnight Sun and Companero's or to the live bands that often appear at **Trail's End.**

DIVERSIONS

Some excellent cross-country skiing is available in the Vail Pass area. Lessons, rentals, and moonlight tours with dinner all are available.

Ice skating is available in the center of the village, as is special racing instruction complete with 2 hours of instruction and video replay ($9 per person; minimum, 5 people).

CHILDREN

Copper is a good place to take children primarily because of the compactness and manageability of the village, where vehicle traffic is at a minimum.

Copper's nursery is at the Base Lodge and takes children one and a half to seven. Hours are 8:30 A.M. to 4:30 P.M., and the cost is $9, including lunch. Reservations are strongly recommended.

The ski school takes children only over five. The cost for two 2-hour lessons plus lunch is $10.50. Parents must pick up their children by 3:30.

COSTS

Prices at Copper are by no means cheap, but certain savings can be effected by those skiers planning to ski nearby Vail. Copper's condominiums, while easily equivalent to many of Vail's, run about 20% less. Thus for anyone willing to make the 30-minute drive over the pass, staying at Copper might work as an alternative to the stratospheric prices at Vail.

19

Keystone

Keystone is tantalizing. For the advanced and expert skier, Keystone is like being given a villa in the South of France on the condition that one eat only turnips during his stay. For the beginner and the very recreational intermediate, though, Keystone may qualify as heaven with a long lift line.

Pampered is what the skier is at Keystone, both at the lovely Keystone Lodge and at the surrounding condominiums (among the most gracious and tasteful accommodations we've found at any resort) and even more so on the mountain. To the delight of the beginner and, we suspect, many intermediates, everything is groomed; nary a bump is allowed to rear its ugly head above the gentle white carpet. The pampering is without restraint, for on any given day the expert is likely to find one or more of the three expert runs on the mountain equally mowed and decimated. Thus, for better or for worse, Keystone is the epitome of the laid-back mountain.

ACCESSIBILITY

Keystone is only 72 miles from Denver. The best access is by either car or bus. By car, drive 67 miles west of the Denver airport on Interstate 70 to the Dillon exit, from which Keystone is only 5 miles east. All major car rentals are available at the Denver airport. Trans Rent-A-Car offers a special rate from Denver to Keystone. The cost is $27, which includes 80 free miles and the use of the car for up to 4 hours. There is no drop-off charge. Driving time from Denver to Keystone is under 1½ hours.

To reach Keystone by bus, Continental Trailways has four trips daily to Frisco which are met by the Keystone shuttle to the ski area. The cost is approximately $10 per person round-trip. Limousine service is also available from Frisco to the Keystone Lodge at a nominal charge.

THE SKIING

"Where do we find the bumps?" we had the temerity to ask a pretty local our first morning at Keystone. "Hey, Keystone is a smooth cruise . . . really," she responded in that mellow way Easterners can only view as lobotomized. Keystone is indeed a smooth cruise and, as such, has become tremendously popular with the legions of smooth cruisers.

Keystone is a relatively small mountain, and its eight double chairs service terrain that is overwhelmingly novice (20%) and intermediate (70%). Much of the novice terrain is at the bottom of the mountain off the very short Checkerboard lift or the Poma, though a nice novice run off the top of the Go Devil lift gently traverses much of the middle of the mountain. The real lure for novices, however, is the 3-mile-long Schoolmarm, which descends all 2,340 vertical feet from Keystone's 11,640-foot summit and is one of the longest and best novice runs around. Beginners who are somewhat more advanced need not be limited to these officially designated novice trails, since the intense grooming at Keystone makes much of the intermediate terrain negotiable for the more secure novice.

Intermediate trails radiate from every lift, but the most popular originate from the summit off the Montezuma and St. John lifts. Don't mistake our lack of discussion of these intermediate runs for any lack of enthusiasm. Trails like Spring Dipper, Flying Dutchman, Jackwhacker, and Wild Irishman are wide, long, beautifully groomed, and classic examples of the "cruise." Nevertheless, they're virtually identical to one another. While this is certainly no sin (witness Snowmass), it does preclude much detailed analysis. One exception is Bachelor, the liftline of the Montezuma chair, which is occasionally left to gather some minor bumps and terrain changes and is the most interesting intermediate run on the mountain. In general, the trails at Keystone will not be taxing enough for the intermediates in search of challenge or wanting to improve their skiing. On the other hand, they're undeniably pleasant—a smooth cruise.

The expert will go nuts at Keystone. The temptation to sabotage a snowcat is nearly irresistible. There are only three expert runs, and often one or more of them is mowed into submission. When we were there, Frenchman, the longest expert run on the mountain and one that had been represented to us as having some bumps, was smoother than the bottoms of a racer's skis and barely of interest to an intermediate—and this was not even on a weekend when crowds had to be accommodated. We turned then to the other choices, which were nice for a day but couldn't hold one's interest for a much longer spell. Go Devil begins with a relatively long cruise and then drops off into a

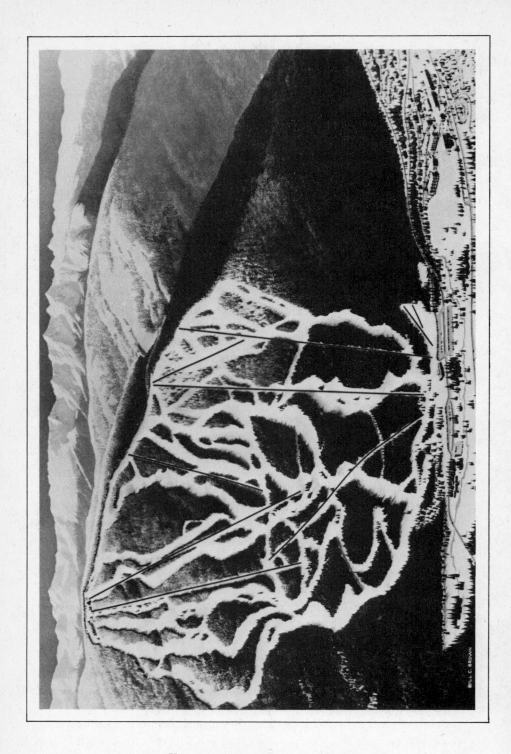

Keystone PHOTO BY BILL C. BROWN

mildly advanced bump run (7) with a steepish pitch at the end. Last Hoot is a short but quite good bump run off of the mid-station of the Peru lift. The bumps are only moderate but they're continuous, as is the pitch of the slope (7.5 with two steeper pitches). Last Hoot is an excellent ratio run, since there's a good deal of uninterrupted skiing for a very short chair ride. Elsewhere on the mountain, ratios are a real problem—especially on the lifts to the summit, which are much too long and flat.

INTEGRATION OF THE SLOPES

Keystone is very compact and easy to get around. Skiers of all abilities can meet up nearly anywhere on the mountain. Eating facilities are found both at the summit in the newly expanded seven-level Summit Lodge restaurant (a huge stone fireplace at Summit House also makes for a great warming hut) and at Mountain House, the pleasantly decorated base lodge, which has both a cafeteria upstairs and Ernie's, for a light sit-down lunch, downstairs.

LIFE IN THE AREA

We were really quite captivated by Keystone, an area where good taste has consistently triumphed over mindless development. The center of the resort is Keystone Village, the group of condominiums, shops, eating places, and nightspots surrounding the Keystone Lodge a few hundred yards from the lifts. As to quality, the shops and other facilities in the village measure up to those of the major Colorado resorts (Aspen, Vail, Steamboat), and aesthetically and compositionally Keystone exudes a grace that in our opinion is nearly unparalleled.

ACCESSIBILITY TO THE SLOPES

Most everything at Keystone is within a half-mile walk of the slopes, and shuttle buses run through the village. For those staying in nearby Dillon, the Ski the Summit shuttle will drop skiers off at the lifts.

ACCOMMODATIONS

Accommodations at Keystone Village consist of the magnificent **Keystone Lodge** and about 15 nearby condominium units. Additional lodging can be found a few miles away in Dillon, which is particularly well located in the Keystone–Copper–Breckenridge–A-Basin access.

The 152-room Keystone Lodge is perhaps the nicest hotel in the Rockies. It has AAA's highest rating and four stars from the Mobil Travel Guide. If Michelin were to visit the area, the Lodge would definitely merit a red chairlift.

Filled with dark wood, plants, plush couches, leather chairs, blazing fireplaces, and seductive bars and restaurants, the Lodge is all tasteful elegance. Only Sunriver at Mt. Bachelor or Topnotch at Stow can compare. The Lodge has a full range of services, including two restaurants. The rooms are lovely ($50).

Many of the condominiums match the taste of the Lodge. The **Willows,** on the shore of Keystone Lake with views of the lake and the mountain, has luxurious 1- to 3-bedroom units. The **Flying Dutchman** and **Wild Irishman** are located a couple of hundred yards farther from the lifts, but both units have pool, Jacuzzi, and sauna (studio to 3-bedroom). The **Tennis Townhouses** adjacent to the courts at the John Gardiner Tennis Club are not far from the Lodge and are tastefully designed and appointed (2- to 3-bedroom). The **Lakeside,** next to the Lodge, also has luxury units. Condominium prices at Keystone vary somewhat, but general approximations are: studio, $60; 1-bedroom, $70; 2-bedroom, $85–105; 3-bedroom, $120–138.

To save some money, note that prices will be lower at the **Holiday** and **Ramada Inns** near Dillon only 5 miles away. In our opinion, however, the real quality of Keystone lies in its environment rather than its skiing; therefore, if you're choosing a base for skiing the Summit areas, Keystone is our recommendation despite the price—which, when compared to equivalent accommodations at Aspen or Vail, is pretty reasonable.

For reservations, call 800–525–5897 (in-state, 332–8037).

RESTAURANTS

In the village, there are two steak houses: the **Navigator** and the **Big Horn Room** in the Keystone Lodge. Lighter meals can be had in the village at the **Brasserie** or **Bentley's.** The main event is definitely the **Garden Room** at the Lodge, which serves impressive but expensive food from a sophisticated menu in a truly lovely setting.

Outside the village, toward Dillon, **Pug Ryan's** is another entry in the steak-and-salad sweepstakes, while **La France** is highly regarded as the local French bistro. The **Old Dillon Inn** has Mexican food.

APRÈS-SKI AND NIGHT LIFE

When the lifts close, most people stick around **Mountain House** for a while, congregating in the level-three bar. Later on, some wander over to **Bentley's** in the village. While Bentley's is primarily a restaurant serving low-priced items like fried chicken and fish and chips, its interior is a more beautiful example of art deco than all the chic attempts at that look currently proliferating in New York. Definitely go over for a drink.

At night, the mellow crowd drinks at Bentley's or the bar at the **Keystone Lodge.** The **Silver Slipper** is the village's fancy disco, but locals and those looking for a little more down-home flavor usually dance at the **Snake River Saloon** (Wednesday–Saturday) or the **Old Dillon Inn** (weekends).

DIVERSION

Keystone is relatively high in this category. There is night skiing every evening 5–10 P.M. at the Checkerboard lift and cross-country skiing in nearby Montezuma Canyon, with trails leading to some old mining towns. A large outdoor skating area offers instruction in both figure and speed skating. For those with excess energy at the end of the day, the **John Gardiner Tennis Club** has two indoor courts.

CHILDREN

Keystone is a good place for kids. The nursery at **Mountain House** takes children one to eight years old (reservations are required for children under two). The cost is $10 per day or $15 if ski instruction is included. Both rates include lunch.

COSTS

Keystone is the most expensive of the Summit areas. But it is also the nicest.

20

Telluride

Telluride is about as undiscovered as any major ski resort in the United States. Isolated in a magnificent, narrow, steep-sided valley in western Colorado, this old mining town has taken on new life. The skiing is a combination of the best and the worst. On the good side, it has two of the best expert 3,200-foot vertical drops anywhere, excellent snow, and no lift lines; on the bad, it suffers from the most ill-designed lift system found anywhere and an inaccessible day lodge. The town is charming and still small. Telluride remains a quiet retreat with problems and potential.

ACCESSIBILITY

One of Colorado's least accessible resorts, Telluride is 127 miles from Grand Junction (a 3-hour drive) and 62 miles from Montrose (about a 1½-hour drive).

From Denver or California, direct air service is provided to Grand Junction, where you can rent a car or reserve a ride with Telluride Transfer (303-728-3961) for $11 per person, minimum of 4 persons. There are two or three direct flights a day from Denver to Montrose, where Telluride Transfer charges $6 per person for the trip to Telluride (again with a minimum of 4 persons). Reservations on this shuttle are necessary.

From the East or Midwest, it takes a full day to get to Telluride.

THE SKIING

Telluride has several dynamite expert runs and many well-groomed novice and lower intermediate trails. In between, something is missing. The area's bottom lift (Lift #1), the Coonskin chair, rises up out of the valley from the town on a steep face that has a 1,836-foot vertical over a length of 4,730 feet. At the top of Coonskin, the ski area lays out to the left and right along a gradual 4-mile ridge running east and west, perpendicular to the Coonskin lift. Coonskin itself and the trails that go down it remind us of the bottom chair at Taos and Al's Run beneath it. These two lifts are the steepest long chairs in North America.

To the right as you get off the Coonskin chair are two novice lifts running in tandem (Lifts #2 and #3). Novices will enjoy these chairs. They have long, broad, immaculately groomed runs which are never crowded. Lift #2 is a beginner's lift and #3 is a novice lift, but the terrain on both is still very gentle. There is more novice terrain on the Lift #4, which starts just below the top of Lift #3. The terrain on #4 is mostly intermediate and again is broad and well groomed. The intermediate will have no trouble with the several steep spots on these trails. The novice can just by-pass these sections.

Once at the top of Lift #4, there are still two more chairs to go before you arrive at the top. Intermediates, even those who are weak skiers, will find good runs off both upper lifts. The Lift #5 is the most frustrating of all the lifts because of its length (5,088') and limited vertical (789'). It is flat at the bottom, steep in the middle, and flat again on top. This lift should be the advanced intermediate area, but the pitch of the runs is too irregular (steep and then flat) to appeal to the advanced intermediate. Finally, from the top of #5, you ski down to #6, the top lift—a superb expert lift (1,024' vertical; 2,708' length). There is one 4-mile run (lower intermediate all the way) down from the top to the day lodge at the western end of the ridge. The chairs back up from the day lodge cover a distance of 18,000 feet, or 3½ miles. It takes about 50 minutes to make this trip up. Lift #6 closes at 3 P.M. Make lunch short.

The lift problem at Telluride results from the number of lifts and their length. It takes five lifts to get from the day lodge to the top or four to come from the bottom of Coonskin to the top of Lift #6. For the expert, this is a drawback; however, once at #6, the expert is home. Four runs are very tough. On the extreme right is Silver Glade, the top of which is a glade and the bottom of which is a steep, bumpy face (8). Then there's Zulu Queen, very steep at the top (about 30–35°), narrow, with huge bumps (9). The liftline, Allais Alley, is like Zulu Queen, and finally there's Apex Glade, a steep, broad face, gladed on top and open at the bottom, which is an excellent run in powder. These are all pure, challenging expert trails.

But the high point at Telluride is the run from the top of Lift #6 back down the face into the valley, to the bottom of the Coonskin chair. This is a 3,200-foot drop, a continuous 25–30° slope, joyous and steep (9). Equivalent to anything at Snowbird, it has almost no letups. It can be done on two trails,

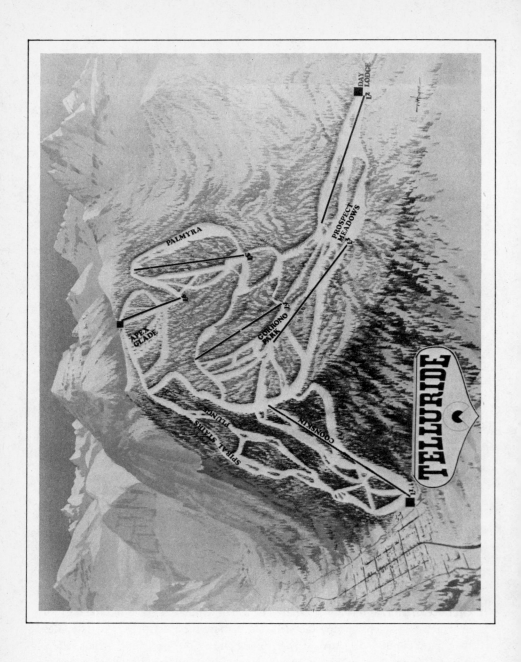

Telluride, with Coonskin chair rising on north face near town   COURTESY
TELLURIDE SKI AREA

the Plunge or Spiral Stairs. Both are bump runs all the way. Spiral Stairs has one continuous face with about a 1,000-foot vertical and a true fall line. The Plunge and Spiral Stairs are both steeper than Limelight at Sun Valley and have a continuous slope as long and challenging as anything at Jackson or Snowbird. Coupled with those on Lift #6 and one equally demanding trail on the Coonskin chair, the runs give Telluride expert terrain comparable to any area in the country, except possibly Jackson.

Though you still have to deal with getting back up to the top, which involves taking 16,000 feet of lifts, this problem has its rewards. The number of skiers on the Plunge and the Stairs is reduced, which in turn helps to preserve the snow.

One final flaw must be mentioned. For the non-expert, the return down the valley face can be difficult. The area did open a trail, Milk Run, down the Coonskin face, which it hoped would be intermediate. Unfortunately, the run is too steep, builds up bumps, and is beyond the ability of most intermediates, particularly at the end of a day. As a result, many skiers are forced to take the Coonskin chair down or to return by road, a 5-mile drive from the day lodge. No transportation is provided. Riding down Coonskin at the end of the day is a bit ego-deflating but at the same time is exciting and beautiful.

The ski school at Telluride has an interesting rate structure. Because of the very few students (or skiers) at the area, the school adjusts the length of lessons according to the number of students. If the class has one student, the lesson is one hour; two students, two hours; three students, three hours; four students or more, four hours—two in the morning, two in the afternoon. Except in holiday weeks, classes, which are divided by ability, usually have less than four students. The classes are expensive ($11, or $44 for five lessons), but the individual attention is maximum.

To end on a positive note, we can say good things about snow conditions at this resort. Telluride gets more snow (400″) than any other resort in Colorado. Because of its elevation (8,700′ at the base), the snow can be very light. The steep, north-facing expert trails are also well sheltered from the sun. This makes Telluride the best bet for powder in Colorado. And the area has good weather. It claims to have an average daily temperature of 30°, second only to Aspen's 32°.

LIFE IN THE AREA

Telluride is an old mining town with a broad main street and small brick buildings built at the turn of the century. The town has attracted the young counter-culture set, which has settled down and adopted the cowboy style of Telluride. The bars, several of which have preserved their historic qualities, are populated by these transplanted locals and are the focus of après-ski and night life. The old style of the area has come together harmoniously with the new.

ACCOMMODATIONS

Telluride has only about 800 beds for visitors. This number is growing, but major expansion will take time. In choosing accommodations, location of the lodging is important. The Coonskin lift is about a half-mile west of the center of town, which means that many of the hotels in town are a 10-minute walk from the lifts. In ski boots, this can be painful.

At the lift is the **Telluride Lodge,** made up primarily of condominiums, which sleeps 360 persons—nearly half the guests in town. The Lodge has serious flaws in construction and maintenance, but the apartments are modern and pleasant and there is an outdoor heated pool and Jacuzzi. The cost is $154 per person, 7 nights, 6 days, 4 persons to a 1-bedroom condominium.

Only a couple of minutes' walk from the lift, across the road from the Lodge, is the **Tomboy Inn,** which has modern, attractive condominiums and a sauna.

Most accommodations are about 7–12 minutes from the Coonskin lift. The Gothic **Victorian Inn,** near the center of town, is the closest to the lifts; it has modern rooms and a lobby with a fireplace, and a sauna and Jacuzzi are planned for 1979. Right in the middle of town on Main Street is the historic **New Sheridan Hotel,** where in 1902 William Jennings Bryan gave his legendary anti-gold speech; describing itself as a "restored Victorian gem," the Sheridan has updated its rooms but preserved its ornate Victorian bar, which is a focus of night life (just drinking) in Telluride. Also in town are two guest houses: the **Dahl House** and, somewhat larger, the **Bushwacker Inn,** with 24 units sleeping 82 persons. Built on the side of the mountain (experts can ski home) on the edge of town, 10 minutes from the lift, is the modern **Manitou Lodge,** a hotel that provides guests with refrigerators in the rooms but does not serve breakfast.

Two sets of condominiums are located west of town. These are the **Brown Homestead** and **Last Dollar,** 2 and 4 miles away, respectively.

A new inn, the **Coonskin,** right at the lift near the Lodge, was scheduled to open in 1978 but at this writing is still not ready.

For reservations at Telluride, the area association number is 303-728-4431.

RESTAURANTS

There are several good restaurants to choose from. Styled after an elegant Old West saloon, the **Senate** serves *haute cuisine* Continental food in small, well-appointed dining rooms. The **Powderhouse** is a good steak and seafood restaurant with the added touch of specialty drinks. **La Paloma** is a good Mexican restaurant serving huge portions in an old, attractively remodeled barnlike building. A less formal restaurant with a good salad bar is the steak house **Silverjack Mining Co.**

The several bars on Main Street, particularly the **Floradesa Saloon** and the **Moon Gypsy** serve simple meals. Finally, there are several sandwich and pizza joints and two delis. The **Flour Garden** and the **Upper Crust** are recommended for breakfast.

APRÈS-SKI AND NIGHT LIFE

Telluride's social activity centers on the bars. Several of these, particularly the bar at the **Sheridan,** have preserved the turn-of-the-century style of exaggerated Mountain West Victorian, with large mirrors and massive wood-carved, ornate paneling. Several bars like the **Moon Gypsy** and the **Roma Bar** (dumpy, informal) have a saloon atmosphere which has been enhanced by the addition of pool tables. The bars are lively from 4 P.M. on. The locals often start earlier.

The sparse dancing in town takes place on weekends at the **Pastime Saloon,** a large basement bar in the cellar of the Bushwacker.

Movies can be seen at the old **Opera House** next to the New Sheridan.

DIVERSION

There is a cross-country skiing center at the day lodge on the mountain, with trails branching out from there. Aside from touring, Telluride offers few diversions other than drinking and enjoying the magnificence of the valley.

In town, crowded into the grotto-like brick cellar of the Opera House, is the **Boiler Room Sauna Baths,** which has coed saunas and Jacuzzi.

CHILDREN

The skiing, with its gentle slopes, is excellent for children. Also, the small number of students in ski school is a real advantage. There are two nurseries at the mountain, at the **Telluride Lodge** and at the day lodge, but check first to see which is open.

The **Alpine,** an excellent game room–3.2 bar for teenagers, offers sandwiches, pinball machines, and pool tables; both local and visiting kids hang out here.

COSTS

Telluride is moderately priced. Lift tickets are $10 per day, $55 for 6 days. Food prices are also reasonable.

21

Vail

Vail has long been identifiable as the resort where the solid, prosperous citizens of American come to ski. It is likely to be crowded with bankers from Chicago, lawyers from Dallas, and dentists from Cleveland. It is *Our Town* in winter, a resort that has appropriately embraced ex-President Ford as a symbol of its devotees.

Vail is a total resort, with every conceivable amenity and facility. It also has a spectacular mountain—one of the very best. What Vail lacks is character. The village is a half-hearted attempt at Tyrolia that combines undistinguished architecture with chaotic planning. Lions-Head, the more recent development adjacent to the village, is nicer but suffers from the same lack of composition and cohesion that gives a "feel" to resorts as disparate as Keystone and Taos.

ACCESSIBILITY

Vail is one of the more accessible major Western resorts. Only 100 miles west of Denver, it is an easy 2-hour drive on Interstate 70. All major car rentals are available at the Denver airport, and Hertz and Avis have offices at Vail. Coming from the west, Vail is approximately 3 hours by car from Grand Junction, where Avis, Budget, and Hertz have offices. Continental Trailways offers bus service daily from Denver.

You can also fly from Denver (on Rocky Mountain) or Grand Junction (on Western Air Stages) to Eagle, some 35 miles west of Vail, but this is not really much of a convenience since you then have to arrange for ground transportation to Vail. Rocky Mountain is in the process of initiating air service to Avon, only 6 miles to the west.

THE SKIING

The key to Vail's excellence is balance. The mountain is vast—the largest ski mountain in North America. There is over 10 square miles of skiing, down 3,050 vertical feet, with 18 lifts servicing a zillion runs. Unlike many of the great Western mountains whose strengths are often diluted by material deficiencies (Snowbird neglects the intermediate, Snowmass has nothing to interest the expert, and novices at Whistler better be prepared to learn quickly), Vail provides superb terrain for every level of skier. Novices can ski top to bottom on scenic 4-mile-long trails; intermediates can find interesting runs all over the mountain; and experts have their choice of the bumps, the steeps, or the powder-laden drops of the back bowls.

Novices will never find more opportunities. They have access to nearly every lift and area of the mountain. From Eagle's Nest, they can ski the entire length of the gondola on Simba—a run of several miles that can even be extended by skiing the Lost Boy trail from the top of Chair #3. Lost Boy winds around the top of Game Creek Bowl and affords spectacular vistas (the best on the mountain), both down into the valley and west over to Mt. Holy Cross. The slightly more confident novice should go over to the Far East at the top of Chair #14 and ski Whiskey Jack, Sour Dough, and Boomer. Real novices stick to the flat areas at the base of Golden Peak. What makes Vail such a treat for the beginner is that it is one of the few mountains whose novice trails combine length, beauty, and diversity.

Vail presents the intermediate skier with a staggering number of choices equaled only by Snowmass. At Vail, however, the intermediate trails (found off virtually all 18 lifts) are generally more interesting than those at Snowmass. Though intermediate skiing is all over the place, the bulk of the cruisers congregate around three areas. Over at the Eagle's Nest–gondola area, long, long runs like Bwana and Born Free travel the entire length of the gondola, with few bumps, alarming pitches, or other obstacles to easy skiing. Moving to the east, the runs off Eagle's Nest Ridge at the top of Chairs #2 and #17 are the best intermediate runs on the mountain. Avanti, Lodgepole, Ledges, Pickeroon, and Columbine are all excellent, long runs, with some bumps, nice pitch, and some terrain changes. These represent the more advanced intermediate terrain at Vail, but they can be handled by most intermediates and really are a must for the spectacular ride up Chair #2, with its views of the Gore Range and Mt. Holy Cross. Further east at the summit of Chairs #4 and #11, there's generally a crush of people fighting for position down popular Swingsville and such runs as Whistle Pig, Expresso, and Cappuccino, which fork off

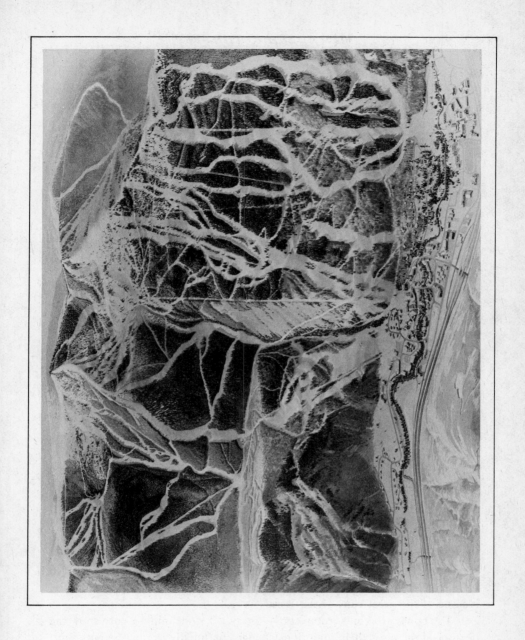

Vail: village at base in center, LionsHead on right   COURTESY VAIL SKI AREA;
ARTWORK BY HAL SHELTON

Swingsville. Other good intermediate runs scattered over the mountain are Riva Ridge off of #11 (marked expert but actually a superior advanced intermediate run); Ruder's Run, a fine, long run down Golden Peak off #6; and the lower section of Prima (do not, unless you are well insured, wander onto the upper portion of Prima).

We have always considered the expert skiing at Vail to be terribly underrated. Somehow, the word has been passed and perpetuated that Vail is an "easy" mountain and the Texans wanted the mountain as flat as an oil field —but it's not true. Vail's expert runs are first-rate. Moreover, Vail's back bowls, the extra and super incentive for the expert and powder skier, have snow conditions that change constantly and make the bowls a different and fascinating place to ski each day, if not each hour.

Experts at Vail have two separate skiing experiences, one when there is powder and one when the snow is packed. The runs off Chair #10 in the Northeast Bowl are a real treat for the good skier. Self-contained and somewhat isolated, these three runs (Blue Ox, Highline, and Roger's Run) provide long and unrelenting bump skiing (8–8.5) all the way down to the base of the chair. This is also nearly the only place on the mountain where a lift line can be avoided. Making these runs even more fun is the fact that the first quarter of each run is a long cruise that allows you to really fly—a much better structure than the usual trail, where the cruise is at the end and your legs are too shot from the bumps to enjoy it.

Chair #11 also offers plenty of challenge. The liftline (8) is very narrow and quite pretty, with some good bumps and a distinct Eastern feeling. First Step is a lot like Red's Run at Aspen, with three steep bump patches (8.25) and flat areas in between. Look for the path off South Rim Run, where you can go nearly straight down through huge bumps and some very tight trees (9.75). If you can ski that fluidly, you're pretty hot. The grand old man of the runs off #11 is Prima, Vail's most famous trail (if you ski it to the satisfaction of your instructor, you're awarded the coveted Prima pin). Prima is a magnificent bump run. Steep (stop for a breather and put your pole horizontally into the hill behind you), wide, and with bumps the size of New York City potholes, it's one of the great runs of the West (9).

The bowls are Vail's trump card—dry powder one minute, corn snow the next, crud the next, their conditions change continually as the elements shift. Only their steepness is a constant. Game Creek Bowl is one of the bowls on the front side of the mountain, and its runs (Faro, Deuces Wild, and Ouzo, for example) are skied mostly in powder. Get there early, since they face west and can't be skied once the sun hits them. From the top of #3 or #7 (or from #11 or #4 if Minturn Mile is open), you can dip down into Sundown Bowl and ski steep Straight Shot or the more moderate Ricky's Ridge. Over in the Sun Up Bowl, try the very steep Yonder, Vail's toughest deep-powder trail.

The nice thing about the bowls at Vail is that they'll *always* have powder. All you have to do is take the elements into consideration in order to successfully locate it. And while the quality of Vail's powder can't measure up to that of Alta-Snowbird, no deep snow enthusiast will be disappointed by Vail's back bowls.

INTEGRATION OF THE SLOPES

The mountain is so big (the trail map looks like a map of the Paris metro) that getting around on it can be time-consuming. Access between chairs is fairly good, however, which satisfies the fundamental concern that once up top the skier can go anywhere on the mountain without having to return to the base.

There are several well-situated places on the mountain at which to rendezvous. Cafeterias and restaurants with table service at Eagle's Nest are at the top of the gondola as well as at Mid-Vail. Down below, the gondola building has a cafeteria and a restaurant, and over toward the east end of the Village is a cafeteria at the base of the Golden Peak chair.

LIFE IN THE AREA

"Complete" is the word for life at Vail. No matter which recreation, activity, or diversion suits your fancy, you're likely to find it within the confines of the Village or LionsHead. There are over 70 restaurants and bars, 62 lodges and condominium units, over 120 shops and boutiques, 20 ski shops, movies, ice-skating rinks, pools—the list goes on forever. But a certain price is exacted. Forget aesthetic surroundings. Forget tranquillity. Forget the unspoiled feel of the Old West (there is both a Burger King and a Baskin-Robbins). Life at Vail is convenient and commercial. Quality, though, has not been overwhelmed by quantity, and many of Vail's accommodations, shops, and restaurants are well above average. On balance, we think all skiers ought to at some point experience Vail.

ACCESSIBILITY TO THE SLOPES

This is one of Vail's high points. Nearly all accommodations are within walking or skiing distance of the lifts. Those staying in the Village can walk out their door and head up to mid-Vail right from the center of town. Advanced skiers can walk a few hundred yards east and beat most of the crowds by heading up via the Golden Peak route. Guests at LionsHead have the gondola at their doorstep.

Vail Village and LionsHead are basically expanded malls where vehicle traffic is for the most part prohibited. About 75% of the restaurants, shops, and accommodations are in the Village, with most of the balance over at LionsHead about a half-mile walk. Continuous free bus service is provided between the two areas. A car is definitely not needed and, depending on the parking facilities of your accommodations, can actually be a hindrance.

ACCOMMODATIONS

As a rule of thumb, the accommodations at LionsHead are newer and more elegant than those in the Village but not as well situated. Prices run the standard Aspen-Vail-Snowmass range: expensive to very expensive. On the luxury end of the spectrum, however, lodging at Vail tends to be slightly nicer than at Aspen-Snowmass. There are a tremendous number of places to stay, many of them of equal quality. Thus, here, more than at any other resort, our recommendations should be read as representative rather than exclusive.

In the Village, the **Kiandra Lodge** and the **Lodge at Vail** are among the most gracious lodges (the Lodge at Vail also has condominium units); both have restaurants, bars, heated pool, and sauna, though we find the Kiandra is the more attractive ($55). The **Holiday Inn** and the **Hilton Inn** both have a full range of services (pool and sauna at Holiday Inn) at a somewhat lower price ($45). Smaller lodges in the Village, such as the **Wedel Inn,** have fewer facilities but are well located and provide comfortable lodging at lower prices ($30).

Over at LionsHead, the nicest lodge is the **Mark,** which also has condominium units; there are two restaurants, a bar, entertainment, a pool, and sauna ($55).

Attractive condominium units can be found both at LionsHead and in the Village. At LionsHead, the **Montaneros** has beautiful aspen-paneled units (1- to 3-bedroom) each of which faces the mountain; there is also a pool and Jacuzzi ($75–140). In the Village, the **Holiday House** condominiums have a pool and sauna (1- to 3-bedroom units, $75–135). For economical condominiums in the Village, try **Apollo Park** (studios to 2-bedroom units, $35–55).

We think **Vail Run,** the newest condominium in Vail, is also its nicest. Unfortunately, its location, directly across from LionsHead on the other side of the highway, is less than perfect. Nonetheless, Vail Run is lovely, with an indoor/outdoor pool, sauna, Jacuzzi, tennis courts, billiard room, restaurant, bar, and shops (studios to 4-bedroom units, $55–160).

For reservations, call 303–476–5677.

RESTAURANTS

Vail has restaurants of every size, shape, price, and ethnic persuasion. Only Aspen has more. If you listen to the regulars, many of these restaurants succeed in their aspirations to match Aspen as the gourmet ski center. Frankly, we've never been impressed with the quality of the food at Vail. This is not to say there are no good restaurants. There are. It's just that once price is taken into consideration, you're probably better off at home—or in Aspen.

The **Left Bank** is French, expensive, and highly regarded, as is the **St. Mortiz,** which sometimes triumphs over a plastic environment. The **Lord Gore** is fancy, attractive, and offers Continental fare and wild game specialties (stick with the Continental fare). The **Watch Hill Oyster Club** is a new addition and the place in town for "fresh" seafood, including lobster. Seafood is also on the menu at **Purcell's** at LionsHead, but the accent here is really on steak and salad. In the Village, the **Ore House** is a wildly popular steak-and-salad joint. Over at LionsHead, the **Wimbledon Room** at the Mark offers quite good gourmet dining.

For ethnic food, **Kosta's Taverna** has Greek fare and is fun. **Ichiban** is Japanese and Chinese and often has good food with dreadful service. **Los Amigos** is a popular Mexican restaurant, and **Pistachio's** is the favorite (but overrated) Italian restaurant.

The best and most pleasant eating experiences at Vail come as a result of the proximity of the town to the lifts. Many restaurants do a big lunch business for skiers who come down the mountain, and during the spring outdoor eating at some of these places can be glorious. Our favorites are **Cyrano's** (great burgers, omelets, and crepes), the **Red Lion, Los Amigo's,** and **Donovan's** in the Village and **Alfie Packer, Hansel and Gretel's,** and **Mr. Earl's** at Lions-Head.

For those who want to eat out but who have some budgetary restraints, a few restaurants (notably **Bully III** and **Watch Hill Oyster Club**) have initi-ated a policy wherein from 5:30 to 6:30 you can order a full dinner from a limited number of items on the regular menu for substantial savings ($3.95 per person at those two establishments mentioned above). We hope this idea catches on.

APRÈS-SKI AND NIGHT LIFE

There is plenty to do at Vail both at night and after the lifts close, though Vail is not nearly as singles-oriented as Aspen or Steamboat and has much less live entertainment and dancing. Vail is much more akin in temperment to Snowmass, and a typical evening is most likely to be dinner and a quiet drink.

The popular Après-ski bars are **Donovan's** (everybody's favorite Vail bar), **Garton's** (for the rowdies), **Purcell's,** the **Clocktower,** and the **Mark.** Garton's and the Mark have afternoon dancing. At night, Garton's and Donovan's continue to be mobbed. The **Red Lion** often has good live entertainment. Disco types head for the Mark, **Tudisco's,** or Vail's newest disco, **Sundance.** For teenagers, the **Cellar** is an under-18 disco.

The more sedate stay closer to home and sip drinks at lounges like the Mark, the **Lodge at Vail,** the **Kiandra,** or the **Holiday Inn.**

DIVERSION

Excellent cross-country skiing is available on over 100 miles of trails throughout the valley. Inquire at the ski school about instruction and equipment. For ice skaters, there is a large rink about midway between the Village and LionsHead. Indoor tennis is available at **Vail Run.** The saunas, pools, and Jacuzzis at many of the lodges and condominiums are open to the public for modest charges. Finally, shopping at Vail is a diversion in itself, with innumerable stores offering apparel and many specialty items of unusually high quality for a ski resort.

CHILDREN

Except for its costliness, Vail is a great place for children. All accommodations are close to the lifts, and kids can wander around the Village with no problem.

There are four separate day-care facilities. The **Small World Nursery** accepts children two to four years old and has facilities both at LionsHead and at the Vail Valley Medical Center. Hours are 8:30 to 5, and a full day is $15 ($1.75 per hour) with lunch included. A 1½-hour ski lesson with equipment included is $5 additional. The **Bratskeller Ski School** is for ages five and up and has facilities at LionsHead and Golden Peak. A full day (including instruction) is $14. Parents must supply lunch money.

Kids at Vail even have their own mountain. Peanut Peak is up in the Eagle's Nest area and devoted wholly to children, complete with Disney characters as slalom gates, an Indian tepee, a silver mine, and a playground director to organize activities.

COSTS

There are not many ways to get around the fact that, along with Aspen, Vail is the most expensive ski resort in North America. One way to try, though, is to take advantage of the early (November 23–December 16) and late (April 2–23) season discounts, which offer savings of up to 23% on lodging and 20% on ski school packages.

22

Winter Park

For most of its nearly 40 years, Winter Park languished as one of the several Denver "day areas." Only 1½ hours from Denver, and with good snow and a decent mountain, Winter Park continued adequately in that incarnation until 1975, when the area did something that hasn't been done in decades of American skiing: it built another mountain. The construction of Mary Jane so radically altered Winter Park that even now, three years later, the area still is in a distinct period of adjustment.

There is no question that construction of the Jane, as it is called, converted a modest intermediate mountain into a vast, well-balanced complex where the expert is genuinely challenged. The real question is whether Winter Park has created a monster. The town still more closely resembles a trailer camp than a resort; accommodations tend to run toward standard motel; and night life is sparse and singularly unsophisticated. Yet Winter Park is a mammoth success (Vail is the only other Colorado ski area that sells more lift tickets). Whether this success can persist without some much needed development is uncertain.

ACCESSIBILITY

Winter Park is wonderfully accessible. Only 70 miles from Denver, it is 1½ hours by car or bus from the airport, on good all-weather roads. All major car rentals are available at the Denver airport, and both Continental Trailway and Greyline buses leave from the airport. Air service is also available on Rocky Mountain Airways from Denver to Granby, 18 miles from the ski area. Transportation is then available to the ski area at between $1.50–14, depending on the number of people. For train lovers, Winter Park can be reached from Denver on Saturdays and Sundays, departing Denver at 8 A.M. and arriving at approximately 10 A.M. Trains return to Denver at 4 P.M. on both weekend days. For those with the inclination, the train ride is a spectacularly scenic one through the Continental Divide, and the mountain offers a $1 discount on the lift ticket for anyone taking the train. Discounts are also available to cars carrying 4 or more people.

THE SKIING

Winter Park now comprises two separate and distinct mountains with excellent access between them. Winter Park, the original mountain, has 8 double chair lifts rising 1,600 vertical feet to a 10,700-foot summit. Mary Jane has 3 double chairs and an access lift rising 1,650 feet to an 11,125-foot elevation. Putting the mountains together and skiing from the top of the Jane to the base of Winter Park extends the vertical to 2,025 feet. The expanded uphill capacity of 14,800 per hour is second in the state (again behind only Vail), though lift lines can still be horrendous on weekends. Substantial snow-making ensures a long season by Colorado standards, with this year's season running from November 19 through April 23.

There wasn't much expert skiing at Winter Park before the Jane, and even that mountain is still overwhelmingly a beginner's and intermediate's mountain. From the Apollo chair lift on Winter Park, advanced skiers can ski Balch, Mulligan's Mile, or Lucky Pierre—all of which are similarly pitched (7) and alternate between cruising and manageable bump skiing.

The intermediate has several choices on Winter Park, but the most popular chairs seem to be the Eskimo and Prospector lifts which service a number of beginner and intermediate runs. Cranmer and Allan Phipps are both long, wide open, and ideal for the recreational intermediate. The vain and intrepid intermediate can try Bradley's Bash, the liftline of the Apollo chair, which has recently been downgraded from advanced.

The beginner has an unusual number of options at Winter Park. Unlike many mountains, Winter Park has a number of runs, including Allan Phipps, where the beginner can ski from top to bottom of the mountain. Also, the new Olympia lift area and the Looking Glass chair lift open up unusually nice terrain for both the beginner and intermediate. The runs off these chairs are pretty, woodsy, isolated, and a little narrow—a terrain combination that the beginner and intermediate seldom get to see. Adding to the variety is a totally different view of the valley and beyond, which is found at the top of the Olympia lift.

Mary Jane is some mountain. In fact, (are you ready for the heresy) it's better than anything at Aspen. Primarily an expert's mountain, it does have three good intermediate runs (Sleeper, Arrowhead Loop, and Mary Jane) that

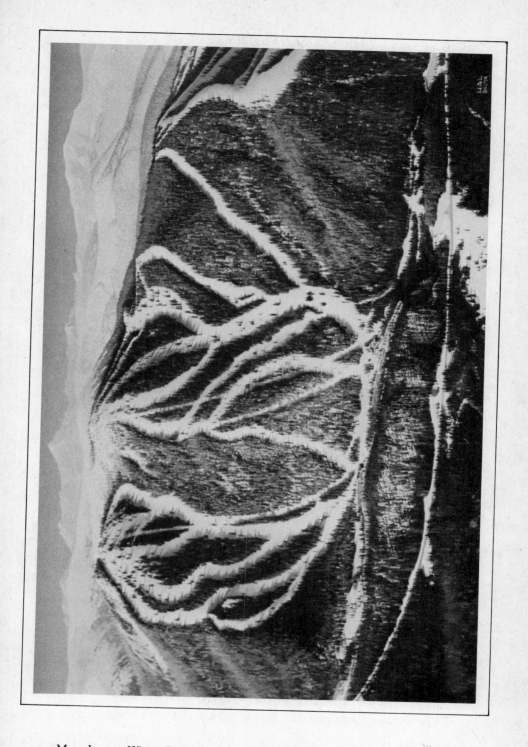

Mary Jane at Winter Park   COURTESY WINTER PARK RECREATIONAL ASSOCIATION

may intimidate the intermediate somewhat because of all the bombers who zing by while taking a little break from the bumps. The trails at Mary Jane are astonishingly similar to those at Vail, another mountain we think very highly of. The Jane's trails are all steep (8–9), bumpy, and long.

For those skiers coming over from Winter Park, the initiation run is Outhouse, a long, steep, unrelenting bump run (8.75). Thankfully, the bumps are well maintained by the mountain's policy of forbidding skiing on Outhouse (and Golden Spike, another good bump run) on skis shorter than 185 centimeters. While we express no opinion on the constitutionality of this policy, it sure does keep the bumps perfect. The biggest bumps are on Drunken Frenchman, while the steepest run is Rifle's Sight Notch (9). When lift lines begin to mount, skiing Rifle's Sight is a good idea because it is a long, constantly demanding run that's plenty of work and from which you can be whisked back up on the Pony Express lift, only a 6-minute ride. Finally, Derailer and Phantom Bridge are excellent steep bump runs (8–8.5), and for the powder days Sluice Box is a good powder chute. For those familiar with Highline, Blue Ox, and Roger's Run at Vail, Mary Jane will be like coming home.

A couple of secrets about Mary Jane: The trails are somewhat layered, so that runoffs can be totally avoided by taking some hard-to-find traverses through the trees from the bottom of one face to the top of another. Ask a local. Also, when skiing back from Mary Jane to Winter Park at the end of the day, the tree route saves time, avoids cut tracks, and is a generally better run.

Snow conditions are standard for Colorado, and Winter Park's new top-to-bottom snowmaking capacity will supplement the 250 inches of annual snowfall. Weather, particularly in March, can be glorious.

Finally, Winter Park has an excellent and unique training and instructional program for the handicapped skier.

INTEGRATION OF THE SLOPES

The ski access in both directions between Winter Park and Mary Jane is very good, so meeting friends for lunch in the cafeteria at the base of either mountain is no problem. Snoasis, a cafeteria and warming hut near the base of the Eskimo and Prospector chairs at Winter Park, provides an alternative to going all the way down.

LIFE IN THE AREA

To be as succinct as possible: Winter Park is not yet a resort.

ACCESSIBILITY TO THE SLOPES

Virtually none of the lodges at Winter Park are within walking distance of the ski area. Most accommodations are about 3 miles away in neighboring Hideaway Park or beyond. This is the cause of some confusion, since "town" is Hideaway Park and not Winter Park. Things are spread out enough so that a car is helpful though not totally necessary, since most (but not all) lodges run free shuttle service to and from the ski area. Check with your lodge in advance.

ACCOMMODATIONS

Accommodations in Winter Park are about evenly split between those places offering straight lodging and those operating on the Modified American Plan, serving two meals. Compared with most resorts, the accommodations at Winter Park, with certain exceptions, are undistinguished.

The places offering no meals are generally motel-type accommodations. Of these, the two nicest are the **Alpenglo Motor Lodge** and the **Olympia Motor Lodge** (both $30). Other motels around town are more or less what one would expect in small Western towns.

A little more diversity and quality are found among the lodges on the Modified American Plan. The closest to the mountain is the **High Country Inn** ($35 per person), one of the only lodges within walking distance of the mountain; the Inn has a pool, a sauna, and a bar featuring entertainment. A possibility for the couple seeking seclusion is the **Devil's Thumb Ranch,** set on 745 acres in neighboring Fraser ($35 per person). Two rustic log lodges look up into the Continental Divide, but modern amenities include saunas and Jacuzzis: the **Tally Ho Ranch** is on 360 acres and is furnished in antique pine by Ethan Allen; it has some of the better food in the valley ($35 per person). **Millers Idelwild Inn** caters to families and gives discounts to children ($25 adults; $18.50 children). Singles generally head for the **Ski Idelwild,** with its pool, steam bath, and cocktail lounge ($23 per person), or the **Woodspur,** with sauna, game room, and bar ($23 per person). **Beaver Ski Chalet** combines a reputation for good food with nice accommodations; it has sauna, Jacuzzi, entertainment, and cross-country skiing on the premises.

Winter Park has several condominium developments that rent to skiers, with prices depending on size. The nicest are **Hideaway Village;** all units have fireplaces and kitchens, and there is a pool and sauna. Other well-appointed units are at **Lion's Gate Pines Lodge;** however, no shuttle service is available from the units to the slopes. Families like **Meadow Ridge Condominiums;** the rates here are moderate, and indoor tennis courts, a pool, saunas, and Jacuzzis are available.

For reservations, call 303–726–5588.

RESTAURANTS

At Winter Park, restaurants are more or less adequate—nothing special in terms of either ambience or cuisine. The best food, and the only place with gourmet aspiratons, is the **Hideaway,** which offers northern Italian specialities. **Corona Station** is the local steak-and-salad emporium, and **C's III** also specializes in steak and seafood.

In the event they're not filled up with their own guests, a few of the MAP lodges may be the best bet for dinner, particularly **Devil's Thumb Ranch, Arapahoe Lodge, Beaver's,** and the **Tally Ho Ranch.**

For something lighter and less expensive, try the **Shed,** where you can get good burgers and Mexican food, or the **Attic,** a crepe and quiche restaurant in a homey atmosphere. The **Pinewood** in nearby Fraser has the best breakfast around.

APRÈS-SKI AND NIGHT LIFE

Various resorts are typified by a certain type of night life. Aspen swings, Steamboat hoots and hollers, and Sugar Bowl is stately. So, too, is Winter Park distinctive: it is tacky.

The social life at Winter Park centers around three establishments. Directly after skiing, people generally head for **Adolph's.** It's not much to look at, but it's the closest bar to the mountain and apparently enjoys its popularity by default; there is often a folk singer in the evening, and a band generally performs on weekend nights. During the afternoon and evening, many locals frequent the **Swiss House** in neighboring Hideaway Park; there is occasional music in this somewhat sleazy rathskeller, but most of its popularity comes from its Advent TV and its continuous telecasting of sporting events—during football season, the Swiss House is the worldwide center for Broncomania. At night, everyone who wants to dance goes to **C's III;** appropriately below the town market, and with its blinking lights and not insubstantial number of polyestered patrons, C's III can only be classified as the K-Mart of discos.

DIVERSION

While various activities are available at Winter Park, including sleigh rides, snow-cat tours of the mountain, snow tubing, and snowmobiling, the major diversion is cross-country skiing. Cross-country trails, equipment, and rentals are provided at several lodges in the valley, including **Ski Idlewild, Beavers,** and **Devil's Thumb Ranch.** Devil's Thumb is devoted exclusively to cross-country, with 50 kilometers of trails laid out in rolling meadows at the base of the Continental Divide.

CHILDREN

There is a nursery open daily at Winter Park. It accepts children from six months to eight years old and is open from 8:30 A.M. to 4 P.M. The cost is $7 for the day and $5 for each sibling. Mary Jane currently has no nursery facilities.

COSTS

Costs are moderate at Winter Park, but then, so is the quality of what is offered. Skiing is the exception: a $10 lift ticket allows you to ski on the best mountain within 2 hours of Denver.

23

Sun Valley

Sun Valley is a centerpiece of American skiing. Started in the 1930's under the auspices of Averell Harriman and the Union Pacific Railroad, the resort has moved gracefully into the seventies. Now a modern ski development, it has lost none its traditional elegance. To this day, the Sun Valley image of a stylish, fashionable resort, the home of "beautiful people," has been preserved. Lift lines are a parade of the well-dressed, well-manicured, and well-tanned. Baldy, the principal ski center, has much more than style. It may be America's best-planned ski mountain. Each of its several faces has numerous trails with excellent intermediate or expert terrain. The mountain is busy and dynamic, and its vitality is felt throughout the resort.

ACCESSIBILITY

Sun Valley is not the most accessible of resorts. The usual approach is through Boise (168 miles, a 3-hour drive) or Twins Falls (78 miles, a 1½-hour drive). The trip from Salt Lake is about 5½ hours by car; from Seattle, it takes about 10 hours.

There are direct flights to Boise from Los Angeles, San Francisco, Portland, and Seattle, but from the East or Midwest the best connections are made through Salt Lake. Bus service is available from these airports to the Sun Valley Village, and arrangements should be made in advance. There are also three or four direct flights a day from Salt Lake or Boise to the Hailey Airport, about 10 miles south of Sun Valley. The trip to Sun Valley from the East or Midwest is likely to take a full day from either direction.

THE SKIING

There are three downhill areas at Sun Valley, but Baldy Mountain, with its 3,400-foot vertical, 11 chair lifts, and an hourly uphill lift capacity of more than 15,000 persons, is the hub. Baldy is a giant—too giant for some. It has several faces. Dividing it in half is Christmas Ridge, with a north and south face each of which is skied. The south side of the ridge is the northern edge of a huge valley that has runs coming down on three sides. There are trails along Christmas Ridge itself, bowls going down the west end of the valley, and trails on the far side (south) on Seattle Ridge. The trails off Christmas Ridge are challenging intermediate-expert runs that usually have bumps. The bowls on the west side are expert terrain (though marked intermediate), often made more difficult by crusted or slushy snow. The runs on Seattle Ridge are good intermediate and advanced novice trails. There are three sets of chairs in this valley. Christmas Ridge has a parallel double and triple chair with 1,350 feet of vertical, taking you to the top of the mountain. If you ski off Christmas Ridge down the bowls, you pick up the lower Cold Springs chair, with 1,000 feet of vertical, that joins the Christmas Ridge chairs. One run off the Cold Springs chair, Inhibition, is rarely skied, mostly unpacked, and has a frighteningly steep (10) bottom section. The Seattle Ridge chair (1,400' vertical) services the trails on that ridge.

On the north side of Christmas Ridge are two valleys, River Run and Warm Springs. These valleys are the two points of entry to the mountain. Several of the trails dropping into River Run are steep and moguled. The most notorious is Exhibition, which starts at the east end of Christmas Ridge and drops down under the Exhibition triple chair (1,322' vertical). Exhibition is very steep at the top (9), with huge moguls but with a fall line that slants off to the right and makes it difficult to maintain a line through the bumps. Intermediates can take one of several routes into the River Run valley, avoiding the steep tops of Exhibition or Upper Holiday. There are even several trail-catwalk combinations to permit novices back down into River Run.

The second valley, north of Christmas Ridge, also has excellent expert and intermediate terrain. Here, experts will find Limelight, the bump run *par excellence.* Limelight comes off the very top of Baldy into the Warm Springs valley. It has an even, continuous pitch of about 25–30°, with large moguls throughout most of its 1,500 feet of vertical. The trail is cut true to the fall line. Limelight reminds us a bit of the National at Stowe—not terrifyingly steep, but always demanding and always moguled. The lift up Limelight has the longest vertical at Sun Valley (2,220') and one of the greatest single chair

Baldy Mountain, top of River Run at Sun Valley   COURTESY SUN VALLEY SKI AREA

lift drops in the West. The rest of the runs in Warm Springs are mainly intermediate or a combination of intermediate-expert.

All in all, Baldy (with the exception of Inhibition) does not have the terrifyingly steep drops of Jackson and Snowbird. The whole of Baldy, however, is skiable, having consistent advanced skiing terrain. There are one or two novice slopes, but these feed into advanced slopes. The novice has to take refuge on catwalks.

One of the pleasures of Sun Valley is following the sun around the mountain. Seattle Ridge has sun early in the day, Christmas Ridge and Bowl have it all day, and Warm Springs has it late in the day in the spring.

The beginner areas of Sun Valley are two small mountains, Dollar (628' vertical) and Elkhorn (550' vertical), that are very close to the village at Sun Valley and about 3 miles from Baldy. Both are treeless hills with broad, packed trails and short runs. A week on Dollar or Elkhorn could be a very long week. Ideally, the novice can graduate to Baldy, though the skiing on Baldy really requires at least an intermediate ability unless the novice is happy with a mixture of trails and catwalks.

A criticism of the lifts at Sun Valley is that the mountain has too many of them. Even so, there are lines on the popular chairs. You can usually find lifts without lines, but those on Christmas Ridge and Limelight are likely to have 10-minute waits during major holiday and some spring weeks. Less popular chairs, like Sunnyside on Exhibition, serving River Run (1,850' vertical), or Flying Squirrel in Warm Springs (1,600' vertical), are good alternatives with tough runs and only occasional lines.

Sun Valley survives on a modest, average annual snowfall of less than 200 inches. White gold does not fall in abundance the way it does in Utah. The winter of 1977 forced the mountain to put in snowmaking, but the capacity is limited. Sun Valley does pretty well with the snow it has. The mountain has been groomed so that a little cover goes a long way. In March, however, the snow is often hard-packed and bare spots are not unusual.

Is Sun Valley really sunny? The name alone has created the image of sun and warmth, and in part the image is accurate. In February and March, Sun Valley gets a lot of sun, though perhaps not as much as Colorado. Despite a northerly location, it has moderate temperature and is warm in February and March.

LIFE IN THE AREA

The resort comprises four centers. The focus is the Sun Valley Village, which has two large but attractive 1930's hotels, condominiums, and shops.

The second area is Elkhorn, which has a large hotel, condominiums, shops and its own novice-intermediate lift. Elkhorn is about 4 miles from Baldy. The commercial center is Ketchum, a small, undistinguished Western town with gas stations in the middle of Main Street. Ketchum has many motels, some good restaurants, night dives, and places for just plain folks. Finally, at the base of Baldy at Warm Springs is a small grouping of hotels and condominiums.

Facilities and services are spread out among the areas, though Sun Valley Village (referred to as "Sun Valley") is the primary resort center. Together, these clusters have the complete range of facilities, including classy condominiums, tacky motels, elegant discos, and raunchy bars.

ACCOMMODATIONS

The two large hotels at the center of Sun Valley are the **Sun Valley Lodge and Inn.** Both were built in the late thirties but have been fully modernized. Each has restaurants and entertainment lounges, an outdoor heated pool, a sauna, and a Jacuzzi. There is an outdoor skating rink right in front of the Lodge. The bus to Baldy starts a few feet from the door of each. (Packages range from $175 to $400 per person.)

The Village has several sets of modern condominiums. The **Lodge Apartments** and **Cottonwood Condominiums** are most convenient to the center but are located in a congested area. The **Wildflower Condominiums** are a 3-minute walk from the center. The **Villager Condominiums, Dollar Meadow,** and **Snow Creek Condominiums** are a 5- to 10-minute walk. (Packages start at $200 per person.) Staying at the condominiums gives you access to the Lodge and Inn facilities.

Elkhorn is an attractive Tyrolian inn-and-condominium center. It is the farthest from Baldy but has bus service. The inn has a good restaurant, an entertainment lounge, and a health club including sauna and Jacuzzi, with package rates starting at $209 per person double occupancy. The condominiums are modern and tasteful. Rates are somewhat less expensive than those at Sun Valley.

For reservations at Sun Valley or Elkhorn, there is a toll-free number: 800-635-8261.

Ketchum has numerous motels. The **Christiana Lodge,** with perhaps the best restaurant around, and the **Tamarack Lodge,** with swimming pool, are elegant, modern motels located right in Ketchum. There is a **Holiday Inn** a half-mile north of Ketchum. About 500 yards from the River Run lift on Baldy is the **Tyrolian Lodge,** a Best Western Motel with sauna ($35 per night per room). An inexpensive, inelegant motel ($20 per room) on Main Street is the **Bald Mountain Hot Springs Motel.** On the road to Warm Springs, one mile from the lifts, is the **Heidelberg Inn,** a two-story motel with a bubbled-in heated pool ($28 per room). All of the Ketchum accommodations have access to the Ketchum bus for rides to the lifts. Reservations at these lodges and others can be made through the Sun Valley/Ketchum Resort Association: 208-726-4471.

For those who want to wake up at the mountain, the choice must be Warm Springs. Most of the accommodations here are controlled by Sun Resorts, which offers elegant modern condominiums at the **International Village,** the **Prospector,** and the **Edelweiss.** All have kitchens, swimming pools, and saunas, there is an excellent restaurant and a disco, as well as access to Elevation 6,000. There are two older, adequate, and inexpensive inns in Warm Springs, the **Aspen Inn** and **Lift Haven Inn.** Reservations at Warm Springs can be made through Sun Resorts: 800-635-4441.

RESTAURANTS

The area has many superior restaurants. The **Christiana Restaurant** has the *haute cuisine* in Ketchum. At the Sun Valley Lodge, the **Duchin Room** also serves good French food. French, small, and good is **La Provence** in Ketchum. There are several steak house–restaurants, the **Ore House** in the Sun Valley Mall, the **Ram,** part of the Sun Valley Inn, and the **Pioneer Saloon** and **Cedars Yacht Club** in Ketchum.

At Warm Springs is **Elevation 6,000,** an excellent Italian-Continental restaurant with a handsome setting.

There are several good informal or inexpensive restaurants, including **Louie's Pizza and Italian Restaurant, Su Casa** (Mexican), the **River Street Retreat** in Ketchum, and the **Fondue Strube** at Elkhorn Village.

APRÈS-SKI AND NIGHT LIFE

Coming off Baldy, for those who need a drink before the bus ride, there is often live entertainment at **Elevation 6,000** in Warm Springs. Otherwise, après-ski life is found back at Sun Valley, where the older set hangs out in the **Duchin Bar** at the Lodge or at the **Village Inn** in Elkhorn. The younger set is at home at the **Ram** in the Sun Valley Inn.

At night, there is real choice. In Sun Valley at the Lodge, the kids (18–30) go downstairs to the **Boiler Room,** a disco; the adults (30–60), upstairs to the somewhat square **Duchin Bar,** which has a "trio." The Ram and **Ore House** also have live entertainment.

Those who prefer more grit and less class can try one of several saloons on Main Street in Ketchum, the **Alpine Saloon, Mulvaney's,** or **Salveys,** where hard rock is in style. There is a pleasant, noisy bar at the **Cedars Yacht Club.**

At Warm Springs is the **Club Dominique,** which, like the bars in Sun Valley, is modern and attractive, and has live or recorded music.

Sun Valley is always lively, even during the week, and provides a choice between elegant and simple entertainment.

DIVERSION

The resort has bars, movie theaters (2), ice rinks (2 outdoors, 1 indoors), swimming pools, indoor horseback lessons (no riding), sleigh rides, a gun club, some helicopter skiing, cross-country skiing, and more. There are several cross-country centers, one at Elkhorn, one at Dollar, and one at the Galena Lodge, 24 miles from Sun Valley, in the national park. Three indoor tennis courts are available in Hailey, 10 miles away, and in Ketchum there is the **Racquetball Club,** with a Jacuzzi and health facilities. The Lodge has bowling, a game room, and a health club.

Each night there are sleigh-ride trips to Trail Creek Cabin, where there is good dining and live entertainment. Sun Valley even has a professional hockey team that plays at the arena in the Village.

For those who may be overwhelmed by the whole experience and just want to stay home, the resort has cable TV that receives on about 10 channels.

CHILDREN

If you stay at Sun Valley and intend to ski with your kids at Dollar, Elkhorn, or Baldy, the resort is fine for the family. There are four child-care centers, two in the Village and one at Elkhorn. You can leave the kids for the day ($2 per hour). The **Lodge** and **Inn** have good play facilities for children. The one difficulty might arise is if you want to ski some but not all of the time with your children and they're not ready for Baldy. Transition back and forth to the mountain or supervision may not be easy. Sun Valley is big and impersonal.

COSTS

Sun Valley is expensive but not outrageously so. Lifts are $13 per day, with little reduction for a 6-day ticket ($72) in high season. Housing is costly, and food is not included in packages. The better restaurants charge between $9 and $12 per entrée; the lesser, $7 to $9.

24
The Big Mountain

The Big Mountain is, according to its own publicity blurb, "Western America's most successful skiing environment." But is it really that big? Well, the answer is no. The mountain is small by Western standards. But once you get there, you'll find it cozy and quiet, unpretentious and friendly. The resort is compact and convenient; the facilities are attractive but very simple. The area is predominantly a family area and because it does have some terrain for all categories of skiers, it is extremely well suited to that purpose.

ACCESSIBILITY

The Big Mountain is in northwestern Montana, about 50 miles from the Canadian border near the town of Whitefish. It is about a 2½-hour drive north from Missoula and a 4-hour drive east from Spokane, Washington, 200 miles away. It is 2 hours from any interstate going either east-west or north-south. The closest large city is Calgary, Alberta, about 3 hours away. Whitefish may not be the center of the interstate highway system, but it is on the main line —yes, the railroad—between Chicago, Minneapolis, and Seattle, and is served by the *Empire Builder,* which makes the run from Chicago in 31 hours. From Seattle, the train trip is about 16 hours; from Spokane, 6 hours.

By air, you fly to the Kalispell Airport, 19 miles from the mountain. There is direct service from Spokane, Missoula, Bozeman, and Salt Lake. From Minneapolis or Seattle, allow about half a day for traveling.

THE SKIING

The Big Mountain is a small mountain with a balanced sprinkling of terrain. The major lift (6,800' long; 2,000' vertical) goes up a round face that is treeless and steep for its upper third. The few trees at the top are covered and bent over by the heavy snow of northern Montana and look like shrouded ghosts. The top third of the mountain is a broad bowl, steep in the middle and on the left side, moderate to easy on the right. Trail skiing begins at the base of the bowl, with several intermediate runs and two expert drops, Heap Steep and Powder Trap, which are generally without moguls and are no longer than 1,000 feet.

A second lift, a double chair (3,840' long; 1,120' vertical), has perfect cruising intermediate terrain, with one broad, open slope just to the left of the chair. This is the most popular trail on the mountain and attracts all the local boomers. To the right is Lower Mully's Run, moguled, marked expert, but with a gentle pitch—a good, undemanding practice area. Finally, there are two beginner-intermediate lifts, a triple chair and a T-bar. These lifts serve an excellent practice area free of interference from speeding kids and experts. The trails at every level of difficulty are broad, open, and well groomed.

Big Mountain rarely has lift lines during the week, except for Christmas or except when the local school system brings children up for the late afternoon. On weekends, the Big Mountain, popular with local skiers and with Canadians, does have lines, particularly on the intermediate chair. The lift lines can be 20 minutes long, though this is unusual.

The resort advertises mild winters (average temperature 23°), and the claim is true. The snow, however, is wet and heavy. It provides a good cover but limited powder skiing. This is a shame, because the mountain, which is steep and open at the top, would be particular well suited for skiing powder. The wetness of the snow results in part from the low elevation of the summit, 6,800 feet, a thousand feet below the *base* of Aspen or Snowbird. The mountain also faces south and is exposed to direct sunlight. The real weather difficulty is the "fog" that seems to cling to the mountain in the winter months. Rumored to come off Whitefish Lake, it can reduce visibility completely on the main chair and make skiing there, with its treeless summit, treacherous indeed.

LIFE IN THE AREA

The resort itself is cute, compact, simple, and most definitely unpretentious. There are three inns, two bars, and a Bierstube within 100 yards of the lifts. The bars have nightly entertainment. The hotels have the American Plan.

Eight miles from the Big Mountain is the town of Whitefish, with a main street that looks like a Hollywood movie set version of a Western small town. Whitefish has several bar-saloons and a freewheeling atmosphere. The saloons have gambling (cards and keno) and dancing. It's not jet-set swank; it's high-country camp.

ACCOMMODATIONS

Of the three inns at the mountain, the **Ski Lodge** and the **Chalet** are simple, the **Apinglow Inn** somewhat more elegant. The Lodge has its own bar and an entertainment spot in the cellar. The Chalet has a homey lounge with fireplace and a plain dining room. The rates are truly inexpensive, but the rooms are generally quite small. At each, the cost per person for 6 nights double occupancy, with bath, a 5-day lift ticket, and three meals a day is $178. One night for 2 persons without meals is $18. The Alpinglow is a modern, four-story chalet-type building with a heated outdoor pool and sauna. It offers the same package for $214. These three hotels are right at the lift. Near the lift are the **Alpine Village Homes,** which are pleasant condominiums rented by the week.

Off the mountain, there are several mediocre motels, hotels, and condominiums. Five miles from the mountain, toward Whitefish, is the **Viking Lodge,** which, while a bit tacky, does have an outdoor heated pool, a coed sauna, and an adequate dining room with a pleasant bar ($19). Next to it are the modern **Wildwood Condominiums.** Two miles from the mountain, in splendid isolation, are the **Ptarmigan Condominiums,** modern with a swimming pool (check to see if it's open) and sauna. In Whitefish are the inexpensive **Cadillac Hotel** ($10) and **Palm Hotel** ($12.50), and the mediocre **Downtowner Motel** ($17). Finally, outside Whitefish, a mile south, are several motels that range from mediocre (**Mountain Holiday**) to just passable (**Allen's Motel, Pine Lodge Motel,** and **Whitefish Motel**).

The number for reservations at the inns on the mountain is 406-862-3511.

RESTAURANTS

If you're staying at the mountain, you'll find the food adequate at any of the three inns. In or around Whitefish, there are more choices. Most formal is **Stump Town** on Main Street, an attractive steak and lobster restaurant. The restaurant at the **Viking Lodge** serves steak, fish, and chicken in a second floor A-framed dining room looking out over the lake. Up the road from the Viking toward the mountain is **Que Pasa,** a good Mexican restaurant, and somewhat nearer town (about 2 miles from Whitefish) on that same road is **The Place,** an informal pizza, sandwich, beer and wine restaurant with pool tables, TV, and an appealing atmosphere popular with students.

APRÈS-SKI AND NIGHT LIFE

You have to smile when you see downtown Whitefish. It has a thigh-slapping, honky-tonk, yet authentic Western old-town quality. There are several bars with wooden floors and red velvet walls, card tables, and pool tables. The **Palm Hotel** adds to this a low-ceilinged disco with high-intensity strobe lighting. The **Hanging Tree,** also on Main Street, is a raunchy bar that has live hard rock three or four days a week.

Five or six nights a week at the mountain, there is live entertainment, usually guitar music, at the **Lodge** and, on weekends, light rock at the **Bierstube.** But the lively activity is found in Whitefish, which is really worth a visit.

DIVERSION

Big Mountain is not recommended for non-skiers. Other than skiing, the choices are limited. In the valley, six miles from the mountain, there is the **Whitefish Nordic Ski Center,** a cross-country center with groomed trails. You can also rent cross-country equipment at the mountain and ski there. Beyond that and a few uninteresting shops in town, you're on your own. Whitefish has night skiing on a novice-intermediate run, Tuesday through Saturday night till 10:30 P.M.

CHILDREN

The Big Mountain is great for kids. It's inexpensive, and if you stay at the mountain, children can be self-sufficient. There's a nice nursery right in the center of things. Game rooms at the mountain are limited to pinball.

COSTS

Probably the cheapest major area in the West, the Big Mountain has 6-night, 5-day packages with lift tickets (without lessons) and three meals a day for $155. One night's lodging at the Ski Lodge and Chalet with adjoining bath and *three* meals is $23.50 per night per person. The day's lift ticket is $8.50. The motels around Whitefish are also inexpensive. Even meals in the area are less expensive than those at most ski areas.

25

Big Sky

Big Sky was built in the early 1970's, at a time when everyone—including its creator, NBC anchorman Chet Huntley—wanted to withdraw from the real world of Vietnam and Watergate. The developers sought a mountain that was as far away from urban America as they could get. Fixing on Lone Mountain, Montana, which in name and otherwise met these requirements perfectly, they built a resort that was consistent with their values. It was small, uncluttered, and remote, and so it remains to this day, with all the advantages and disadvantages of seclusion. Big Sky is quiet and does not have lift lines; it has little entertainment and is hard to get to. The skiing, unfortunately, is flawed: the novice and intermediate trails are good; the expert trails are almost nonexistent. But for those who want to "mellow out," this attractive resort is there, in the middle of nowhere, inviting you to "ski the sky."

ACCESSIBILITY

Big Sky is 40 miles south of Bozeman and 50 miles north of Yellowstone National Park. The distance from Salt Lake is about 380 miles; from Spokane, 450; and from Billings, Montana, 180 miles. Fortunately, there is air service to Bozeman from Billings, Minneapolis, and Chicago, and from Salt Lake, Boise, and Seattle. Since service can be rather disjointed, if you miss a connection you'll lose half a day. There is sporadic bus service from Bozeman. If you rent a car, don't expect to drop it off at Big Sky. You'll probably have to keep it for the week and drive it back.

THE SKIING

Big Sky is a novice-intermediate area, with almost no terrain that will challenge the advanced skier. As usual, the length-vertical statistics tell the story. The major lift, a 4-person gondola going up the center of Lone Mountain toward its peak, is 8,670 feet long with a 1,500-foot vertical. This approaches a 6:1 ratio, making it difficult indeed to design balanced runs. The top of the gondola has some moderately steep (intermediate) drops and even a short expert drop, but once off the top third of this lift the terrain is novice-flat all the way to the bottom. In fact, it's worth noting that the Explorer chair (3,745′ long; 620′ vertical), a pleasant novice chair on the bottom right that serves three broad trails, has a ratio not terribly different from the gondola's.

Above the gondola is a triple chair going to an elevation of 9,800 feet, about 1,200 feet below the peak of Lone Mountain. This chair (833′ vertical over 3,000′) is entirely above the tree line and serves a broad, concave bowl that's steep at the top and flat at the bottom. The top is a good, treeless powder area and in the right snow can be exhilarating. This area including the gondola (a total run of 9,700′ over a 2,300′ vertical) is an intermediate area, though the top of the Lone Peak Chair is marked expert.

At the bottom to the left of the gondola is Big Sky's "expert chair," the Andesite chair, with a length of 4,800 feet and a vertical of 1,150 feet. Again, the ratio tells the story. The trails, marked expert, are broad, pleasant, advanced intermediate runs. Two trails, Ambush under the chair and Tippy's Tumble at the bottom, have sections that are somewhat steeper than the ratio would suggest. Because of their consistent terrain, these trails are fun to cruise for experts and intermediates.

Except at Christmas, Big Sky does not have lift lines. Day skiers could come from Bozeman, but for whatever reason (cost?) they choose not to. There are days in January when you can have the whole lift to yourself. Things may change, but except for winters like 1977, when Colorado and Utah had no snow, Big Sky is never crowded.

Big Sky is in snow country. Its annual snowfall is around 400 inches. The mountain faces northeast so that the snow stays fresh. The limited number of skiers helps to maintain powder conditions a day or two longer than at more crowded resorts.

LIFE IN THE AREA

The inns and hotels, bars, and shops at the resort are almost the only manifestations of life to be found for 40 miles around. The resort is made up of two villages, one at the mountain and one in the canyon below. Both, built in the 1970's, have two or three inns and several condominium developments. In the Mountain Village there is, in addition to the inns and condominiums, a handsome indoor, modern four-story commercial mall, with ski shops, a deli, two bars, a restaurant, a cafeteria, and ski school and ticket counters. The gondola terminal is part of the mall.

The guests and staff (sometimes the latter outnumber the former) are the whole community (there are no locals and almost no day skiers). They patronize the restaurants and populate the two entertainment bars at night.

ACCOMMODATIONS

At the center of the Mountain Village is the **Huntley Lodge,** a 204-room modern hotel with handsome lobbies and dining rooms but a rather stark exterior. The Lodge was completed in 1974. All rooms have twin queen-size beds, color TV, and telephones. There is a heated outdoor pool just off the mountain's slopes, a Jacuzzi, sauna, and skating rink. The Lodge is expensive, $247 per person at the height of the season (double occupancy, 7 nights with 6-day lift ticket, no meals) or $219 in low season (December, except Christmas, January, and April). One night at the Lodge is $42 for two.

Just below the Lodge are the **Stillwater** and **Deerlodge** condominiums. Both are attractive and modern, but the Deerlodge is more elegant, with a lounge, indoor pool, and sauna, and unlike Stillwater has 2- and 3-bedroom units. A per-person, double-occupancy, 7-night, 6-day ski package at Stillwater in a 1-bedroom unit is $212 ($230 with loft) and at Deerlodge is $212 for a 1-bedroom unit, $247 for 2 bedrooms. Somewhat less expensive are the **Hill Condominiums,** all studios, about a 10-minute walk from the lifts. The packages are $151 per person for 4 persons, or $168 for a studio with a loft that sleeps four.

The other inn in the mountain village is the **Lone Mountain Lodge.** Formerly the Hostel, it was modeled after the inn with the same name at Jackson Hole. It is a great facility designed for students. This lodge has small rooms with four built-in beds (one a double-decker), a private shower, toilet, and sink. There is a lobby with pool tables. The area does not advertise this bastard child, perhaps because it is inexpensive and attractive. The cost is $18 a room for two, $21 for three, and $24 for four. Unlike the Hostel at Jackson, which is right on the slopes, the Lone Mountain Lodge was stuck in a corner about a 10-minute walk from the slopes.

The **Meadow Village,** 8 miles below in the canyon, also has two inns, several condominiums, and a former hostel called the Meadow Lodge Motel, with the same rates as the Lone Mountain Lodge but with no game room. The condominiums in the Meadow Village are slightly less expensive. There is only infrequent bus service to the mountain, so if you stay in the Meadow a car is necessary.

There are three places to stay near Big Sky which are not a part of the development. The most interesting of these is the **Lone Mountain Guest Ranch.** Dating back to 1927, the Ranch is composed of many charming heated 2-bedroom log cabins that surround two central chalets in which there is a lounge and dining room. The Ranch, now run by Bob Schaap and his family, is a cross-country skiing enthusiast's Valhalla. It is located in splendid isolation a half-mile off the access road to Big Sky, about 7 miles from the area. It has its own 30 miles of trails, marked and groomed, and for the adventurer, all the mountainside that can be reckoned with as well as ready access to Yellowstone National Park. The Ranch has 7-day package plans that include 1- to 7-night stays in Yellowstone, with guided tours through Yellowstone's back-country trails. A 7-day package, double occupancy (3 days, 2 nights in Yellowstone) is $278. The same package without the Yellowstone trip costs $225 per person, double occupancy. These prices include three meals a day. The Ranch food is good, emphasizing a healthy diet, and is served family-style at large tables. Transportation is available to Big Sky for its downhill skiing guests.

In the canyon, 10 miles south off the Big Sky entrance, is the **Almart Lodge,** which has simple propane-heated cabins and a nice restaurant ($25). North of the Big Sky entrance is a second group of wood-heated cabins, **Karst Ranch.**

For reservations at Big Sky, call 800-548-4486 or 406-995-4211.

RESTAURANTS

There are three restaurants at the Huntley Lodge, one with a general menu, one a steak house, and one a fondue "stable." All are adequate; all are expensive.

In the mall, at the lifts next-door to the Huntley Lodge, there are four restaurants. Three are principally daytime restaurants: a cafeteria, which serves dinner; **Ernie's Deli;** and the **Brass Bell,** a luncheon sausage and pizza spot. Finally, the best restaurant at the mountain is **Ore House** in the mall, a small, attractive steak house.

The other two restaurants, not at the mountain, are the **Four Seasons Restaurant** in the Meadow Village and **Bucks,** a good, moderately priced chicken, steak, and Alaskan crab restaurant on the Canyon Road, 1 mile from the Big Sky entrance. Bucks provides free transportation to and from the mountain.

There are several attractive bars right in the mall. The **Saloon** and the **Caboose** both have live entertainment, usually folk or light rock. There may also be live music at **Chet's Bar** in the Lodge. The locals—that is, the staff—go down the mountain to **Bucks,** particularly on two-for-one night. There is also entertainment at the **Almark.**

All of these spots except Chet's Bar attract the college 20's crowd. To have fun, others should follow the age-old prescription, b.y.o.f.—bring your own friends.

DIVERSION

There are two cross-country ski centers at Big Sky, one in the Meadow Village, the other at the Lone Mountain Guest Ranch. The Meadow has an abundance of easy terrain. Cross-country skiing can also be done at the mountain.

The principal diversion at Big Sky is the trip to West Yellowstone, 50 miles south. From here, you can take day or overnight trips into the Park by sled, cross-country skiing, snowmobiles, or snowshoes. The most popular trip is by snowcoach into Old Faithful, where you can stay overnight at the Snow Lodge. Snowmobiles, which can be rented, may use the Park but are limited to the 150 miles of "groomed roads" (unplowed). The back country is reserved for ski tourers or snowshoers.

Snowmobiles can also be rented at the **Three Twenty Ranch,** 12 miles south of Big Sky in the Canyon.

CHILDREN

Big Sky is an excellent resort for children. The skiing itself will appeal to all novices and intermediates. The area, if you stay at the Huntley Lodge, Stillwater, or Deerlodge, is compact, and children can be left on their own.

There is a nursery in the mall that charges $10 per day or $2 per hour for children ages two to seven. No special ski school program is available.

COSTS

Big Sky is moderately expensive. The gondola lift ticket is $12, $8 for children, but a chair lift ticket allowing two gondola rides a day is also available for $8. This is the best deal in town. Housing, food, and drink are all comparable to major Colorado resorts. The two former "hostels," the Lone

Mountain Lodge and the Meadow Lodge Motel, provide an excellent inexpensive housing choice for the young or young at heart. The rates at the Huntley Lodge and the condominiums do not include food, so actually the week's package is expensive. And if you add the cost of getting there, Big Sky is no steal.

26

Taos

Taos Ski Valley is a very special small corner of American skiing. The mountain itself is not expansive like Vail or Jackson, but it is one of the four or five toughest in North America. The Ski Valley is tiny, with a handful of inns and condominiums, and gives a feeling of being removed and sheltered from the everyday world. Perhaps the most European of all American resorts, Taos is quiet and, except for holiday weeks, intimate. Go with family and friends, settle in, join the ski school, and enjoy an unpressured week of undistracted, uncluttered, very challenging skiing.

ACCESSIBILITY

The best approach to Taos from East or West is to fly to Albuquerque. From the East Coast, this usually can be done by a direct but not nonstop service. From the West, Chicago, or Texas, there is nonstop service. Once in Albuquerque, you can rent a car or use the limited bus service to the Valley. The 150-mile drive takes 3 hours. You won't need a car at Taos, and you can arrange to drop it at the Valley (though you may wish to keep the car for trips into town). There are limited scheduled flights from Albuquerque or Denver to the Taos airport, 18 miles from the Ski Valley. From the East, it almost invariably takes a full day to get to the resort, there being few evening flights to Albuquerque. The alternative route through Denver offers better air service but requires a 5½-hour drive. Relax, take a morning flight, and enjoy the drive across the fascinating desert of the Southwest on your way to the snow-covered slopes.

THE SKIING

Every description of Taos starts with a report of the awe experienced by the newcomer who looks up from the base of the mountain and sees Al's Run and Snake Dance cascading down into the Valley. (Are those the only runs? How will I get down?) Well, as the customary story continues, a sign at one of the lifts states, "Don't panic," since there's a lot more to Taos than these two overbearing slopes.

And indeed there is more—a lot of additional expert terrain, some excellent intermediate terrain, and some very limited novice terrain if you're good enough to get to it.

In general, the skiing at Taos is trail skiing, not unlike in the East, though Ernie Blake, the founder, father, and shepherd of the valley, would quickly add that the weather, the snow, and the open areas in Kachina Basin are in fact very Western. Trails on the mountain have been broadened and glades have been opened on many of the steep faces.

The principal mountain has two sets of overlapping chair lifts with a total vertical of 2,600 feet and a peak elevation at 11,819 feet. The bottom chair, which runs up notorious Al's Run, is the steepest we know of anywhere (1,800' vertical, 4,000' long, a 27° slope). Al's Run itself, and the combination of Al's Run to Inferno or Spencer's Bowl into Snake Dance, are steep, moguled, demanding expert runs (9's)—as tough or tougher than Limelight at Sun Valley, Silver Fox at Snowbird, or the Ridge of Bell at Aspen (and considerably longer than the Ridge). The second set of parallel chair lifts going to the summit have a vertical of 1,100 feet over a distance of 3,600 feet. The liftline here, Reforma, and the run to the left, Blitz, are also very steep, moguled runs. To the right on this second set of lifts are five chutes, narrow and heart-stoppingly steep (10's), comparable to the chutes at Jackson or Snowbird. Taking these, you ski, or perhaps slide, into the open flat bowls of West Basin, which allows you to catch your breath, your confidence, and your friends, who went around. There is still more expert terrain off to the left of both of these chairs. Two glade trails, often unpacked, drop steeply from the middle of the second lift off to the right to the bottom of the first chair.

But don't despair: Taos has some good, wandering intermediate terrain on these two front chairs. Perhaps the most interesting run is Porcupine, which is broad on top and then twists and turns through the trees to the bottom. The trails on the bottom half of the second chair are relaxed intermediate runs that are entered by taking a trail off the top and then a short catwalk through the steep liftline of this chair. The Whitefeather trail, on the bottom lift, is a

Taos: Al's Run chair at bottom left, upper chair and steep bowls on right
(Kachina chair is to extreme left, not visible in photo) COURTESY TAOS SKI AREA

novice-intermediate run with uneven terrain. The problem with Whitefeather and other novice-intermediate trails at Taos is that they also serve as expert catwalks and are skied by all at every imaginable speed. Other than Whitefeather, there is no novice terrain in the area served by the front lifts.

Behind the main mountain in a bowl of its own is the Kachina chair. This chair has an interspersing of novice, intermediate, and occasional expert terrain. The top is a large gentle bowl, fun for all skiers. The bottom is a mixture of trails. It is the dessert after the stiff main course of the principal mountain.

There is a small novice area at the base of Taos that is short and not well suited to beginners. The best novice trail is found at Kachina, but this can be reached only on novice-intermediate runs. It is preferable to have some trail confidence before attempting survival at Taos, but don't stay home for lack of it.

Taos promises no lift lines. It keeps the promise, even in holiday weeks. With its handful of accommodations and its distance from any major urban center, the lifts are almost never crowded.

Taos has an average annual snowfall of 327 inches. Its base elevation of 9,000 feet produces light powder, but its southerly location and warm weather reduce the number of light powder days. In the late spring, the cover may also be a little less good than at the more northerly resorts. On the other hand, the sun is warmer.

Taos Ski School. A special note is added here about the Taos Ski School because it is central to a week's vacation at this resort. Everyone from the raw novice to the hardened expert joins the school. In the past, Jean Mayer, the owner and manager of the Hotel St. Bernard and the 1954 Junior National French Downhill champion, led the top class at full speed down the steep trails and around the mountain. Now there are often several mountain classes. All classes have from eight to ten skiers, chosen on the basis of ability, and meet each morning with the same instructor. No particular technique is stressed beyond an emphasis on being over the skis in a natural, relaxed position. The classes keep moving, so you get in a lot of skiing. You also meet companions of equal abilities with whom you can ski the rest of the day if you choose. All join in at Taos, and the ski school tradition gives a structure to the morning and the week that all guests seem to enjoy.

LIFE IN THE AREA

Taos is special; Taos is European. These are the claims and they are true. First, the Ski Valley is very small. The principal inns in the Valley are 50 to 300 feet from the lifts. One's life is limited to the inn and the slopes. The buildings have an Alpine appearance, and managers and inn owners are European; Ernie Blake, founder of Taos Ski Valley, is Swiss-German; Jean and Dadou Mayer, French; the chef at the Thunderbird, also French; the owners of two other inns, Austrian. It is customary to eat all three meals at your inn, and the mainstays of other American ski area cuisine—hamburgers, sandwiches, French fries and Cokes—give way to beefsteak, pommes frites, and wine, even at lunch.

The town of Taos, 18 miles away, and the surrounding area have an interesting blend of three cultures: American, Spanish, and Indian. The Ski Valley adds a fourth: European. The impact of each culture is felt in the architecture, art, food, and, more generally, the ambience of the area.

ACCOMMODATIONS

At the base of the bottom chair, a ski pole's distance from the first lift's stanchion, is the **Hotel St. Bernard,** owned and operated, managed, and with food served by Jean Mayer, *qui est très français.* The rooms of the hotel are simple, small, and plain, but the lounge–dining room is charming and warm, with large wooden family tables and a hearth. Excellent French food (though not always *haute cuisine*) is served on platters for twelve, both at lunch and dinner. Dinner is a group occasion for the entire inn.

Next-door to the St. Bernard is the **Edelweiss,** owned by Jean's brother, Dadou. The rooms at the Edelweiss are more modern and spacious. Guests eat lunch and dinner at the St. Bernard, a 200-foot stroll away. Breakfast is taken in the small breakfast room at the Edelweiss and is excellent.

A few feet behind the St. Bernard is the modern **Hondo Lodge,** a plain, pleasant inn with sauna and Jacuzzi and an undistinguished dining room. The rooms are bigger and more plush than those at the St. Bernard, but the ambience is lackluster compared to its neighbor's. Across the Valley—that's 300 feet—is the **Thunderbird Lodge,** a three-story chalet building, with small rooms and an informal dining area. The food is excellently prepared French cuisine. The inn offers a sauna and a pleasant bar. Also, there is the **Innsbruck Lodge,** which is the least expensive, is convenient to the lifts, and has a Jacuzzi, a game room, and an Austrian atmosphere and cuisine.

The Valley has three condominiums that rent to guests by week or day, all convenient to the slopes, all modern, all with saunas. The **Rio Hondo** has a Jacuzzi.

That covers the accommodations in the Ski Valley itself. On the road to Taos are several other inns. Foremost among these is the luxurious **Hacienda de San Roberto,** which has a Spanish ambience, advertises the absence of telephones and television, and has a heated pool. Nine miles away is the **Abominable Snow Mansion Ski Hotel,** a $9 per night dorm with sauna and game room. Just before the town of Taos, there is the **Tennis Ranch of Taos**

(12 miles away from the Valley), with eight outdoor courts, two indoor courts, an attractive dining room and lounge, and heated swimming pool. The Tennis Ranch claims to have as little as 20 inches of snow a year while the Ski Valley has 327 inches. In Taos itself, there are other motel-lodges including the elegant **Sagebrush Inn,** which has live entertainment and a handsome lounge.

For reservations, call 505–776–2206.

RESTAURANTS

The hotels in the Ski Valley have the American Plan, including three meals a day. Food, then, is centered in these hotels. The best, as indicated, are the **St. Bernard** and the **Thunderbird,** which serve French food. Outside the hotels, there is the **Chalet Suisse,** located right on the beginner hill slope and serving steak and lobster dinners. Toward the town of Taos are several small restaurants with a Mexican adobe ambience, including the **Hacienda de San Roberto** and the **Casa Cordova** (perhaps the best). In Taos, there is a Mexican restaurant, **La Cocina.** Food at the **Tennis Ranch** is also good.

Among the hotels and restaurants out of the Ski Valley, the range of choices is varied and interesting, even if limited in number.

APRÈS-SKI AND NIGHT LIFE

Après-ski life at Taos depends largely on the type of crowd each week. After skiing—not to mention before and during skiing—skiers return to their lodges for a shot, a nip, or whatever. The St. Bernard has a lively bar, the **Rathskeller,** which is always active after the lifts close.

At night, the inns sometimes have movies, occasionally a local band, or often disco music in their small lounges. At Taos, to find out what's happening you "ask around"—in ski school in the morning, on the slopes, in the ski shop. This is what is meant by the phrase "small and friendly."

DIVERSION

The principal diversion at Taos is a trip to the town itself. The atmosphere created by the coexistence of three cultures makes this a special trip. The Taos Indians still occupy a multistory red adobe pueblo dating back more than seven centuries. The pueblo is open to visitors. The Spanish influence, dating back to 1615, is also very strong. Taos is an important art center of the Southwest and also a shopping center for silver and turquoise jewelry as well as paintings. For those unfamiliar with the Southwest, the trip to the village of Taos gives an exposure to the remarkable contrast of the green and white snow-dominated mountains and the brown, arid plains with their expansive views. Five miles north of Taos, at the edge of the mountains in San Cristopher, is the last home of D. H. Lawrence; now owned by the University of New Mexico, the former ranch has a wonderful site, though it is not otherwise interesting. Beyond sightseeing and shopping, there is tennis at the **Tennis Ranch.**

There is no formal cross-country ski center, but you can rent cross-country equipment at the central ski shop and set off on trails in the Valley.

CHILDREN

Taos is a good valley for children, except that the skiing can be difficult for them. Inasmuch as all activities are in the lodges and the lodges are small and personal, with meals served at large tables and at set times at some inns, children present no inconvenience. There is a nursery, the **Kinder Kafig,** for three- to eight-year-olds, which does an excellent job supervising the children in and out of ski school. As stated, the novice slopes are extremely limited, but with the help of the ski school the difficulties thus presented can be overcome. The primary advantage of Taos is the immediate access to the slope for all staying in the Valley.

COSTS

Taos is moderately expensive. In reviewing quoted prices, be aware that they include three meals a day, room, a 6-day lift ticket, and 6 morning lessons. At the St. Bernard, such a package is $350 per week per person, double occupancy, and $380 at the Thunderbird or $310 at the Innsbruck Lodge. A 6-day lift and lessons ticket is $110. Per-day double occupancy without skiing at the St. Bernard is $40. A day's lift ticket is $12.

27
Alta

Alta exceeds the sum of its parts. Though the combination of a very good mountain, distinguished lodges, and unbeatable snow makes Alta's popularity easy to understand, the essence of Alta really is tradition. The Brahmin of Western skiing, Alta inspires loyalty in skiers all over the world. A remarkable example lies in the fact that the recent development of nearby Snowbird, an instant success and perhaps the most formidable mountain in the world, never made a dent in Alta's popularity. The same skiers return to Alta again and again, and the old guard at the Alta Lodge measure status by the number of years they had skied the mountain prior to the construction of the first lift.

Alta shares Snowbird's mining history. Between 1860 and 1900, the area thrived and bustled with saloons and hotels. Remains of the old buildings can still be seen while skiing or hiking on some of Alta's upper trails. After the decimating effects of the Depression, Alta remained a ghost town until its development as a ski area in the thirties. The lift, completed in 1938, became one of the first in the country to transport skiers up the mountain in the luxury of a chair.

ACCESSIBILITY

Alta is only 26 miles south of Salt Lake City, which is accessible directly by air on United, American, Western, Air West, Frontier, and Texas International. There is service between the Salt Lake airport and Alta, about a 40-minute drive, via regularly scheduled bus, taxi ($20–25 per cab), or rent-a-car. Direct helicopter service is also available through Hosking Helicopter ($120, 4 to a bird).

THE SKIING

The statistics on Alta are really fairly ordinary by Western standards: 2,000-foot vertical, 10,500-foot summit, 6 double chairlifts, uphill capacity of 5,000 skiers per hour. But Alta is no ordinary mountain. There is an annual snowfall of over 500 inches of near-perfect powder, and the mountain is very well balanced between novice, intermediate, and expert skiing. Almost no mountains, except those with vast amounts of skiable terrain like Squaw Valley or Vail, offer the degree of choice found at Alta. The ability to choose between skiing the steeps or the bumps, or simply cruising, is one of the great attributes of Alta and a leg up on its neighbor Snowbird, where the recreational skier is often sentenced to tribulation and terror.

For the beginner, the Albion and Sunnyside lifts provide some long and scenic runs. Particularly helpful is that even during the heaviest of snowfalls the runs off these chairs are machine-packed and groomed. Albion-Sunnyside also gives access to the Sugarloaf chair, which allows skiers in that mid-range between intrepid beginner and reluctant intermediate to see the top of the mountain and try some gentle intermediate skiing.

With the exception of Extrovert, a not very challenging expert run off the Sugarloaf chair, advanced intermediates and experts will find their skiing off the Collins, Wildcat, and Germania chairs. There is some great intermediate skiing off the Germania chair, which is reached from the top of the Collins chair and has a 1,125-foot vertical. For a great cruise in a nice bowl with no bumps, ski Ballroom into Mainstreet. Mambo is another nice run off the Germania chair that is perfect for the intermediate as well as great fun for the expert who wants to do some high-speed skiing. The liftline of the Germania chair, unmarked and unnamed, is a good advanced run.

The Collins chair (1,100′ vertical) and the Wildcat chair (1,250′ vertical) both originate at the base of the mountain near the main ticket office. Most of the runs off these chairs are marked expert, but virtually all of them can be comfortably negotiated by the advanced intermediate. A nice route down the Collins chair is to take the cruise on the top down to Schuss Gulley or Nina Curve. Schuss Gulley is a fairly narrow, mild gulley, not very steep, with moderate rounded moguls. Nina Curve is steeper, narrower, bumpier, and a good advanced run. Also off the Collins chair is Collins Face, rated expert but really a mild face offering a long, good run.

The Wildcat chair has a series of interesting, tough runs. A good challenge from the top is Punch Bowl, a short, very steep face (9), into Waterfall and finally Bearpaw. Waterfall is unmarked on the map, but just stay directly under the chair. It's a narrow, steep run (8.25) with substantial moguls that converges with Bearpaw, another well-pitched bump run. Staying left off the Wildcat chair opens up the Westward Ho side of the mountain, with some excellent uncut powder runs for the expert as well as good advanced trail skiing on Rock Gulley or Wildcat Face.

For the expert looking for the steeps, the high traverse off the Germania chair opens up a series of faces and chutes that come at you in ascending degrees of pitch. Any of them—Stone Crusher, Christmas Tree, Sun Spot, Race Course—are good steep smooth runs (8–9) reminiscent of Jackson. The last of the runs along the high traverse is really something. High Rustler is one of the great trails in the country. Very long, very steep (10), and moderately moguled, it is a must.

The real Alta loyalists will scorn the above description of Alta skiing for its reliance on cut trails. You can recognize Altaphiles by their boast that they haven't been on a trail in ten days. To many people, what Alta is all about is eschewing the lifts and hiking to the vast amount of open untracked terrain to ski the powder, the corn snow, the crud, or whatever. The backside of the high traverse slopes down into the Greeley and Eagle's Nest areas in a beautifully pitched drop to a huge bowl that has spectacular powder skiing. Also, there is wide-open untracked skiing off High Rustler in the North Rustler area, as well as on the other side of the mountain in the Westward Ho area. As yet, you can't ski from Alta to Snowbird, but as one Alta regular put it, "Why would anyone ever want to?"

Alta gets a good part of its more than 500 inches of annual snowfall in major storms that settle over the range and "dump" for several days. A single storm accumulation of over 50 inches is not uncommon. It is those storms, along with the lesser ones, that create the famous Alta powder days. For those who choose not to ski the powder bowls during the storms, there is plenty of tree skiing that affords good visibility. The average daytime temperature is 20–25°. Like Snowbird, weather moves quickly through the canyon, and a beautiful blue sky can turn into a white-out in 15 minutes. Having yellow lenses with you at all times is advisable.

INTEGRATION OF THE SLOPES

Meeting friends or eating lunch on the mountain is easily accomplished. The Watson Shelter, accessible from the Germania, Collins, and Wildcat chairs, and the Alpenglow Inn, which you can reach from the Albion and Sugarloaf chairs, both have cafeterias. At the base of the mountain, the Gold Miner's Daughter and the Snowpine Lodge also have food service.

LIFE IN THE AREA

We describe life at Snowbird as being quiet and comfortable. That being the case, we would call Alta sedate and serene. Alta describes its ambience as being one of the last where the skier can experience the lodge life. Depending on your predilections, that translates either as an intimate and relaxed week where new friendships are struck or a week with nothing to do.

ACCESSIBILITY TO THE SLOPES

You can ski directly from any of Alta's lodges to the lifts. A series of rope tows called "transfer tows" bring you directly back to your lodge after skiing and provide transportation during the day from one lodge to another. Shuttle buses provide regular service down the road to Snowbird ($.25). A car is definitely unnecessary for guests at any of Alta's lodges.

ACCOMMODATIONS

There are five lodges at Alta. In descending order of elegance and price, they are: the **Alta Lodge, Rustler Lodge, Alta Peruvian, Goldminer's Daughter,** and **Snowpine Lodge.** It's important to note that all of the Alta lodges run on the Modified American Plan, wherein the price of your room includes breakfast and dinner. Also, all lodges add a 15% service charge and there is no tipping. The Alta Lodge is the oldest lodge at Alta. It is AAA-approved and rated excellent. It has an older crowd than the other lodges, and the sight of guests dressed up for dinner is not unusual. The dining room serves what some people think is the best cuisine at any ski resort. There are 56 rooms in various kinds of accommodations: dorms, suites housed in the old lodge, and a new wing completed in 1968. The rooms in the old lodge are small but wood-paneled and nicely appointed. The new wing has large carpeted rooms facing the mountain. Prices in the old lodge range from $25 per person for a dorm (4 to a room) to $38 per person for a bedroom–sitting room combination. Rooms in the new building (it has no dorms) range from $36 to $42 per person. There is no sauna or swimming pool.

The Rustler Lodge is more modernly elegant. It has a comfortable lobby area with fireplaces and comfortable couches, a game room downstairs, and a large dining room with an ideal view of the mountain. The food rivals that at the Alta Lodge. There are saunas and a big outdoor pool facing the mountain. The crowd here is younger and dominated by young professional couples. The staff is exceptionally pleasant and accommodating. There are 55 rooms of every permutation ranging from dorms to small bathless rooms to suites.

The per-person price ranges from $24 to $68, with a double room and bath costing $40 per person.

The Alta Peruvian is slightly more rustic. It has comfortable areas in which to socialize and relax, as well as a game room, sauna, and large outdoor swimming pool. The dining room is attractive and informal. The ambience here is quite congenial and the crowd is youngish. Rates range approximately from $25 to $35 per person.

The Goldminer's Daughter is the closest lodge to the lifts, and its bar provides what precious little après-ski action there is at Alta. The lodge is somewhat barracks-like on the outside and standard motel inside. There are saunas, game rooms, and a dining room. Rates range from $21 to $37 per person. This is the only lodge that has rooms with kitchen facilities.

The Snowpine Lodge holds 34 people in dorms and offers good economy for the skier who wants to stay at the mountain ($18.50 per person, including two meals).

There are also two condominium developments at Alta. The **Hellgate Condominiums** have 13 units from studios to 2-bedroom units. Prices range from $35 to $120 per unit and include no meals. The **Blackjack Condominiums** are new, and many have views of the mountain; sizes range from studios to 3-bedroom units, and prices from $45 to $145 without meals. The virtue of the condominiums is that one can cook at home. An important caveat, though, is that most shopping is at the bottom of the canyon 8 miles away.

The alternatives to lodging at the various Alta inns are either to stay at Snowbird (equally costly but without meals) or to economize by staying in Salt Lake and hoping for good weather and open roads.

For reservations, call 801–742–2040.

RESTAURANTS

All of Alta's dining is centered around the lodges, which take great pride in their ability to serve up gourmet cuisine. The **Alta** and **Rustler** lodges have imported fine chefs and take great pains with their menus. The **Alta Peruvian**'s meals are simpler but fairly good. The fact is, however, that none of the dining at Alta is particulary distinguished. Breakfast is actually the best meal, with unlimited amounts of eggs, pancakes, waffles, ham, bacon, and whatever else you can imagine. Dinners are a time for leisurely conversation with new acquaintances.

Alternatives to dining at the lodges are the **Shallow Shaft,** an Alta steak house, or the Snowbird restaurants (pp. 185–86). If you decide to dine elsewhere, a credit of approximately $6 per person is available at most of the lodges on 24-hour notice. Finally, **La Caille,** a French restaurant at the bottom of the canyon, provides the most ambitious fare in the area.

APRÈS-SKI AND NIGHT LIFE

Next topic. There is not much to do at Alta. Après-ski means a trip to the bar at the **Goldminer's Daughter,** a ride down to the tram room at Snowbird, or a sauna and swim at your lodge. At night, the schedule is usually dinner, a drink, and bed. There may be a guitar or two in front of the fireplace or an occasional ski movie at one of the lodges, but that's about it. The emphasis is on talk among those you've come with or those you've met. Alta is a good place to make friends.

Singles who have anything more than skiing in mind should avoid Alta. There is the tram room down at Snowbird, but singles will clearly be happier at Aspen, Vail, Squaw Valley, or, for that matter, almost anywhere else.

DIVERSION

Most of the diversion is found down the road at Snowbird, including cross-country skiing, ice skating, and tennis (pp. 186–87). The most exciting skiing diversion is helicopter powder skiing, available through **Wasatch Powderbird Guides.** Groups are limited to 8 skiers, and popularity and fickle weather conditions require advance reservations (at least the day of your arrival and preferably earlier). The cost is $25 for the first run and $15 for each additional run. A full day's skiing is six or seven runs.

CHILDREN

Alta is better than Snowbird for children but is still not ideal. The lodge system allows for convenient family meals, and most lodges give a discount to children under twelve. Also, lodges with pools provide good afternoon diversion. Meeting skiing children on the hill during the day is not difficult; however, for younger and non-skiing children no nursery or day-care facilities presently exist.

COSTS

The actual skiing at Alta is one of the last great bargains. A full-day lift ticket is just $7 (compare this with $15 in New England). Lodging prices, though meals are included, are substantial. Snowbird lodging is equally expensive, and the only real alternative for the budget-minded is staying in Salt Lake City.

28

Park City

Park City is a resort oriented toward relaxed skiing and good times. Unlike ominous and architecturally cold Snowbird, or traditional, ascetic Alta, Park City has a warm, inviting Victorian ambience, a comforting, predominantly novice-intermediate mountain, and an active after-ski life.

The area attracts families and adult groups, but usually not the inveterate skier or the social single.

ACCESSIBILITY

Park City is as accessible as any resort in North America. It is about 50 minutes from the Salt Lake airport. Cabs are available to the resort for a $25 fare, which can be split among several passengers. Rental cars are also quite cheap in Salt Lake, but you won't need a car in Park City. There is bus and limousine service from the airport or from downtown Salt Lake, with prices starting at $4.50 on the bus and slightly higher for limousine service, which is available by reservation only. Getting to Salt Lake is easy. Even from the East, you can leave in the early evening and arrive 6 hours later at the resort, in time to join in evening entertainment. Returning to the East, you'll lose at least half a day of skiing. From the West or Midwest, transportation is also problem-free.

THE SKIING

Park City developed a reputation as an unchallenging mountain. This was well deserved and remains so, though the addition of a new chair has greatly improved skiing for the expert.

The reputation may well have evolved from the area's main lift, a four-passenger gondola, 12,620 feet in length with a 2,400-foot vertical, a 23-minute ride to the top. It is pleasant in the morning when you want to digest breakfast, but taking this trip twice a day can be dull. In fairness, most skiers, no matter what their ability, stay up top all day and ski several chairs that serve the upper runs. (The principal day restaurant is at the top of the gondola.) Prospector and Lost Prospector, the two most popular chairs, are parallel to one another and conterminous with the gondola. The trails under these chairs are predominantly intermediate, with a touch of expert terrain. Below these chairs is a triple chair (length, 4,960′; vertical, 1,245′) that serves trails which are very gentle on top, with short drops at the bottom. These trails are broad and, like many of the trails at Park City, well-groomed. They are great cruising terrain, manageable by lower intermediates but entertaining for stronger skiers.

Just above the top of the gondola is the expert Thaynes double chair (length, 2,763′; vertical, 886′). Thaynes has three demanding, short bump runs (8's). The steepest, Hoist (perhaps a 9), is theoretically restricted to skiers with skis longer than 190 cm. Prior to the winter of 1977, these three trails were the principal expert terrain on the mountain and were hardly sufficient to hold the expert's attention for more than a day or two. Park City has now added the Jupiter Bowl chair, which is accessible from the top of the gondola and which extends the mountain to a 10,000-foot elevation, giving Park City a total vertical of 3,000 feet. Again, Jupiter is short (3,400′), but it has a good vertical (1,100′) and the top half of the Jupiter Bowl is steeper than that ratio suggests. There is one bump run off Jupiter, but in general the bowl has a broad, very steep, smooth face, dotted with evergreens. Jupiter reminds us of the upper portion of the Peruvian Bowl at Snowbird. It is ideal for powder skiing.

A bottom lift, the Ski Team double chair (length, 5,985′; vertical, 1,600′), does serve steep runs such as the Ladies' and Men's Giant Slalom trails, which are extremely steep on top and flat on the bottom. The trouble with these runs is that they are skied infrequently, are not groomed, and are often covered with unpacked, heavy snow. Their partially southern exposure does not help the snow conditions.

The soul of Park City is found in its long novice and intermediate runs from the top of the gondola down. Intermediates can ski all over the mountain. The trail under the gondola is very gentle. It goes along the top of a ridge, with trails falling off to the skier's left back to the Prospector and King Con chairs. Novices can go to the bottom along the ridge or drop off the ridge on Claimjumper and come back up any of these chairs. If they wander to the bottom, they can ski three bottom chairs. Intermediates can leave the ridge a little higher up and connect back onto the Prospector chairs. For intermediates, Park City has limitless terrain.

Park City also has good snow. It does not get as much as Alta or Snowbird, a few air miles away, but it does average about 300 inches per year. On

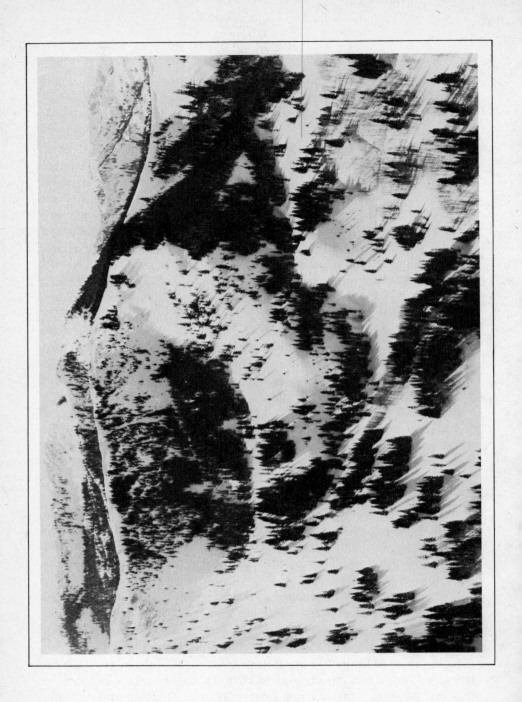

New Jupiter bowl at Park City   COURTESY PARK CITY SKI AREA

the upper chairs, the cover is always good, and the powder, when it comes, is light Utah gold. Jupiter Bowl now gives Park City legitimate powder terrain. The weather is mild, and the days are often sunny.

Despite its proximity to Salt Lake, Park City has few lift lines. On weekends, the Prospector chairs can have 15-minute lines. These occasionally spill over to the King Con triple chair. The Thaynes chair and Jupiter, however, are lift-line free, and the bottom chairs have no lines. The gondola will have lines in the morning, but these are easily avoided by taking a series of chairs to the top starting with the Ski Team chair. If you're an expert, or at all flexible about what you're willing to ski, you need not worry about lift lines at Park City.

LIFE IN THE AREA

Park City is a somewhat revitalized old mining town. The ski resort, about 2 miles from Main Street, has its own little Victorian square, with a hotel, restaurants, bars, and a few shops. Scattered about within a half-mile of this center are many new condominiums. Main Street, in town, is a little dumpy but also comical (if we were charitable, we'd call it "charming"). It has several plain-folks bars (3.2 beer only), a couple of 1890's hotels suddenly reawakened, and some good restaurants or "clubs" with entertainment. The combination of town and resort works well and gives Park City greater after-ski diversity than any other resort in Utah.

ACCOMMODATIONS

Park City has the only hotel in the middle of the mountain in the Rockies. This is the **Mid-Mountain Lodge,** an old wooden mansion with simple rooms. Packages here include breakfast and dinner and cost $230 with lift tickets, double occupancy. The common rooms are plain, and there is little to do at night.

The principal accommodations at the resort (rather than in the town of Park City) are in condominiums. Right at the resort center are the **Village Plaza Condominiums,** built into the mall above the shops. The rooms are pleasant, and restaurants are readily available. The other condominiums are a 5- to 10-minute walk from the lifts. They are all modern town house structures that are comfortable but not luxurious. Of these, the **Three Kings** and **Crescent Ridge** are the most accessible to the slopes; the **Payday** and **Park Avenue** are less so. The **Claimjumper** and **Homestake Condominiums** are a 12- to 15- minute walk from the lifts. Without maid service, the 7-night, 6-day package is about $300 per person, double occupancy.

Park City has continuous shuttle bus service that starts in town and goes past the condominiums. Buses come about every 15 minutes in the morning, so that all the accommodations have access to the slopes without private transportation.

There are several hotels within 2 or 3 minutes' walk of the lifts. Largest of these is the **C'est Bon Hotel,** modern but undistinguished with a restaurant and lounge. Next-door is a small chalet-type hotel called the **Innsbruck.**

Two small, not luxurious lodges within 2 minutes of the resort center have swimming pools. These are the **Chateau Après Lodge** and the **Silver King Lodge.** The Chateau Après has a dorm ($104 for 7 nights, 6 days). Right across the parking lot from the resort center is a dorm called the **Miners Hospital** (a former hospital), which while clean is otherwise badly run. The **Tramway Lodge,** about 3 minutes' walk from the lifts, has accommodations with kitchens.

There are several hotels in town that are accessible to skiing by a 15-minute shuttle bus. One old hotel, the **Treasure Mountain Inn,** has been converted to modern condominiums. The **Alpine Prospector Lodge** is another old hotel with a good, plain American restaurant, a bar, and small, inexpensive rooms without baths; it attracts a college crowd. A third, on Main Street, is the turn-of-the-century **Claimjumper,** which has a good restaurant and a bar. There will soon be a luxury **Holiday Inn** in Park City at the resort end of town, a 3-minute bus ride from the lifts.

Finally, at a drive 5–10 minutes from the lifts but also served by a free shuttle bus, are two modern condominium developments, the **Park City Racquet Club** and the **Prospector Square Condominiums.** The former is well located if you want to play tennis. Both are somewhat removed from other services and from nightly entertainment.

The reservations number at Park City is 801-649-8266.

RESTAURANTS

Park City is not a gourmet's delight, but it has several good restaurants and a sufficient range of choices. In town, there is the **Car 19** restaurant, which features seafood and shish kebob. There is also an extremely popular seafood restaurant, the **Mountain Fishery.** Three steak restaurants are recommended: the **Claimjumper, Prospector's Sirloin** (plain but good), and the **Cattle Company.** The **Mainstreet Express Company** is a moderately priced steak house. The **Ritz Cafe,** also in town, serves crepes and fondue in unpretentious but attractive surroundings. There is also a simple but adequate Italian restaurant, the **Miletis,** and two Mexican restaurants, the **Utah Coal and Lumber Restaurant** and **Durdy Annie's,** are in town at the resort plaza. The **C'est Bon** at the C'est Bon Hotel is more elegant and serves Continental cuisine. Also Continental is **Adolph's** at the Park City golf course and the **Christopher** on Park Street near the mountain. There are sandwich shops in town and at the resort. The **Eating Establishment** in town is recommended for breakfast.

Remember, Park City is in Utah. Don't expect to enter a bar and order a drink. You'll quickly be reminded where you are. At bars, you can have 3.2 beer or wine only, or, at some places, you can bring your own bottle and they'll provide setups. Still other bars qualify as "clubs." For a small fee, you can become a member and then can order hard liquor. You may end up paying a few membership fees ($5 for 2 weeks) and bringing your "guests" along, but having made this adjustment, there is life in Park City.

After skiing, you can choose between two bars at the resort plaza: the **Rusty Nail,** a large disco upstairs above the base cafeteria, and **Potato John's,** a small bar with a badly located 7-foot video screen that shows television sports and replays of the day's Nastar. Both bars are open at night, and the Rusty Nail has live music on Fridays and Saturdays. Across the parking lot is a small bar–snack spot, the **Ski Connection Bar.**

In town is the elegant **Car 19,** a club with a small membership fee and nightly entertainment for the over-thirty crowd. At the mountain is the **Silver King,** also a club, featuring raucous music and dancing. This is the liveliest spot in the area. There are several other small clubs—**Milet's Social Assoc., Prospectors Sirloin Club** and **Down Under**—that have occasional entertainment, such as a guitar group, and from time to time there is also entertainment at the **Racquet Club.**

Park City is not an area for singles. It appeals to couples and groups, with a scattering of college-age kids on weekends.

DIVERSION

Park City has cross-country skiing at the **White Pine Ski Touring Center** several miles from the mountain. You can also cross-country ski on the mountain itself. Night skiing is available on intermediate and novice slopes. The **Racquet Club** has four indoor courts. There are some shops in town and an art center with exhibits and workshops.

CHILDREN

Park City is a good mountain on which to learn. Expert and novice slopes converge at the top of the gondola, so it's easy to check out the children's progress.

There is a nursery right at the lifts ($2 per hour, $12 per day with lunch). The ski school gives lessons to children two and half years old and up. The one drawback at Park City is that even those condominiums that are near the slopes are a 10-minute walk.

COSTS

Park City is an expensive resort. Lift tickets are $11 a day. All-day lessons are $11; a 1½-hour lesson, $8. A package in a condominium (7 nights, 6 days), 1 bedroom, double occupancy, ranges from $200 to $320.

29

Snowbird

Uniquely, Snowbird is a ski resort whose limitations stem directly from its excellence. Descriptions and brochures on Snowbird can be misleading. There has been a tendency to portray Snowbird as a mountain for all skiers. It is not. On the other hand, a strong argument can be made that what the area offers is so spectacular that its deficiencies are gladly ignored for the privilege of skiing the "best."

What Snowbird has is the best mountain for the truly expert skier in the United States, a very accessible location, over 500 inches of annual snowfall, and unusually tasteful accommodations. What Snowbird lacks is après-ski and night life, intermediate skiing, and adequate facilities for children.

Snowbird is 30 minutes from Salt Lake City, in the Wasatch National Forest's Little Cottonwood Canyon. The canyon was settled in the mid-nineteenth century as a mining community, and by 1873 the population of Alta had risen to 8,000. By the Depression, the boom town had been virtually deserted. It was not until 1938, when the first ski lift was constructed at Alta, a mile up the Canyon, that the area began to revive. Alta was the only developed ski area in the canyon when a group of investors, impressed by the possibility of developing the bowls and valleys below Alta, launched Snowbird.

ACCESSIBILITY

Snowbird is perhaps the most accessible of the major ski resorts. It is only 26 miles south of Salt Lake, which is serviced by six major airlines: United, American, Western, Air West, Frontier, and Texas International. There is service from the Salt Lake airport to Snowbird, about a 40-minute drive, via regularly scheduled shuttle bus, taxi ($20–25 per cab), or rent-a-car.

THE SKIING

Snowbird is a big, steep mountain even by Western standards, with a vertical drop from its 11,000-foot summit of 3,100 feet. There are five double chair lifts and a spectacular 125-passenger tram that whisks you up to the summit in 8 minutes. The lift complex provides an uphill capacity of 6,600 skiers per hour, a figure which can be sorely tested on weekends because of the proximity of Salt Lake City. The season is long, with the lifts in operation from mid-November till the first of May. The average snowfall in March and April is an incredible 121 and 117 inches, respectively, so Snowbird is still having its famous powder days while its Colorado neighbors struggle to hold their snow in bikini weather.

For intermediate skiers used to the family area back home or the groomed forgivingness of a Snowmass, Snowbird can be a painful experience. Trails like the ostensibly intermediate Chip's Run, which wanders down the Peruvian side of the mountain from the top of the tram, would unquestionably be marked expert on any other mountain. Similarly, the runs off the Gad II chair, designated intermediate, all have a few fairly steep faces as well as sizable moguls. This is not to say, however, that recreational skiers have a choice at Snowbird between a week on the bunny slopes or a month in the hospital: some pleasant intermediate skiing can be done off both the Gad II and Wilber Ridge chairs. There is just not nearly as much of it as the 40% advertised. The presence of Alta a mile up the road, with some really excellent intermediate skiing, greatly lessens this problem.

While intermediate skiers may be somewhat neglected at Snowbird, novices have their own chair lift. The Chickadee chair, with its 142-foot vertical drop, allows the novice to practice out of the way of speeding hot-doggers. Also for the advanced novice is Big Emma, a long, wide, gentle run off the Gad I chair that is one of the best runs of its kind.

It is for the experts, the super-experts, the hot kids, and other assorted crazies that Snowbird defines "going for it." The first tram up in the morning will have a conspicuous absence of short skis and high styles, but watch them coming down (the best skiers we've encountered in our travels have been at Snowbird and Stowe). If you want a tough run, take the tram or pick a chair; you'll find challenges all over. The most famous run off the tram is Regulator Johnson, a huge bowl with a steep fall (8.25) and a 1,100-foot vertical drop. Packed or in powder, it is a memorable run. Three or four other runs come down under the tram through the Gad Valley. Each of these in places is steep (8–8.9), narrow, moguled, and tough. Coming down the Peruvian side, you

Snowbird: Peruvian Gorge to left of tram; Regulator Johnson and Gad chairs
on right   COURTESY SNOWBIRD SKI AND SUMMER RESORT

reach lower Primrose, lower Silver Fox, and Blackjack—all now served by the new Peruvian chair, which greatly expands the mountain, and all at least 8.5's. These runs are Snowbird's "bump runs," and an afternoon of skiing the Peruvian chair will weaken the best of knees. Even for the expert, skiing the tram can be grueling. The length of the runs, coupled with standing in the tram on the way back up, takes a real toll on the legs. Better to wander over to the Gad chairs for a while, though runs like the steep Gadzooks and S.T.H. will not be much of a breather. Finally, of course, there are the chutes. Suffice it to say that there are about five or six of them, incredibly steep (10), off the ridges to the right of the tram. To most mortals, these chutes will be unthinkable except under the soft leveling protection of powder.

Snowbird has an extraordinary annual snowfall of over 500 inches. The range in which Snowbird and Alta is nestled is prone to major storms that stay over the area and "dump," so 3-day storms with accumulations of over 50 inches are not uncommon. There is cause for rejoicing when this happens, since Snowbird-Alta claims to have the driest, best powder in the world. Heavy snowfalls, however, can sometimes close the mountain for short periods for avalanche control. On cold, windy, or snowy days, skiing the chairs will provide some protection from the weather. Average daytime temperature, though, is a comfortable 20–25°. Weather moves very quickly through the canyon, and a beautiful blue sky can turn into a white-out in 15 minutes. Having yellow lenses with you at all times is advisable.

INTEGRATION OF THE SLOPES

All trails at Snowbird lead to the base of the tram, the Plaza area, where there are places for lunch, rendezvous, and après-ski. The Mid-Gad restaurant on the mountain provides an alternative to returning to the tram at midday.

LIFE IN THE AREA

Life at Snowbird is basically quiet, comfortable, and devoted to skiing, though a relatively wide range of diversions exists at the area.

ACCESSIBILITY TO THE SLOPES

All the lodges at Snowbird are within easy walking distance of both the tram and the chairs. Shuttle buses also provide regular service up the road to Alta's lifts ($.25). A car is definitely unnecessary if you're staying at the mountain.

ACCOMMODATIONS

Lodging at Snowbird is particularly luxurious. There are four lodges right at the mountain: the **Cliff Lodge, Iron Blosam, Lodge at Snowbird,** and **Turramurra Lodge**—all of which have lovely, modern, well-appointed rooms. There are few distinctions between the lodges. All have floor-to-ceiling windows, with most rooms facing the mountain and affording exciting views. All have saunas and heated swimming pools. All have kitchen units and fireplaces, and suites are also available. Turramurra, with 68 rooms, is slightly cozier than the others, which have between 160 and 181 rooms. The Iron Blosam has three indoor tennis courts ($12 per hour). The Cliff Lodge and the Lodge at Snowbird both have restaurants. Prices are the same at all the Snowbird lodges and are relatively high. Rooms range from $40 to $50 per night; suites and studios, both of which include kitchen facilities, range from $65 to $90. Important to note is that lodging at Snowbird includes no meals, unlike that at Alta, where breakfast and dinner are included.

For economy, it is possible to stay in or around Salt Lake City, which has hotels, a **Holiday Inn, Hilton Inn, Ramada Inn,** and the **Travelodge,** as well as a score of smaller motels. The main disadvantage, of course, is the 30- to 45-minute drive up the canyon, which renders one a slave to road and weather conditions. The road up the canyon is steep though well maintained. Snowbird boasts that the road has never been closed on a day when the lifts have been open, but since there are days when both the lifts and the road do close, you may be able to get up the canyon but not back down. Powder lovers will tell you that it's only bad to be stranded *without* your skis.

Another alternative is to stay at Alta, which definitely provides an experience and ambience different from Snowbird (pp. 171–73).

For reservations, call 801–742–2000.

RESTAURANTS

Restaurants at Snowbird are perfectly adequate, though they clearly lack the diversity of the larger areas. Prices run fairly high. Like everything else at Snowbird, the restaurants are centered in the tram building—that four-level monolithic structure that actually houses the tram along with 90% of everything else. The mainstay of the tram is the **Plaza Cafeteria,** which serves breakfast, lunch, salads, and homemade soups. Popular for lunch between tram rides are the **Birdfeeder** and the **Forklift,** which also serves dinner. Skiers wishing to stay on the mountain to avoid crowds can eat at the **Mid-Gad** cafeteria, at the top of the Gad I chair, from 10 A.M. to 3:30 P.M. For snacks, sandwiches, and fountain specialties, the ice cream shop on level two of the tram is popular. On spring days, nothing is more pleasant than just sitting in the plaza area outside the tram, eating hamburgers cooked on a makeshift grill and getting tan.

For dinner, there is the **Steak Pit** (steak and seafood) in the tram building. The Cliff Lodge has a Mexican restaurant, the **Mexican Keyhole and Greenhouse Restaurant,** and the elegant **Golden Cliff** restaurant, which offers the only Continental cuisine at the mountain and on Fridays has a special all-you-can-eat buffet of fresh seafood. On Wednesdays and Thursdays, things liven up when the waiters and waitresses star in a musical cabaret patterned after the show at the Crystal Palace in Aspen. A new restaurant is being opened at the Lodge at Snowbird which is to offer an eight-course prix fixe dinner in a small, lush setting. Up the road are the Alta lodge restaurants, where you can reserve for dinner, and the **Shallow Shaft Steakhouse.** Finally, down the canyon, is **La Caille,** a French restaurant that offers the most ambitious food in the area.

APRÈS-SKI AND NIGHT LIFE

You go to Snowbird to ski. A brochure guarantees that Snowbird is a place where singles will feel at home. True enough—if home is a monastery. Go with someone you really like or bring the reading you've been meaning to get done. Snowbird is *not* the place for the swinging single.

After skiing, everyone goes to the tram room (swimming at the various lodges is the only après-ski competition) in the bowels of the tram building, where through one of the glass walls you can watch the gargantuan machinery that propels the mammoth tram. After about 3 P.M., the tram room begins to fill up for drinks and dancing. Also after skiing, the tram room serves popcorn and pizza, and shows ski movies. In the evening, the tram room becomes the main diversion, with disco nightly and live entertainment on most Monday nights. The crowd tends to be made up of young people, many of whom come up from Salt Lake (a commentary on what's going on down there). A quiet alternative for après-ski is the **Eagle's Nest,** a nice lounge in the Cliff Lodge.

DIVERSION

The diversions found at Snowbird are related primarily to skiing. While there are ski shops, boutiques, and some specialty shops in the tram building, these are fairly ordinary and shopping cannot be the pastime it is at Sun Valley, Aspen, or Vail.

Ice skating is available throughout the winter at the rink near the **Turramurra Lodge.** For cross-country skiing, a number of trails twist through Little Cottonwood Canyon. Lessons and equipment are available from **Timberhaus** on 24-hour notice. Tennis can be played at the **Iron Blosam.**

There are two major ski diversions of note. The first is a novel and excellent concept called the Snowbird Mountain Experience. This is a program for advanced skiers. For $14 for the day or $30 for 3 days, an instructor will act as your guide to the mountain. The "experience" is that your instructor's role is to push you as far as you can go. While some view the Experience as a cross between est and a forced march, the skier willing to really go for it for a day will ski runs he never knew existed and have first-rate instruction at a modest price.

The other diversion is helicopter skiing, which allows the skier to get off into the untracked powder for which Snowbird is famous. If you're a serious powder skier, this is a must. Helicopter skiing is available through **Wasatch Powderbird Guides.** Since groups are limited to eight skiers and weather often grounds the helicopter, advance reservations (at least the day of your arrival, preferably before) are required. The cost is $25 for the first run and $15 for each additional run. A full day's skiing will get you six or seven runs.

CHILDREN

Snowbird is not particularly good for children, primarily because of the difficulty of the skiing. Only two lodges have restaurants, so children will have to go out for breakfast. And only the **Cliff Lodge** has a play area. The day-care center at the Cliff is free but is restricted to guests of the four lodges (children must be toilet-trained). The ski school will take children four years old and up.

COSTS

Lodging and food at Snowbird are quite expensive. Lifts, though, are a bargain. An all-lift ticket costs $11, and a ticket for the chairs only (a good buy for non-experts) is $8.

30

Grand Targhee

Don't feel like a fool because you've never heard of Grand Targhee. Even those who have, refer to it as "the resort on the backside of the Tetons behind Jackson Hole." The area is a haven for the powder skier and has lots of fresh snow from December through May. Beyond the snow it adds few frills for the vacationing skier. The basic needs are met in a tiny resort complex right at the base of the two chair lifts that serve the mountain. It is very small and cozy. The staff and ski school teachers greet visitors with friendly spirits and by the end of the week know all the guests. For the ski devotee who shuns wine, women (or men), and song, Targhee is well suited. Others are advised to bring their skis and anything else that they might need along with them.

ACCESSIBILITY

Targhee is on the western edge of the Tetons in Wyoming, just east of the Idaho state line. The approach is from Driggs, Idaho, about 12 miles west. The resort is about 90 miles from Idaho Falls, 80 miles from West Yellowstone, 300 miles from Salt Lake, and 600 miles from Spokane, Washington. By air, you can fly either to Jackson, about 1½ hours away by car, or to Idaho Falls, about 2 hours away. Be sure to check the weather before booking through Jackson, since the airport shuts down frequently and the pass over the Tetons from Jackson is often closed. Idaho Falls has direct air service from Billings, Boise, or Salt Lake. There is no public transportation to the area from these airports. Rental cars are, of course, available.

THE SKIING

Targhee is known for its snow, 500 inches a year. It even had snow in 1977. The snow is no better than in Utah, perhaps not even as good, but because Targhee is hard to get to and is not as popular as Utah's major resorts, the fresh snow stays around longer.

The mountain is well designed for skiing powder, though Snowbird devotees will find it insufficiently steep. The major lift, the Bannock double chair, has a vertical of 2,000 feet over a 6,000-foot length. The top of the mountain, at 10,000 feet, is entirely open and skiable and has a 25° slope or more at points. Two hundred yards off to either side of the lift are short, steep trails that descend between patches of trees. Nothing at Targhee is as steep as the drops off the tram ridge at Snowbird, High Rustler at Alta, or various chutes at Jackson.

Because of its openness, Targhee will appeal to the intermediate skier. The Bannock chair services trails to the extreme right and left that are of intermediate steepness. A second chair, Blackfoot, has still more intermediate terrain, with some expert steepness near the top that is nonetheless easily traversed and skied by intermediates.

Novices need not be frightened away by the presence of powder. The area grooms the bottom slopes and has two beginner chairs and a baby rope tow that provide short runs and sufficient novice terrain. The adventurous beginner-intermediate can ski off the Blackfoot chair down broad parts of the face that are packed.

Targhee has an uphill chair lift capacity of 3,000 persons per hour (it lists the rope tow at 800 per hour), and during the week crowds are handled without difficulty. On weekends, skiers do come from Idaho Falls, so that 10-minute lines are not uncommon. Since the housing capacity of the area is very limited, lines remain the exception.

Targhee ski area: ski terrain in foreground. Teton Peaks at back   COURTESY
TARGHEE SKI AREA

LIFE IN THE AREA

The resort is very small, totally unpretentious, friendly, and fun. *The* restaurant and bar are likely to close early on quiet (most) nights. In fact, the resort is like a small camp for all ages, with day visitors who drop in from Driggs, Idaho, or Idaho Falls. By the end of a week, you should know most of the campers.

ACCOMMODATIONS

Upon arriving at Targhee, you'll find a visitor's registration desk. It serves all three lodges. The **Targhee Lodge** has 16 modern rooms, each with two queen-size beds, a color TV that gets one channel, and a view of either the slopes or the valley ($28). There is no lounge; rooms are entered from outside walkways. The second inn is the **Teewinot Lodge,** a simple four-story structure with modern rooms, two queen-size beds in each, and a lounge with a fireplace. The third accommodation is the **Sioux Lodge Apartments,** condominiums, again with no central lounge. All guest rooms are right at the lifts and have access to the outside heated pool and game room found at the cafeteria building to which the Lodge is attached. The buildings have a contemporary design and are pleasant, simple, and modern.

Off the mountain, there are several places to stay. Most of these accommodations are mediocre motels in Driggs, 12 miles away. One exception is the **Teton Teepee,** in Alta, Wyoming, on the Targhee access road 8 miles from the mountain. This inn is centered around a 40-foot-high wooden teepee structure that encompasses a large, circular central fireplace and lounge–dining room, with piano, pool tables, and a dance floor. Around the teepee are 18 tiny rooms with double beds, each having a double door opening onto the common room. A floor below, there are two dorms (a girls' and a boys') with 14 double-decker beds in each. Teton Teepee has no liquor license, so you must bring your own, but otherwise everything—room, two meals a day, lift tickets, and entertainment—is included in the prices: $113 per person, double occupancy, for 3 days, $226 for 7 days; or, in the dorms, $50 for 3 days. The inn provides transportation to the mountain.

The reservations numbers for Targhee are 800-443-8146 and 307-353-2308.

RESTAURANTS

The one restaurant other than the cafeteria at the mountain is an adequate, simple steak restaurant with a salad bar. Away from the mountain, across the street from Teton Teepee, is **Lost Horizon,** a good Chinese-Japanese restaurant that is open Wednesdays through Saturdays and has a $10 minimum.

APRÈS-SKI AND NIGHT LIFE

The village facilities include a downstairs bar but no live music. There is a swimming pool and a game room. The **Teton Teepee** has recorded music, piano music, and a lively ambience. If you think the town of Driggs will provide the extra spark, think again. Driggs does not have a bar! Targhee offers movies on Tuesday, casino nights on Wednesday, and dinners with friends the rest of the week.

DIVERSION

There is cross-country skiing and lessons, but the resort does not maintain or groom its trails. On this side of the Tetons, cross-country skiing is rigorous.

In Driggs, for those with courage, there is gliding with the **Red Baron Flying Service**—great "mountain waves and fantastic ridge lift"—on the west-facing slopes of the Tetons.

A third diversion is a trip to Yellowstone, 80 miles north. In the park, there are day or overnight trips to Old Faithful by snowcoach, ski touring, and snowshoeing, or you can rent a snowmobile and cruise the 150 miles of roads.

Finally, there is Jackson Hole. Targhee advertises a joint 7-night, 6-day ski package which includes an Avis rental car. You can start at either area and stay at the **Teewinot** at Targhee and the **Hilton** at Jackson. With a 3-day car rental, the rate is $255 per person for two.

CHILDREN

Targhee is a great place for children who like to ski, since there are few other distractions. There is a nursery, $1.25 per hour or $1.50 in diapers, and a small-fry ski school for $4 per hour or $15 for the day (2 hours of lessons, balance in the nursery). The small game room beneath the cafeteria has a ping-pong table.

COSTS

Targhee is an inexpensive–to–middle-priced area. The day's lift is inexpensive: $10, children (12 and under) $6.50. The lodge packages are $143 per person, double occupancy, for 5 days, including lifts, or $188 for 7 nights, 6 days. Two meals per day on the package cost an extra $12 per person. The Teewinot is a few dollars more. The condominiums can be less expensive if you share with more than 4 persons.

31

Jackson Hole

Jackson Hole, on the slopes of the Grand Tetons in northwestern Wyoming, is one of the giants of American ski resorts. With its 4,136-foot vertical, the greatest vertical drop in the United States, Jackson is a massive mountain with 2,500 acres of skiable terrain and innumerable steep faces, as well as excellent, intermediate slopes. There are long drops all over the mountain, any one of which would be the expert plunge at other areas.

This mountain draws the skiing purists and the powder nuts, all of whom are serious skiers indeed. But it is also an excellent family area, and families not frightened by its awesome reputation enjoy the week at Jackson Hole. Teton Village, built at the base of the mountain in 1965, is compact, convenient to the slopes, and well suited to families. Each of the handful of inns is within a snowball's throw of the lifts. The Village has a pleasant après-ski ambience that is centered on attractive bars with live guitar and group music. Jackson is not glamorous and elegant like Aspen, but for those who want to concentrate on skiing, it has better fundamentals and fewer distractions.

ACCESSIBILITY

Jackson is not exactly on the beaten track. It is situated about 250 miles north of Salt Lake City and about 200 miles southwest of Billings, Montana. For those who wish to fly to Jackson, no route is really convenient. Even allowing a full day to travel from the East, you'll find the trip a difficult one. From the East or Midwest, you can fly to Denver or Salt Lake and transfer to Frontier Airlines, but the Frontier flights from those cities into Jackson leave no later than early afternoon. There is a late-afternoon flight out of Billings, but this route requires a change in Chicago and then has an unsatisfactory, tight connection in Billings that may well result in the loss of skis and luggage for at least a day. From the Far West, the best connection is through

Salt Lake, and the trip can take a good part of a day. Perhaps the most satisfactory way to get to Jackson from the East Coast is to fly to Salt Lake and rent a car for the week. The drive is 5 hours, but you're certain to get there —even if late in the evening.

THE SKIING

Jackson is a huge mountain with broad trails, wide-open faces, bowls, and chutes. The principal lift is a tram, a 15-minute, 2½-mile, 4,100-foot vertical lift that takes you to the top of the Tetons at an elevation of 10,450 feet. The tram's top is restricted to experts. (There is a station two-thirds of the way up where intermediates can get off.) The area accessible from the top is truly vast. Starting with Rendezvous bowl, one of the great bowls accessible to lift skiers anywhere, the run down branches out into other steep bowls, tree skiing, long scenic traverses, and broad ridges. Rendezvous itself has a 25–30° pitch but is so big that it rarely has moguls and is an 8. Coming off to the right of the tram is one of the most terrifying trails at any area. This is Corbett's Couloir, which is entered by jumping off a 10- to 15-foot vertical lip (the length of the drop depends on snow conditions) or by being lowered by rope. After the entrance, the Couloir is a 10 all the way. Catch an edge and the run is over. Corbett's is but one of several breathtakingly steep chutes. The skiable area on the left side of the mountain stretches a half-mile south of the tram. It is has broad faces and bowls that can be traversed for 500 feet. This is all excellent powder terrain. Because of the size of the mountain and the relatively limited uphill capacity, these bowls and faces are never heavily moguled. The Jackson skier characteristically descends in broad traverses and smooth giant slalom turns, and covers great vertical distances without a stop. It is not the home of the hot-dog skier. It appeals to those who like long, steep descents without interference from moguls. Underneath the tram halfway up the mountain is the Thunder chair (length, 3,770'; vertical, 1466'), an expert chair that has Jackson's only expert bump run, Thunder. The Thunder trail has one good, steep, bumped face with a true fall line (9).

Jackson skiing is by no means limited to expert terrain. Intermediates will enjoy runs off the Thunder chair and two other chairs. The principal intermediate chair, Apres Vous, is long (5,000') and serves several trails that have varying intermediate pitches, are broad, and are excellent practice runs. The bottom of Apres Vous starts not far from the tram base, but its top is almost 2 miles from the top of the tram. Between the two lifts are innumerable intermediate traverses and runs. There is also, between the two, a short triple chair, Casper, starting halfway up the mountain, with some gentle intermedi-

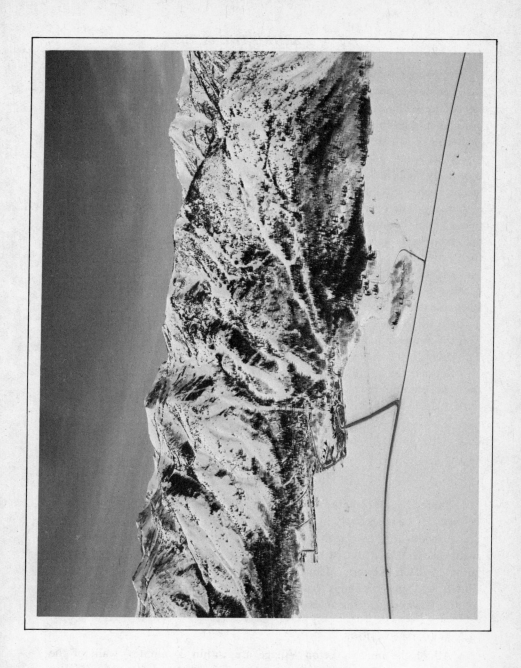

Jackson Hole: Teton Village at base; tram rising at center left, Apres Vous
chair on right   COURTESY JACKSON HOLE SKI AREA

ate terrain and a couple of advanced intermediate bump trails.

The novice areas are limited to two bottom chairs with lengths of 2,500 feet or more. These are also excellent practice areas. Novices, after a few days' work, should be able to handle Campground and Easy Does It on the Casper chair and return to the bottom on wandering catwalks.

Most vacationers stay away from Jackson because they think its weather is brutally cold. Jackson can be colder than Colorado, but it is by no means brutal. It often has long stretches of sunshine and moderate temperatures, even in January. The average daytime temperature is 21°. Jackson's snow is less reliable than the snow at many areas. It averages better than 450 inches a year, but the easterly and southerly exposure can turn light snow into "cement," then crust, and back into slush within hours. When you hit good snow at Jackson during the week, however, you'll find unsurpassed powder skiing because of the vertical, the ease of access to the terrain off the tram, and the steepness of the faces.

Crowds at Jackson are small, but still the tram can have 30-minute lines. There is a reservations system, however, that allows you to ski while you wait. The chairs rarely have lines longer than 5 minutes.

Because the uphill lift capacity is so limited and the mountain so huge, the trails coming down are invariably empty. It's nice having a friend to ski with at Jackson, if only for safety.

LIFE IN THE AREA

There are two centers at Jackson: Teton Village at the lifts and the town of Jackson, 11 miles away in the valley. Teton Village has a Tyrolean charm and provides the basic accommodations, restaurants, and limited entertainment. Jackson is a tourist cowboy town and a major resort center in the summer. It has Western saloons, half-dollar bars, some good and some tacky motels, and souvenir shops. Its bars have rock or country-and-western music and are always good for an evening's fun.

ACCOMMODATIONS

All of the inns in Teton Village are within 3 minutes' walk of the tram and other lifts. All are on the edge of the slopes and can be reached on skis. Foremost among the inns are the **Alpenhof** and the **Sojourner**, both attractive and modern. The Alpenhof has a heated outdoor pool, a game room with ping-pong and pool tables, and an attractive bar and restaurant ($30–44). The Sojourner has an attractive lounge that offers live music and serves inexpensive Mexican food. A touch less elegant is the **Hilton**, a large lodge with restaurant and lounge. There are two simple hotels with modern rooms but without further amenities, the **Crystal Springs Inn** and the **Village Center** ($34 each).

Jackson has one of the best student lodges there is, the **Hostel,** which is on the slopes and has rooms with 4 beds and a simple bathroom with a shower. The rooms cost $14 for 1 or $22 for 4 persons. The entire basement of the Hostel is a large ski repair room that doubles as an informal but attractive lounge. There is no food served. In addition to these inns, there are studio apartments and condominiums in the Village. In Jackson, there are countless motels, most of which are inexpensive in winter.

For reservations in Teton Village, phone 800-443-6931.

RESTAURANTS

Restaurants in Teton Village are necessarily few but are more than adequate. The **Sojourner, Alpenhof,** and **Hilton** all have formal restaurants. The Sojourner also has an informal Mexican restaurant in the cellar. The **Mangy Moose** is a good steak-and-salad restaurant. In its cellar is a snack bar that is open in the evening and serves hamburgers and health foods. This is an excellent place for kids. It has pinball and pong machines.

APRÈS-SKI AND NIGHT LIFE

Après-ski at Jackson Hole revolves principally around several bars with live music and no dancing. It begins at the **Rendezvous** bar at the base of the tram. The **Mangy Moose** bar often has live music, folk or rock, both après-ski and at night. The bar in the **Sojourner** has musical groups. The more sedate entertainment takes place at the **Alpenhof,** which has an attractive, elegant bar often with guitar music.

Jackson has several saloons that try to capture the air of the Old West. These are decorated with silver dollar bar tops, barstools in the shape of saddles, and red velvet Victorian decor. They have old wooden floors and pool tables, and often big bands play rock or country-and-western music. Dancin' and thigh slappin' are very much in style.

DIVERSION

The Tetons are magnificent, and you may want to take a day off from downhill skiing to enjoy their beauty. The area encourages cross-country skiing, starting right at the mountain and going on to trails in Teton National Park.

There are trips to Yellowstone National Park, 50 miles to the north. The resort organizes tours that go into the Park by sled. In the spring, helicopter skiing is available out of Jackson Hole. There is also horseback riding year round south of Jackson at **Scott's Horse Palace.** Guests and staff at Jackson often join in broom hockey, played on the ice-skating rink right next to the tram in front of the Rendezvous bar après-ski.

Four miles from Teton Village is the Jackson **Racquet Club,** which has two bubbled indoor tennis courts for those whose battered knees can take another kind of pounding.

CHILDREN

The resort is an excellent area for children. They should be careful not to try trails beyond their abilities or to ski alone, but after taking these precautions, they'll find the skiing very manageable. The Village can also be fun. Children can be left entirely on their own. There is a good game room at most of the hotels and a nice, informal snackery with pinball machines downstairs at the **Mangy Moose.** The **Hostel** runs a nursery for very young children.

COSTS

Jackson is moderately priced. Day tickets for the tram and chairs cost $14; for the chair without the tram, $11. Six-day tickets for the tram cost $78; for chairs only, $60. The lodges have rates without meals. Rooms at the best places cost $30–40 per night. Meals at the Mangy Moose or the cellar of the Sojourner are quite inexpensive.

32

Banff—Lake Louise

Banff is western Canada's most complete "our-west-is-best" resort. On the eastern edge of the magnificent Rockies, Banff is a tasteful modern town with a few touches of Victorian grandeur. It is surrounded by Banff National Park for 50 miles to the north and south. In close proximity to Banff, there are three principal downhill areas: Lake Louise, Mt. Norquay, and Sunshine Village. In addition, there is ready access to helicopter skiing, winter camping, hot springs, cross-country skiing, and other outdoor winter activities. Once glamorous, the area is now more family-oriented. Its night life, governed by the somewhat restrictive laws of the province of Alberta, is tame; bars and restaurants close early. Banff has a healthy aura. You'll feel like getting up early and going outdoors. The resort projects an air of fun—good, clean fun.

ACCESSIBILITY

The area is a 1½-hour drive west of Calgary (75 miles) and about 2 hours from the Calgary International Airport. There is direct bus service from the airport to Banff or to the Banff Springs Hotel by Calgary Grayline or Greyhound. Since the service is not frequent, the connection should be checked prior to leaving home. Alternative bus service is available from downtown Calgary. Car rentals are available at the airport.

Calgary airport has direct flights from Vancouver, Salt Lake, Denver, Winnepeg, Toronto, Montreal, and New York. From the Midwest, connections are best made through Winnepeg. The flight, with a plane change, will take 6 hours from New York, 4 from Chicago, about 4 from California, and 2 from Salt Lake—depending, of course, on the number of stops involved. United States airline excursion rates are applicable to flights into Calgary.

In short, Banff is highly accessible because of the frequency of flights to Calgary and the resort's proximity to that city.

THE SKIING

To go to any of the three downhill areas around Banff, you must take a car or bus from town. The closest area is Norquay, 4 miles away. Sunshine is 15 miles away; Lake Louise, 35 miles. There is bus service to each from downtown Banff or from the Banff Springs Hotel every morning at about 8 and 10, with return trips in the afternoon. The bus ride, with intermediate stops, takes about a half-hour to Norquay, 45 minutes to Sunshine, and 1¼ hours to Louise.

Lake Louise is the major mountain of the three. By car, it is a 45-minute drive west on the Trans-Canada Highway, which runs through a flat valley with towering mountains topped by rock spires on both sides. In the morning light, this trip can be absolutely beautiful.

The mountain at Lake Louise is a big one, with a good balance of novice, intermediate, and expert terrain. In fact, Louise advertises itself as having three mountains—a slight exaggeration of the facts but a true indication of its size. The principal face (south) has two sets of chair lifts: one to the top left peak of the mountain, the other to the right cornice. The major chair is the Olympic chair (length, 7,000'; vertical, 2,134'). From its top you can transfer to the Summit T-bar (length, 3,670'; vertical, 1,345') or to the Eagle chair, which goes up the right side. The total vertical from the base to the top of the Summit T-bar is 3,300 feet. The Olympic chair and Summit T-bar areas are mostly for advanced skiers. Off the Olympic chair are two expert runs, the Men's Downhill and Ladies' Downhill, which are long but not difficult (7's). The Men's Downhill often has good bump patches. Both can be handled by strong intermediate skiers. There is a short, moguled face, Grizzly Bowl, to the right off the top. Olympic also has one intermediate trail, Juniper, which runs in and out of the Men's Downhill. The novice will find friendly terrain on the Wiwaxy trail, which comes down from the top of the Olympic chair, or at the bottom of the south face, which has its own triple chair and a short T-bar.

The Summit T-bar, as indicated by its length and vertical, is steep. The lift starts at the tree line and goes up a broad, treeless face, which when skied in flat light can be treacherous. There is one intermediate run off the Summit on the south side, but the balance is open expert terrain.

The backside (north) of the Summit is also skiable. There are four chutes plunging into a huge, treeless bowl. These are usually closed because of avalanche hazards or danger resulting from steepness (10's). There is also an intermediate entrance into this area. After its initial steepness, this bowl flattens out into a long runoff that returns you to the Ptarmigan chair.

Back on the front face, to the right at the top, the short Eagle chair serves several trails that are classified expert but are really advanced-intermediate terrain.

From the top of the Eagle chair, there is access to Louise's "second mountain," the northeast face. This side has a novice trail, two intermediate trails (marked expert), and an expert run under the Ptarmigan chair (length, 3,430'; vertical, 1,045'), which serves the area. The novice run, Pika, is a long, gentle trail, very broad at the bottom. The expert trail, Exhibition, has modest moguls, making it a challenging 8. There is also a chute off Ptarmigan (9.5 bordering on 10) that is rarely open and some good tree skiing.

Finally, there is "the third mountain," to the east of the Ptarmigan chair. This is the Larch chair area (length, 4,800'; vertical, 1,463'). It is a predominantly intermediate area with two novice trails.

In summary, Louise has a complete mix of terrain, trails, and bowl skiing. There is novice skiing off all lifts except the Summit T-bar. Aside from several chutes that are mostly closed, the expert terrain is modest in challenge.

Norquay. Only 6 miles from Banff, Norquay is small and steep. The principal lift goes up a steep, narrow face and has a 1,300-foot vertical. The top of this lift serves three precipitous descents that flatten out about halfway down. The other lifts—a short chair, two T-bars, and two rope tows—serve broad novice slopes. Norquay is a tough expert practice area with novice slopes at the bottom. (Occasionally, Norquay is listed as having a 2,400-foot vertical. It does have one trail with this vertical, going well below the bottom of the lifts, but the lift area vertical is 1,300 feet.)

Sunshine Village. Sunshine is in itself a complete resort (accommodations and all) 12 miles west of Banff. Of the three downhill areas, Sunshine gets and keeps the most snow. Of the three areas, Sunshine is the best powder area. Unlike Norquay, Sunshine spreads itself out across a broad, gentle bowl with three separate lift systems going up to three summits. Also unlike Norquay, it is predominantly a novice-intermediate area. The principal mountain, Lookout, rises 1,820 feet over a distance of about 7,500 feet. The skiing throughout Sunshine is mostly open bowl skiing on intermediate to novice terrain, with occasional short steep drops for the expert.

None of the areas will have lift lines during the week. On weekends, you'll discover that Banff is not the end of the world and that all Canadians do in fact ski. This does not create long lines, but you can expect 10- to 15-minute waits—on perfect days, perhaps even longer. At Louise, with an uphill lift capacity of 7,600 people per hour, there is ample choice of lifts so that lines can be avoided if you're willing to keep away from popular slopes. In the morning, the lifts at the bottom on the south face will be crowded. At 11:30, the crowd moves to the Ptarmigan chair. In the afternoon, the Larch chair is popular. The Summit T-bar usually has no lines. Except for holiday weekends

(Canadian) and sunny weekends in March, lift lines are likely to be less than 10–15 minutes.

Because Banff is so far north, one would expect it to be cold. For unfathomable reasons having to do with ocean currents or whatever, Banff has an average daily high of 22° F. in January, 29° in February, 38° in March, and average lows of 4, 7, and 15°. This range is well below Colorado's, but it does provide perfectly tolerable daytime temperatures. Days are short in Banff, particularly in January, and often cloudy. Banff reports an average 57 hours of sunshine in January, improving to 99 hours in February.

The snow conditions vary enormously even within the region. Banff itself averages a barren 73 inches of snow per year, while Sunshine Village, within 10 air miles of Banff, gets 350 inches of snow and holds it well, in part because of its elevation (base, 7,200'; summit, at 9,000'). Sunshine is a good bet for powder, even late in the season. Norquay, on the other hand, faces south, has a peak elevation of 7,000 feet, and gets much less snow. Its conditions are unreliable. Lake Louise is somewhere in between, getting less than 250 inches. Because it faces south, it is not a powder area, the snow becoming packed or heavy quickly. The bottom of the south side of Louise can have a very thin cover. The top holds pretty well.

LIFE IN THE AREA

Banff is a major resort town in both winter and summer. Tourists aside, it has a population of 4,000 people and a life of its own. The town has shops, restaurants, and nightspots. None of these is distinguished. The shops are pleasant; the restaurants, adequate to good; the nightspots, oriented toward the college and twenties crowd, closing at midnight or 1 A.M.

ACCOMMODATIONS

Banff grew with the Canadian Pacific Railroad, which built several massive chateau hotels that to this day remain landmarks. Foremost among these is the **Banff Springs Hotel**, an extraordinary structure that stands in a mountain setting above the town. Begun in 1886, expanded at the turn of the century, rebuilt after a fire in the 1920's, the hotel is a massive 10-story mixture of Romanesque, Gothic, French Renaissance and Victorian architecture which together create the appearance of an unfortified Scottish castle. It has marvelous lobbies with beamed ceilings, huge fireplaces, and elegant traditional furnishing. There are several restaurants, including a formal *haute cuisine* restaurant, an informal steak house, and a Japanese restaurant, as well as lounges and a disco. Many recreational facilities are available in or at the hotel, including an indoor (unheated) pool, sauna, skating rink (lighted and just outside a lounge), cross-country trails, and a game room with ping-pong and pool tables. The rooms—one does sleep there—are adequate. It is a hotel from another era, and it lives on in a gracious manner ($32–45).

In Banff, there are many motels and a few inexpensive hotels. The better modern motels are the **Voyager Inn,** with outdoor heated pool, sauna, and restaurant; the **Charlton Cedar Court** (from $26 per room), with pool but no bar or restaurant; the **Ptarmigan Inn,** with attractive rooms and a sauna; and the **Travellers Inn.** These and several others are all on Banff Avenue, the main street, about two blocks from downtown, and are close to the ski area pickup bus stop at the Voyager Inn.

In the center of town are several inexpensive hotels that are plain but clean ($14–20). These include the **King Edward Hotel,** the **Mount Royal Hotel,** and the **Cascade Hotel.** Above Banff, 300 yards from the hot springs baths, is the **Rimrock Inn,** a modern motel-like accommodation with restaurant, bar, and a magnificent view down into the valley ($30–40). A car is absolutely necessary here. Outside Banff on the way to Norquay is the **Timberline Hotel,** which is modern and has a good restaurant and bar.

There are also accommodations at Sunshine Village and Lake Louise. At Sunshine, the **Sunshine Inn,** an attractive though not luxurious hotel, is right on the slope, with a pleasant lounge, good dining room, sauna, and occasional dancing. At Louise, the village is located a mile from the ski area and has three simple hotels. The **Kings Domain** is modern, with a lounge and kitchens in the rooms ($27). The **Post Hotel** and **Pipestone Lodge** ($32) are run jointly and share a bar and restaurant in the Post. Seven miles east of Louise is the isolated **Wapta Lodge,** just off the Trans-Canada Highway; it offers motel-like rooms, chalets, and a good restaurant. There is no night life in Louise.

About 3 miles south of the town of Lake Louise is the lake itself, a small glacial lake tucked into the side of the mountains. Next to the lake is another Canadian-Pacific giant, the **Chateau Lake Louise;** the Chateau is presently being renovated and is scheduled to reopen in the winter of 1980.

There is no central reservations number in Banff.

RESTAURANTS

In Banff, there is a broad choice of average to good restaurants. The major hotels—the **Banff Springs, Voyager Inn, Rimrock,** and **Timberline**—have restaurants offering the traditional steak, chicken, and veal. The Banff Springs has both a formal Continental restaurant and a less formal steak restaurant. The restaurant at the Rimrock has striking views. In town, there are several steak houses, the best of which is **Bumper's** at the end of Banff Avenue near the Voyager Inn. The **Caboose** is also a good steak and lobster spot. **Grizzly House** is an attractive, darkly lit restaurant that serves fondue, crepes, and steak.

Guido's Spaghetti Factory is a good informal Italian place. There is a Japanese restaurant at the **Cascade Hotel,** and finally there is our favorite, but only for its name: **El Toro.** It is, of course, Greek.

APRÈS-SKI AND NIGHT LIFE

Après-ski activities are centered in the lounges of the many inns throughout the area. At the **Banff Springs** and **Voyager,** there is often music in the lounges. In town, there are two bars which, on weekends, have music after skiing and at night. There is the bar and disco at **Silver City Emporium** and the bar at the **Cascade Hotel;** both attract primarily the twenty-year-old crowd, made up largely of locals or weekenders from Calgary. The Banff Springs has a disco in its least formal restaurant in the evening. The lounge at **Bumper's** has live music both after skiing and in the evening. The **Rimrock** and **Grizzly House** may also have live, quiet music at night. In Lake Louise, the **Wapta Lodge** has a lounge that provides an occasional lift to the otherwise silent nights.

DIVERSION

Banff has access to North America's best-organized helicopter skiing run by **Canadian Mountain Holidays** (see THE BUGABOOS, pp. 206–10). CMH has a trip leaving each morning from the Banff Springs Hotel at 7:30 A.M. for the 2-hour journey to Radium, where the heli-skiing begins. The drive itself is magnificent in the morning and tiring on the way back. The cost of a day's skiing is $75 in low season, $100 in high season. Sunshine has an "Introduction to Heli Skiing Week" run by CMH, which gives a good skier who lacks confidence about powder a chance to step into heli-skiing one foot at a time.

The Banff National Park has infinite cross-country trails for the adventurous tourer. Guide service is available in Banff and Lake Louise. Less exotic but no less beautiful are the many trails at Lake Louise near the lake itself and at Lake Moraine, Ross Lake, and the Wapta Lodge. In Banff, there are trails at the Banff Springs Hotel along the Spray River.

For the hardy, there is winter camping in tents or recreational vehicles both near Banff and at Lake Louise. For those who are not quite so hardy, there is an outdoor hot springs pool above the town of Banff. You can rent a bathing suit. The baths will be crowded after skiing, particularly on weekends.

CHILDREN

The children's facilities at Banff are adequate. The Banff Springs Hotel is a complete community with a broad range of recreational activities, and baby-sitting is available; however, there is no nursery. The motels in town generally do not have game rooms. Only at Sunshine Village can you walk to the slopes. There is a nursery at Lake Louise ($.50 cents per hour, ages two through six).

COSTS

Prices in Banff and Louise are in Canadian dollars, which means that everything starts with a discount. In addition, prices are modest. A day lift ticket at Louise is $9, and lessons are $7. Sunshine offers packages with 6 days' room and board, three meals a day, a 6-day lift ticket, 5 days of lessons, for $260–275 per person, double occupancy. Lodging is less expensive than at major United States resorts. Food is comparable.

33

The Bugaboos— Helicopter Skiing

"Skiing the Bugaboos" is the dream of every skier who has experienced the exhilaration of cruising through bottomless powder with the snow flowing up over his head. In the dream, the skier is all alone on a vast, precipitous, untouched, white face, with endless mountains stretching in every direction, unbroken by even the merest sign of human existence. The face is infinite, the skiing effortless, the feeling almost orgasmic.

Well, the real thing may not be quite like the dream. The face is never infinite, and for very few of us is deep powder skiing effortless. But once the helicopter has dropped the group, you're alone with ten other skiers in an apparent endless expanse of mountains. There are moments, hours, even sometimes days, when the skiing seems like work, but then for a few minutes, or perhaps an hour, you, the snow, and the weather all come together and your skis seem to cut without resistance through a cloud. There is a feeling of excitement, of joy, and of ecstasy. It is the moment you had in mind when you bought your first pair of skis!

That can be helicopter skiing anywhere, but in the Bugaboos, "heli-skiing" is organized for weekly trips, and it is that experience on which we report.

Heli-skiing in the Canadian Rockies on a commercial basis was started by Hans Gmoser in the Bugaboo range in 1965. It has since been expanded into several ranges. The name "Bugaboos" has become a label for skiers who talk about and plan a week of powder skiing in the unblemished wilds of the Northwest. We have chosen to report on Gmoser's Canadian Mountain Holiday (CMH) program because of its preeminence, but there are competitors—particularly Mike Wiegele's program run out of Radium.

CMH now runs ski weeks in six areas: the Bobbie Burn, the Bugaboos, Cariboos, Monashees, Radium, and Valemont. The programs have some differences, but they all have the one great plus: untracked snow.

ACCESSIBILITY

The four major programs—the Bobbie Burn, Bugaboos, Cariboos, and Monashees—are all 7-day packages that begin on Saturday morning with bus transportation from Calgary or Edmonton, depending on the resort. For the Bugaboos or Bobbie Burn or Radium (which has day packages), bus transportation begins in Calgary. If you go to the Bobbie Burn or the Bugaboos, you must be in Calgary on Friday night. CMH will book you into the hotel from which the bus leaves. For the Radium program, CMH provides bus service from Banff (the Banff Springs Hotel). Banff is 2 hours west of Calgary and there is frequent bus service from Calgary or its airport. You can also drive to Radium, about 3½ hours from Calgary.

If you're skiing the Cariboos, Monashees, or Valemont, for which bus service is provided from Edmonton, you must meet the bus in Edmonton on Saturday morning or choose an alternative route. For the Monashees, you can fly to Kelowna, British Columbia, through Vancouver or Calgary, and drive up in a rent-a-car. For Valemont or the Cariboos, you can take the Canadian National Railroad from Vancouver to Valemont, where CMH will meet you.

CMH bus departures differ each year, so you should check with the organization when booking.

THE SKIING

The six programs run by CMH differ slightly, but the skiing is pretty much the same throughout. Each week (except in Radium, where people come in and out), there are 25 to 44 skiers in each area. At 8:30 A.M., weather permitting, the first group of 10 to 13 skiers, led by a well-trained guide, meets at the helicopter pad and is taken up for the first run of the day. While they descend, the other groups, perhaps as many as three, all with guides, are brought up—perhaps to the same mountain, often to different ones. Descents, of course, differ in distance, time, and conditions. Each run can be a new experience. Throughout the day, the helicopter shuttles the groups up different mountains.

The verticals of runs vary from 2,000 feet to 5,000 feet (and occasionally more). A descent can take 10 minutes or 2 hours, but it is not uncommon to ski 10 to 15 runs on a good day.

In most of the ranges, there is a great deal of glacier and broad, open-face skiing, combined with some woods skiing at lower elevations. On days with low visibility, you ski mostly in the woods. The Monashees are generally acknowledged to have the steepest runs and the most snow. Most of the skiing there is done in the trees and gullies. The Monashees have many drops with verticals of 5,000 feet or more.

This is true adventure. Days rarely pass without a hitch. Imagine the guide pointing out the best general area in which to ski, instructing his group to "stay to the right of my tracks," and then dropping off through the powder and woods. While you pick your line down this foreign terrain, you soon realize that the guide's track is indistinguishable from those of others in your group. "Is this track the one farthest to the left or can I go over a little farther?" Soon you find no other tracks and a large knoll between you and the group.

But problems aside, the skiing can be unsurpassed. There are many days when the snow is not fresh, but there are few if any days when you won't be taken to untracked faces. You can't have your own track on every drop, but on almost every run there will be some terrain where the snow is unbroken.

CMH estimates that the snow is "very good 70% of the time." Our experience confirms at least that percentage. On most days, your guide will be able to find some good snow. Late in the spring, there will be days when the bottoms of runs will have snow like cement; given the feasibility of a helicopter, however, if you do not like the snow on the first ten mountains, you can always try an eleventh.

The weather is relatively dependable. You should expect to ski every day, but there may be days when bad visibility will prevent the helicopter from flying. Again, CMH states that, on the average, only 3 days are lost during a 20-week season. The week's costs are based on skiing 100,000 vertical feet in the week, which is about 16,000 feet a day. The weather is sufficiently reliable to assure most groups at least that vertical. Some days you may take 12 to 15 runs, about 25,000 to 35,000 feet. Others may be half-days, constricted by the weather. On good days, you eat out, sitting next to the helicopter in the snow. Those who want to quit can do so if a few others agree to do the same.

The skiing is not cold. At most downhill resorts, you get cold standing in line or riding up. There are no such problems in heli-skiing, though there are occasions when you have to wait for the chopper. The ride up is warm, friendly, noisy, and, on clear days, magnificent.

Heli-skiing is definitely for advanced skiers, but you don't have to be a hot skier or a super-expert. Some past success in powder will do. If you have doubts about your abilities, there are several approaches. You can try helicopter skiing in the Rockies or the Sierra Nevadas, or you can go to the Radium area with CMH. At Radium, heli-skiing can be done on a day-to-day basis, and there's a small downhill area, Panorama, with a 3,000-foot vertical nearby, for more conventional lift skiing. Alternatively, you can ski at Sunshine near

Banff (pp. 00–00), where there's an introduction to heli-skiing package.

Heli-skiing requires no special ski equipment, but the equipment you have should be good. It's nice to have skis that you find comfortable in powder. Over-the-cuff ski pants are important. Goggles are crucial and must have double lenses. Two pairs of mittens or gloves and a scarf are also helpful. The extra pair of gloves can be left on the helicopter so you can change during the day.

LIFE IN THE AREA

Expect to have a quiet week. In the Bobbie Burn, Bugaboos, and Cariboos, which have their own lodges accessible only by helicopter, you'll see the same 50–60 people (guests and staff) for 7 days. In the evenings, you can play cards, talk, read, or drink. In general, lights out comes at 10:30 P.M. and the rising bell is at 7 A.M.

ACCOMMODATIONS

The lodges in the Bugaboos and Cariboos are substantial four-story Tyrolean inns, each with a pleasant lounge and dining room. Rooms sleep 2–4 persons. There are a few rooms in the Cariboos with private baths. Each of these lodges has a ski repair shop and a sauna. The food is good, down-to-earth cooking and is ample.

The Bobbie Burn has an elaborate temporary camp with double rooms, a bar, and a dining room. This program takes only 27 skiers per week and uses 9 rather than 14 passenger helicopters. In the Monashees, skiers are lodged at the very simple **Mica Village Hotel.** The Village is comprised of temporary homes for dam-construction workers. There is a small store, a snackery, and a post office. At Radium, CMH guests stay at the **Radium Hot Springs Lodge,** which has modern rooms with TV, a whirlpool, and access to an outdoor hot springs pool. Finally, at Valemont, CMH uses the **Sarak Motel,** which now has an indoor pool and sauna but is not luxurious.

The complete isolation of the Bugaboo and Cariboo lodges (and to some degree the Bobbie Burn) nurtures a special feeling of togetherness during a week's stay. The absence of cars, telephones (radio communications only), newspapers, and streets makes the experience unique.

COSTS

Prices for the 7-day package are based on skiing 100,000 vertical feet. If you ski less, you get back $4.50 per 1,000 feet. If you ski more, you pay $4.50 per 1,000 feet. (Most groups ski more.) The basic rates are different for low season (December, early January, and late April) and high season. Prices are in Canadian dollars and do not include air fare. In the Bugaboos, the low season costs around $800 per week; the high season, $1,200–1,400. The Cariboos are similarly priced. The Bobbie Burn and the Monashees have only a high season, which costs $1,140 per week. Radium, at low season, costs $865 per week; at high season, $1,000. Valemont costs $785 at low season, $900 at high. These prices include all expenses except liquor and ski equipment costs from the time you get on the bus to the time you return on the bus. If you ski by the day at Radium, the cost of skiing alone ranges from $75 to $100, again depending on the season.

The central office of CMH is in Banff. The number is 403-762-4531.

THE EAST

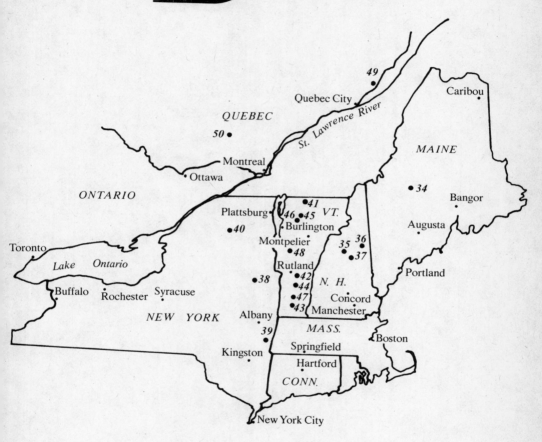

QUEBEC

● 49

Quebec City

St. Lawrence River

QUEBEC

50 ●

Montreal

● Ottawa

ONTARIO

Toronto

Lake   Ontario

Buffalo   ● Rochester   Syracuse

NEW YORK

Kingston

Plattsburg

● 46 ● 45   ●41   VT.

● 40   ● Burlington

Montpelier

● 48

Rutland

● 42

● 38   ● 44

● 47

● 43

Albany

● 39

N. H.

● 35   36
        ● 37

Concord

Manchester

MASS.

Springfield

Hartford

CONN.

New York City

MAINE

● 34

Bangor

Augusta

Portland

Boston

Caribou

34

Sugarloaf

Sugarloaf is the crown of Maine skiing—a huge, broad mountain, which, with the right snow conditions, is one of the top three or four downhill areas in the East. The ski village at Sugarloaf is a simple New England town, with scattered inns and several lively bars and discos that fit harmoniously with the young families and college students who come here to ski. Sugarloaf is as true to Maine as Aspen is to Colorado, or Mammoth is to California, and if you like the tradition and style of the folks "down East," you'll like Sugarloaf.

ACCESSIBILITY

Sugarloaf is about a 5-hour drive, or 230 miles, from Boston. You take Route 95 north to either Lewiston or Waterville. From Lewiston, you exit on Route 4 and drive north for 2 hours on two-lane roads. Alternatively, you can leave Route 95 just north of Waterville, taking Routes 201, 8, and 16 to Sugarloaf. It's also a little under 2 hours by road from Portland, 5 hours from Montreal, and 3 hours from Quebec City.

By air, about the best you can do is fly to Portland or Augusta; then you must rent a car to make the rest of the trip.

THE SKIING

Sugarloaf is a major mountain, rising above 4,200 feet with a skiing vertical of 2,600 feet—the third highest overall vertical in the East and arguably the highest skiable vertical. (Whiteface, which has a 3,200-foot vertical, is often closed at the top. Killington's 3,000-foot vertical extends over a 3½-mile gondola.) The mountain is shaped in a concave curve, steep at the top, gradual in the middle, and flat at the bottom. It has a good range of trails, though a substantial percentage of them are novice or intermediate. The lift system is very symmetrical. There are T-bars in tandem on either side of the mountain, going about three-quarters of the way to the top, and a 4-person gondola going 8,550 feet from bottom to top right up the middle. On the right of the gondola is a chair lift, the Spillway chair, that parallels the top T-bar.

Three tough expert trails, Raindown, Wedge, and Bubble Cutter, start at the top in Sugarloaf's famous Snowfields—a large barren, rocky expanse at the top of the mountain above the tree line. The area is steep and broad, and provides an exciting challenge for experts. Unfortunately, because of the exposure, the treeless Snowfields open only when the snow base is substantial, usually late in the year. (Sugarloaf does get 180 inches of snow annually, which is above average for the East, and its lower runs remain well covered; they also benefit from snowmaking.) Below the Snowfields is further expert terrain (7's; at points, 8's) on Raindown and Boom Auger. These lower portions can be skied off the King Pine T-bar, the top T-bar on the left. Narrow Gauge, the mountain's central top-to-bottom run and the course over which the downhill race is run, is not steep enough and is too well-groomed to be designated as expert. It does have a short, steep drop in the middle called the Headwall. The real problem in skiing Sugarloaf's hardest runs is that the expert has to go all the way to the bottom to get back up. The last half of that run takes the skier through the heart of the intermediate and novice areas.

Strong intermediates will enjoy most of the terrain on the upper T-bars, including Sluice and Narrow Gauge, and the very long trails that sweep down from the top of the gondola on the right side. Once tired out by the upper region, they can drop down to the middle of the mountain where it begins to flatten out. There is also ample terrain for the novice. The bottom of the mountain across its entire width is really all novice, perhaps intermediate-novice. On the left side, there are long, flat trails that snake through the woods and are uncrowded. To the right is a new bottom chair, the Bucksaw chair, which, though it adds some intermediate terrain, is pretty mild.

Sugarloaf remains uncrowded and has lift lines less frequently than any major area in the East. The gondola has lines on weekends, but the T-bars generally do not.

Sugarloaf: gondola rising to left and T-bars on either side PHOTO BY CHIP CAREY

LIFE IN THE AREA

The Sugarloaf area, if there is one, stretches out along Route 27 between two small Maine towns—Kingfield, 16 miles to the south, and Stratton, 8 miles to the north. In the valley, known as Carrabessett Valley, running between these towns, there are two clusters of inns and shops which supplement the accommodations found in Kingfield and Stratton.

ACCOMMODATIONS

Right at the lift, and almost a part of the day lodge, are the modern, stylish **Mountainside Condominiums** in a small complex with a restaurant, bar, and shops. The **Sugarloaf Inn,** just below the ski area, has its own lift to the base; a modern, two-story, motel-like lodge with dining room, lounge, game room, and even a dorm, it is pleasant but not luxurious, and you pay for the location. Back in the woods only a quarter-mile from the slopes is the **Blue Ox Lodge,** with inexpensive condominium studios that have kitchens and sofa convertible beds.

There are several inns a couple of miles from the lifts, including the **Lumberjack Lodge,** which offers kitchens; the somewhat more stylish **Capricorn Lodge,** which has a sauna and game room, as well as occasional live entertainment at night; and a bit further on, the **Narrow Gauge Inn,** an older lodge (1950's) with a dining room and a disco lounge.

At "the Crossing," as it is called (two roads meet!), about 6 miles south of the mountain, there are two accommodations, the **Left Bank Condominiums** and the **Red Stallion Inn,** and a small boutique shopping center. The Red Stallion is a late-nineteenth-century inn and is now the center of college night life at Sugarloaf. In Kingfield itself, 20 minutes from the mountain, is the old nineteenth-century classic, the **Hotel Herbert.** There is also a small guest house, the **Country Cupboard,** which serves home-cooked dinners to its guests at the family table. Also in Kingfield is the **Sugarloaf Ski Dorm,** with a capacity of up to 600 skiers, and the log cabin **Deer Farm Camps,** which have their own cross-country trails. North of Sugarloaf toward Stratton or in the town itself are several modern motels, including the **Mountain View,** with housekeeping units, the **Stratton Motel,** with TV in every room, **Roger's Motel & Lodge,** and several others.

Reservations are most easily made through the area association, 207-237-2861.

RESTAURANTS

Well, it's not New York, but you won't starve. At the crossroads, you'll find the **Truffle Hound,** which serves good French food in an elegant dining room. Next-door in the same boutique complex is **Tufulio's,** a bar with Italian food and light entertainment. Downtown, in Kingfield, there are two places for dinner, the **Frozen Lager,** which serves inexpensive and good Italian pasta and fondue, and the old **Hotel Herbert,** which has an American menu. For breakfast or lunch in Kingfield, try the **Country Cupboard,** right next to the Herbert.

APRÈS-SKI AND NIGHT LIFE

Après-ski starts right at the mountain, in **Maxwells** bar upstairs in the Base Lodge, where you'll find rock sounds, dancing, and Nastar prize presentations.

At night, the college crowd goes to the **Red Stallion,** which is as crowded, noisy, and lively as other leading ski resort night clubs like the Rusty Nail (Stowe), Gallaghers (Mad River–Sugarbush), and the Red Parka (Wildcat); the Red Stallion is at the crossroads on the right. For the more mature and sedate, there is often live sound at the **Capricorn Lodge** near the mountain or folk music at the **Sugarloaf Lodge** at the mountain and **Tufulio's** at the crossroads. In the basement of the **Herbert,** there may be country music, with the audience made up mostly of local folk.

DIVERSION

Sugarloaf is for skiing. If you want tennis, try Florida; shopping, New York; ice skating, Mt. Washington; horseback riding, Maryland, drinking— well, yes, there is drinking.

There is also cross-country skiing. The **Deer Run Ski Touring Center** in Kingfield has 20 miles of trails. The **Carrabessett Valley Recreational Center,** a mile south of the Sugarloaf access road, has 80 miles of marked trails. At both, there are lessons and rental equipment, and at Carrabessett there are waxing rooms, a wine and cheese store, and, once a month, moonlight tours. Neither area has much vertical.

CHILDREN

If your children ski, the area is good. The skiing area is large but well connected. There is a dollar-an-hour nursery at the base of the mountain for children two and a half years old and up. For children three to seven, there is a little cub ski school. Not a lot else is offered for kids, though some inns do have playrooms—most, unfortunately, featuring pinball machines.

COSTS

The Sugarloaf area is inexpensive, even by New England standards. Adult tickets for 1979 are $12 on weekends, $11 on weekdays. There are reductions for 5-day lift tickets. Food can be cheap, and accommodations are mostly inexpensive.

35
Cannon Mountain

Cannon Mountain is New England's oldest major resort. A ski school was established in the area in 1929, a racing trail was cut in 1932, and its aerial tramway, the first in the United States, was built in 1938. Cannon, often referred to as Franconia, has changed slowly, preserving and guarding many of its old ways. The mountain, with its long, tricky runs, is the most interesting in New Hampshire. The town of Franconia remains a quiet settlement with touches of life on weekends. Old New England inns still predominate, though recently modern motels have intruded.

ACCESSIBILITY

Cannon is a 3-hour, 150-mile drive from Boston straight up Route 93. From New York, the drive is more than 6 hours, either by way of Route 91 to Wells River, Vermont, across Route 302 to Lisbon, New Hampshire, to Route 117 to Franconia, or, traveling east from Hartford, by way of Route 86 to the Massachusetts Turnpike, to Route 495, to Route 93, and up. Cannon is 3 hours south of Montreal by way of Routes 10 to 55, to Route 91 and across Route 18 at St. Johnsbury to Route 93 at Littletown.

The best choice by air is through Boston. The alternative is to fly to Manchester, New Hampshire, which is about 1½ hours by car.

THE SKIING

Cannon has a reputation as a tough mountain. The challenge comes not from the mountain's steepness, but from twisting trails and challenging conditions—not uncommonly, wind and ice.

Skiing starts with the Tramway, a 27-passenger tram with a vertical of

2,022 feet over a length of 5,350 feet. (The old tram will be replaced in 1979 by an 80-passenger vehicle.) This is one of the most efficient lifts in North America; however, the skiing down does not reflect the above ratio. The tram rises on the east face of the mountain. You ski down the north face. Therefore, the runs are long. With a 6-minute ride up, you have a 2-mile run down. The trails at the top are not steep, but they are curvy and have banked turns and ever-changing fall lines. Under good conditions, Cannon is a fascinating cruiser's mountain. The challenge of catching the same tram car back up, 8 minutes later, is an exhilarating experience best reserved for the young. After cruising two-thirds of the way down the north face, the skier drops back down the east face on Avalanch, Paulie's Folly, or Zoomer—all expert trails, steep (8–9's), bumped, and short, about 2,000 feet long with 25–30° slopes. This is the expert area and can be skied directly on the 1,800-foot Zoomer chair that parallels the tram on the east face at the bottom. There is also an intermediate run from the north face back to the tram.

The north face of the mountain is also served by a series of chairs and T-bars. The bottom, called the Peabody slopes, has a 5,000-foot double chair, rising about 1,500 feet, and a shorter 3,200-foot chair. The longer chair connects with two upper T-bars (2,200' and 500' vertical) to the top of the mountain at the tram station. The upper runs off the T-bars (described above) are a combination of not-steep expert-intermediate terrain. The bottom runs on the two chairs are of intermediate to novice difficulty.

Novices can ski the bottom chair and a 1,500-foot T-bar located near the tram. With improvement, they can just keep going higher.

On weekends, Cannon has lift lines comparable to those in most Eastern areas. A 30-minute line at the tram is not unusual, and whether the new 80-passenger tram will decrease lines is doubtful. The nicest feature of the tram is that you can reserve a place on a particular trip and have a cup of coffee while you wait. During the week, the area rarely has lines and you can get in a lot of vertical on the tram.

Cannon's greatest flaw is its weather. The mountain is located on the west side of Franconia Notch, which acts as a wind tunnel. The wind sweeps over the mountain, ruining the cover and icing up the trails. The bottom of the mountain—particularly the intermediate-novice area, which has snowmaking throughout—is better protected and with grooming holds its cover well. The top is unreliable but is always open. The conditions are made to order for the New England skier (called "the Cannon skier" at Franconia) who rises to adversity and excels in tough going.

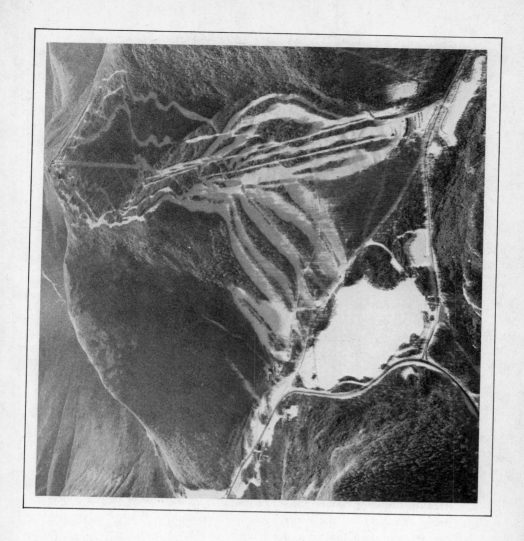

Cannon Mountain, featuring north face and Peabody slopes; small tram lift-line barely visible to left of slopes on east face   COURTESY CANNON MOUNTAIN SKI AREA

LIFE IN THE AREA

The small, peaceful town of Franconia constitutes Cannon's social center. There is no lodging or entertainment at the mountain itself, though one inn has ski trails that connect to the slopes. Franconia is below the ski area, 3 miles from the lifts. The town has several nice old inns and few romping-and-stomping joints. Liquor laws in New Hampshire require that drinks be served only at restaurants. There are pleasant bars at the inns, but these are quiet particularly during the week.

ACCOMMODATIONS

On the western side of the mountain, a half-mile from the bottom chairs, is a fancy resort called the **Mittersill Inn.** A hotel with chalets, Mittersill has its own ski lifts and its trails connect into Cannon's. An Austrian ambience prevails, with Tyrolean entertainment, shops, and restaurants.

Further down, you come upon **Lovett's,** a 175-year-old, very attractive inn with modern cottages, a cocktail lounge and restaurant. (Five-day packages with food range from $140 to $85.) Just above Lovett's on Wells Road is another old inn, the **Horse and Hound,** with 9 rooms and an excellent restaurant, and just beyond, still before the town of Franconia, is the **Flintlock,** a small inn with a pleasant bar-lounge and dining room and a separate building with motel units. The area's most traditional inn is the **Franconia,** 2 miles south of the town, about 10 minutes' drive from the mountain. The Franconia has relaxing drawing rooms and libraries, as well as indoor tennis courts (generally closed during the winter) and a cross-country skiing center with sixty-five miles of trails that go to the doors of Lovett's, the Horse and Hound, and the Flintlock, and for those who are strong, to the trails of Cannon Mountain.

In the town of Franconia, there is the **Hillwinds Motor Inn,** a modernized facility with added motel rooms, a rustic dining room–bar, and a game room with a pool table, and **Raynor's Motor Lodge,** an attractive but conventional motel. Additional motels can be found to the north and south, but part of the charm of skiing Cannon is to stay in the old inns of Franconia.

For reservations in Franconia, the number is 800-258-0366.

RESTAURANTS

The principal places to eat are in the inns of Franconia. The **Franconia Inn** serves a full-course New England dinner with Continental frills in a traditional dining room. The **Horse and Hound** has a more formal Continental dinner menu. The rustic restaurant at the **Hillwinds** is a good steak house. In the middle of Franconia, there is the **Village House Restaurant**, which is plain but serves Continental food. The **Flintlock** and **Lovett's** have traditional New England menus. **Mittersill** serves Austrian food against a background of Tyrolean music.

APRÈS-SKI AND NIGHT LIFE

Cannon is quiet during the week. On weekends, **Mittersill** and the **Flintlock** have slow music and dancing, or sometimes guitar music. The younger folks will find rock music at the **Hillwinds.**

DIVERSION

The major inns near the village—the Flintlock, the Franconia Inn, and Lovett's—are all connected by cross-country trails. The touring center is at the Franconia. There is also ski touring on marked trails right at Cannon and at Mittersill.

CHILDREN

Cannon is uncrowded during the week and is therefore a good mountain for children. Families should ski out of the Peabody slopes base lodge on the north face. (There is a nursery at Peabody.) The bottom trails are gradual and become more difficult with the longer lifts. There is no lodging at the Cannon lifts, however, so you must drive to the slopes.

COSTS

Franconia is inexpensive. Weekend lift tickets are $12; weekday tickets, $8. The inns all offer meal packages ranging in cost from $100 to $180 for 5 days, double occupancy. In the Barn, a dorm at Lovett's, the 5-day package with meals is $85. At the Franconia Inn, the prices range from $108 to $180 per person, double occupancy.

36

Mt. Washington Ski Valley

At the top of the East, in the shadow of white-capped Mt. Washington, is one of New England's largest, most diverse ski valleys. The Mt. Washington Valley offers five ski areas joined by a single lift ticket; inns, motels, and restaurants of every sort; and a range of activities as broad as can be found anywhere. None of the five downhill areas has terrain that can compare with the ultimate Eastern expert challenges at Stowe or Mad River, but Wildcat, with its 2,100 vertical feet, has some expert trails and to a more limited extent so do the other areas. The Valley provides a choice of atmosphere and life styles ranging from the charming, unspoiled old New England town of Jackson to a modern motel-ridden "Strip" in North Conway. The Valley also offers spring skiing for the venturesome. At the Headwall at Tuckerman's Ravine, you can ski as late as the 4th of July.

ACCESSIBILITY

Mt. Washington Valley is a 2¾-hour drive from Boston up Route 95 to Route 16; the last half of the distance is a two-lane road, which lengthens the trip. An alternative is to take Route 93 to Route 104 at Meredith, then drive across Route 25 to Route 16. From New York, the drive is almost 7 hours, through Hartford onto Route 86, the Massachusetts Turnpike, Route 495, and up Route 93.

The area is accessible by air through Boston. The closest major city other than Boston is Portland, Maine, about 1½ hours away.

THE SKIING

The major mountain of the area is Wildcat, located at the northern end of the Valley directly opposite Mt. Washington. Wildcat has a vertical of 2,100 feet, a top elevation of 4,050 feet, and an overall distance to the top (the length of the gondola) of 6,800 feet. This ratio, not the strict 3:1 ratio of several Vermont areas, gives a tough intermediate-expert rather than top expert quality to even the roughest runs on the mountain. The mountain offers intermediate runs from top to bottom, with even some novice terrain from the top. There are several expert trails—Lynx at the top, Lower Catapult in the middle, and Lower Wildcat at the bottom—which are narrow but neither very steep nor heavily moguled. Nothing on the mountain is a challenge beyond an 8.

The intermediate and novice runs are good and varied. Lower Lynx is the picture of an intermediate run, wide with changing steepness and a vertical of 1,000 feet or more. The lower half of the mountain is predominantly intermediate, with varying terrain. Novices can go to the top at Wildcat and come down Polecat, which is broad and gradual and has spectacular views of the Presidential range. Polecat is also accessible from a double chair that goes up two-thirds of the distance to the top.

There are four other ski mountains in the Valley, all of which may be skied on the same midweek ticket ($40 for 5 days) and which provide further variety but not much more than a touch of expert terrain. Mt. Cranmore, located just above the town of North Conway, is one of the oldest areas in the country. Dating back to 1938, it was nurtured by Hannes Schneider, a giant of early American skiing, and is now run by his son. Cranmore has wide, open slopes, skiing on two sides of the mountain, a vertical of 1,500 feet, and snowmaking from base to summit. The mountain is fully developed, with three chairs, a poma lift, and the unique skimobile—a wooden track raised above the slope with mini 1-person cars going up the track. It has extensive intermediate terrain but limited expert trails.

Attitash, with a 1,525-foot vertical, is the newest area and was the first in New England to establish a limited ticket sale and reservations policy. Day ticket sales are stopped at 1,500 persons, and lines on the chairs rarely exceed 10 minutes. One or two trails deserve expert rating (7), but Attitash is principally for the family, with a heavy emphasis on intermediate runs. There are four chairs, one going to the top with a length of 5,200 feet. The area has limited snowmaking capacity but is a touch more challenging than Mt. Cranmore.

Finally, there is Black Mountain and Tyrol, both above the town of

Jackson. Black faces south, which may make it warmer than the other areas on sunny days. It also has a lodge, Whitneys, and a night club at its foot, and can provide a carless vacation once you get there. Both Black (1,100′ vertical) and Tyrol (1,000′ vertical) are small, gentle mountains, again oriented to the family. Black has an $8 weekend day ticket and a $6 weekday ticket. Tyrol sells 2-hour lift tickets that vary from $3 in the early morning and late afternoon to $4 in midday. Tyrol employs gimmicks such as races, contests, festivals, and photographing to help liven up the routine. Give a call in the morning and find out what's scheduled.

Candor compels us to report that the Valley can be windy and cold. Somehow, the proximity of the Presidential range does not produce stable, mild weather. Wildcat, in particular, has a lot of wind. The top, with a 4,000-foot elevation, is often wind-swept or icy. The snow conditions are no worse than those at its New Hampshire neighbor, Cannon Mountain, but they are not as reliable as in Vermont.

Tuckerman's Ravine. Eastern skiing cannot be covered in full without mentioning Tuckerman's. In the spring, when the lifts close, it's time to hike up the side of Mt. Washington. Put your skis and boots on your back, pack some wine and cheese, take warm clothing (just in case), and try the Headwall.

The trip requires endurance and dedication. Starting at the Appalachian Mountain Club, 11 miles north of Jackson, it is a 2½-mile walk to the slopes up a stone-strewn path that looks like a creek bed. According to the Forest Service, the average climbing time to the Headwall is 3 hours. Three-quarters of the way up is a ranger station (affectionately known as Howard Johnson's), with lean-tos where you can camp out overnight. The lean-tos are taken on a first-come-first-served basis, and by Friday afternoon in April, May, and June the spaces will be filled.

From Howard Johnson's, you can hike 40 minutes to the bottom of the Headwall or 20 minutes to the bottom of Hillman's Highway, a broad, steep pitch with a vertical of 1,500 feet and a 40° slope at the top. The trip from Howard Johnson's to the Headwall is up a narrow, rocky trail which opens into a vast bowl with the broad, curved Headwall looming above. Even in June, both Hillman's and the Headwall have many feet of snow. (The Headwall may have a 75-foot depth.) The snow softens up during the day and becomes slushy and granular.

At the bottom of Hillman's or the Headwall, you change from hiking boots to ski boots and continue up the snow face. Both slopes get progressively steeper, the Headwall becoming an unbelievable 55°. As you walk in the notches formed by skiers, the tips of your skis, which are still on your shoulder, can touch the snow in front of you. When you reach a point where you no longer feel comfortable, or when exhaustion sets in, find a ledge and put on the skis. While you catch your breath, look from the 5,200-foot elevation across mountains and green forests toward the coast of Maine. Then push off the ledge, and for 30 seconds to a minute, shoot down the 800-foot vertical of the Headwall into the floor below. How many runs to make a day is up to you, your legs, and your conditioning.

Tuckerman's is not the wilds. On a sunny day, thousands of college students and some families hike up the ravine to ski the Headwall and bask on the hot rocks in the sun. There is an air of revelry not unlike that at Aspen in late March.

In April, there may be snow below the Headwall and even below Howard Johnson's on the Sherburne trail. If so, you can ski a good part of the distance down toward the AMC; if not, you face the real challenge—a 3-hour walk down at the end of the day, again carrying skis and boots. An overnight stay is preferable, but whatever your schedule, you'll feel fulfilled by a trip to Tuckerman's.

LIFE IN THE AREA

The exciting part of Mt. Washington Valley is its diversity of facilities. You'll find great cross-country skiing, super tennis, several night clubs, and innumerable restaurants.

ACCOMMODATIONS

The Valley is 30 miles long, and you should choose your lodging according to where you intend to ski. Only Black Mountain has an inn right at the base. The other ski areas have some inns or condominiums nearby, but in general all must be reached by car. Mt. Cranmore is a mile from the center of North Conway. You can hitchhike the mile's distance from the Appalachian Mountain Club to Wildcat, but be prepared for an occasional walk. More important, if you plan to ski Wildcat, it's recommended that you not stay in North Conway, 15 miles away; rather, stay in Jackson or Glen, which are at least 10 to 15 minutes closer. You might run into bad 4:30 traffic jams at North Conway, particularly if your hotel is south of the center of town.

The choices of accommodations are endless. There are several traditional inns in Jackson, a charming New England hamlet which you enter by crossing a covered bridge. In the center of Jackson is the **Jackson Lodge and Pub,** with small inn rooms, a ski dorm, and its own restaurant. Nearby is the folksy **Village House,** located next to the Jackson Ski Touring Center. Up the hill away from the Village is the **Thorn Hill Lodge,** an old inn that stands by itself on the hill and faces Mt. Washington. All the way up the hill, by itself at Black Mountain, is **Whitneys,** which has small rooms and its own restaurant and nightspot, the Shovel Handle. The **Dana Place Inn, Christmas Farm Inn,** and **Stone Fox Guest Lodge,** also above Jackson, are very attractive retreats, with immediate access to cross-country skiing. More lively but less quaint are the inns on Route 16 near Jackson, such as the inexpensive **Iron Mountain House,** with its 1,000-foot lighted ski tow and an elaborate recreation room offering ping-pong and pool, or motels such as the **Linderhof,** which is modern and has a lounge and nightly entertainment, and the **Covered Bridge Motel.**

Up at Wildcat, for the hardy skier, is the **Appalachian Mountain Club.** Located in Pinkham Notch, the Club consists of bunk rooms and simple common rooms ($10.50 per person with breakfast) and is a center for winter hiking and cross-country skiing.

To the south of Jackson, in the town of Intervale, is the **Idlewild Inn,** dating back to 1795. Further south, in the center of North Conway, is the magnificent white clapboard **Eastern Slopes Inn,** which thrived with the once-prosperous, now-defunct railroad, and to the north of town is the more elegant **Scottish Lion Inn** with its much-recommended restaurant. On "the Strip," south of the center of North Conway, is the still-charming **Oxen Yoke Inn** as well as motels, the most deluxe of which is the modern-style **Red Jacket Mountain View Motor Inn,** which offers an indoor pool, pool tables, sauna, and lounge. The **Airport Motor Lodge** has a pool. The simple and pleasant **Arend's Motel and Inn** serves breakfast to guests only.

Reservations can be made through the Mt. Washington Valley area association (603-356-3171), or, for accommodations near Wildcat, call 603-466-3326.

RESTAURANTS

There are a number of different kinds of restaurants to choose from. The Strip has several fast-food places, and undistinguished steak houses. All of the Valley inns serve good American fare. Most favorably mentioned is the charming **Scottish Lion.** The more pretentious **Bernerhof** in Glen serves Continental food. The **Smiling Ox** in North Conway, a part of the Oxen Yoke Inn, has good traditional New England food.

More informal is the **Red Parka Pub,** a hangout for the younger crowd that offers steak and salad, or the **Shovel Handle** at the foot of Black Mountain, which has sandwiches and chili.

APRÈS-SKI AND NIGHT LIFE

The Valley is full of activity. College kids and young singles can find swinging rock sounds at the **Red Parka Pub** in Glen; it is spunky and often very crowded. For hard rock, try the **Alpine Inn** near Cranmore in North

Conway. Other lounges with live music are the **Shovel Handle,** a charming old barn at the foot of Black that offers folk music and movies during the week; the **Dana Place Inn** and the **Wildcat Tavern,** both with a warm ambience and folk music; and the **Linderhof Motor Inn,** a modern lounge with live music and a zesty après-ski atmosphere. In North Conway, there's more music at the **Oxen Yoke Inn** and at the pleasant **Up Country Saloon** on the Strip. The lounge of the **Red Jacket Motor Inn** also has music.

DIVERSION

There are two centers that offer topnotch cross-country skiing. The **Appalachian Mountain Club** on Mt. Washington provides workshops for beginners; 30 miles of ungroomed trails, much of it expert terrain; and, most exciting, two huts on the mountain open all winter to cross-country skiers and hikers alike. The huts provide shelter only ($3 weekdays; $6 weekends). The skier should bring along food and sleeping bags.

Connected to the AMC trails are the 90 miles of trails of the **Jackson Ski Touring Foundation.** These run through the White Mountain National Forest, connecting the three downhill centers of Black, Tyrol, and Wildcat, and cover elevations of from 700 to 4,000 feet. They also run past inns in Jackson. Wildcat encourages cross-country skiing by offering a special gondola rate for touring skiers. From the top of Wildcat, there is a 13-mile trail with a 3,400-foot vertical descent to the town of Jackson. These trails are well maintained, and some are groomed.

The area also has two four-court indoor tennis facilities: the **Mt. Cranmore Tennis Club** at Mt. Cranmore in North Conway, with whirlpool bath and saunas, and the **Mt. Washington Valley Racquet Club** in Glen, with indoor heated pool, lounge, sauna, and nursery.

There are also ice-skating rinks in Conway, North Conway, and Jackson; ice climbing; ice fishing; snowmobile rentals; hiking with overnight stays at the Appalachian Mountain Club cabins; and even an all-year-round stables (**Bald Ledge Stables** in East Madison) for sleigh or indoor riding. The **Eastern Mountain Sports Shop** in North Conway provides rental and guidance for the hiker and snowshoer who wants to brave the winter cold.

CHILDREN

There's a lot for children to do, though they may have to be taken from place to place by car. Wildcat has day care at the mountain. If you stay at inns away from Route 16, the kids can go out to play, sled, and hike. If you stay at a more modern inn, they can play in the game rooms.

COSTS

The area is inexpensive. Lift tickets at Wildcat are $12.50 on weekends, $9 on weekdays. The other areas cost even less. A 5-day ticket at Wildcat is $35; a 5-day, 5-area ticket costs $40. Accommodations generally include meals and range from $15 to $30 per night per person, often in the lower range. New Hampshire is a playground for Boston, not for New York, and the prices reflect that difference.

37

Waterville Valley

Conceived and developed in the 1960's, skiing's era of expansion, and quietly reflecting the prosperity of that decade, Waterville Valley has emerged as one of the more elegant "new" resorts in the East. The village, the center of all activity, is modern and, if not lively enough to suit all needs, functional for a week's ski vacation. Accommodations are tasteful and well-located. Life in the village, which initially carried a certain aura of glamour because of its early association with the Kennedys, is pleasant and sedate.

The mountain itself, Mt. Tecumseh, has a good distribution of trails for skiers of all abilities, though its runs tend to be less challenging and interesting than those of its neighbor, Cannon Mountain.

ACCESSIBILITY

Waterville is the closest major resort to Boston, 2½ hours away on Route 93, 11 miles north of Exit 28. Route 93 goes directly from Boston to the resort, making it the easiest 1-day ski trip available from that city. From New York, the best access is through Hartford, traveling east toward Boston on Route 86 to the Massachusetts Turnpike, to Route 495, and finally from Route 495 to Route 93; in all, it's about a 6-hour drive.

By air, Boston is probably the best bet, though Manchester (1½ hours by car) and Lebanon (1 hour by car), are possible alternatives.

THE SKIING

Mt. Tecumseh has a summit just above 4,000 feet. The trails, developed on the tightly confined eastern face of the mountain, provide terrain for the entire range of skiers, though they are primarily for intermediate and to a limited extent for experts. The mountain has a total vertical of 2,000 feet. The principal lift is the White Peak double chair (length, 5,265′; vertical, 1,580′), which forms the mountain's central axis. Almost all the trails ribbon off this chair to the right and left. Intermediates will enjoy the trails to the right, which are broad and of moderate steepness, follow the fall lines, and have a continuous pitch. Intermediates can also ski three undemanding runs on the short summit "High Country chair."

The expert terrain begins with the liftline under the White Peak chair, which has two steep drops but is generally unchallenging (7). The toughest terrain is farther to the left near the Sunnyside chair (length, 2,920′; vertical, 900′), starting one-third of the way up the mountain to the left of the White Peak chair. Sunnyside has two steep trails that are 8's on the scale when moguled. The toughest of these is True Grit, the liftline of Sunnyside. The lower part of Bobby's Run is steep but very short.

Two lower chairs, one a 5,000-foot triple chair, serve a somewhat crowded intermediate-novice area. The stronger intermediate will enjoy more peaceful runs on the White Peak chair. Finally, there are two small novice-only areas, well-segregated from the rest of the mountain with a chair and a J-bar. The adventurous novice can ski the "High Country chair" as well. Tecumseh has a racing slalom slope with a steep T-bar (length, 1,482′; vertical, 500′) and gates set up for all who wish to practice. The course is authentic; it usually has deep, icy, unyielding ruts.

Across the Valley from Tecumseh is Snow Mountain, a second mountain for the novice or lower intermediate, which has a double chair and almost 600 feet of vertical, and is a quiet spot away from the often busy Tecumseh area.

There are eight lifts at Waterville, with an hourly lift capacity of 8,700 skiers. During the week, this system is unlikely to have lift lines, but on weekends 30-minute lines are not uncommon at the White Peak chair. The lines on the expert Sunnyside chair are shorter, but given Waterville's proximity to Boston, you have to anticipate crowds.

Probably the most reliable snow in New Hampshire is found at Waterville —though unfortunately this doesn't say much. The Valley claims an annual snowfall of 150 inches, about average for New England, but it tends to be somewhat icier than its competitors in Vermont. It has snowmaking on six of eight lifts, including the White Peak chair. The mountain is less windy than neighboring Franconia or Wildcat across the state.

Waterville is part of an association of ski areas, called "Ski 93," which offers interchangeable lift tickets that can be used at Loon Mountain, Cannon, and Bretton Woods, all within an hour's drive. On weekdays, these tickets are also good for all Mt. Washington Ski Valley areas.

Loon Mountain, about 10 miles to the north as the crow flies, deserves more than a passing reference. Primarily a family ski area, with single-family

Waterville Valley COURTESY WATERVILLE VALLEY SKI AREA

houses located on the mountain itself, Loon has a vertical of 1,850 feet, a gondola, ample intermediate terrain, and two short moguled runs that can entertain the expert. Developed by Eisenhower's chief aide Sherman Adams (Waterville was developed by Thomas Cochran, son of Roosevelt's aide Tommy the Cork), Loon has inn accommodations right at the base. Best of all, Loon's policy of limiting the sale of lift tickets provides some assurance against endless lift lines.

LIFE IN THE AREA

The village in the ski valley is a quiet center made up of a few lodges, two restaurants, and a night club with occasional live music. Most of the evening's activity during the week takes place in the lounges and game rooms of the lodges.

In Campton, 11 miles away, there are several dance places that are active on weekends and cater to college students. In general, however, Waterville is a quiet resort.

ACCOMMODATIONS

The village itself has six lodges and four condominiums, constructed of wood in a contemporary style. These accommodations are all within a 5-minute walk of the centrally located Fourways Restaurant. The newest and most luxurious lodge is the **Valley Inn.** All rooms have two double beds, a private bath, and terrace. Some rooms have lofts for children. There is also a heated indoor-outdoor pool, platform tennis, a game room, sauna, massage, and a setup (b.y.o.) bar.

The other lodges are similar in style if a bit less complete. The **Snowy Owl Lodge** has a pleasant lounge, an elaborate game room with ping-pong table, a pool table, and saunas. The **Silver Squirrel Inn** is less expensive but offers similar extras. The **Pfosi Lodge** and the **Landmark Inn** have Jacuzzis and saunas. All of these inns are within 2 minutes' walk of the village's center. A few hundred yards beyond these inns is the **Waterville Valley Bunkhouse,** a modern dorm with 6 beds to a room, a limited game room, and an adequate lounge.

Of the four condominiums, the most luxurious are the **Mad River** and **Settlers Waterville Condominiums,** but all are modern and are located in the village itself.

There are several small inns in or near Campton, 11 miles away. Between Waterville and Campton, about 7 miles from the Valley, is **Amity House,** a late-nineteenth-century private house converted into a lodge, offering inexpensive accommodations including dorm rooms with meals. A mile farther from the Valley is **Anderson Inn,** an informal, inexpensive lodge. Just off Route 93 is the modern, rather plain **Scandinavi Inn,** with restaurant, rathskeller, sauna, and outdoor pool (infrequently open). There is also a **Holiday Inn** in Campton with an indoor heated pool.

The central reservation number for accommodations in the Valley is 603-236-8371.

RESTAURANTS

The principal restaurant is the **Fourways Restaurant,** which has a good Continental menu and a salad bar. During the week, the Fourways offers a package meal plan with two meals a day for as little as $8. Also in the village, a 5- to 10-minute walk from the inns, is the **Finish Line Restaurant,** an informal steak house that also serves sandwiches.

Six miles from the Valley is a lively Swiss restaurant and lounge, the **William Tell,** and in Campton is the rathskeller at the **Scandinavi Inn,** again principally a steak house. Also in Campton on Route 3 is **O'Malley's,** a steak house, the noisiest nightspot around, and the **Mt. Blanc Restaurant,** which offers both sandwiches and full-course French meals.

APRÈS-SKI AND NIGHT LIFE

Life at Waterville suffers from New Hampshire's legal constraints against bars without restaurants. A night club cannot have a liquor license unless it serves food. Thus there are no simple bars and no informal entertainment. The best nightspots are restaurants that have already been mentioned. The **Fourwinds** has a pleasant lounge with disco and occasional live music. The **William Tell** bar has a good drinking spirit. **O'Malleys** in Campton is popular with college kids and young persons and has live hard rock on weekends. The **Scandinavi Inn** sometimes has live music.

DIVERSION

Waterville has an active cross-country skiing program that originates out of the **Village Cross Country Center** located 5 minutes from the Fourways. The Center has workshops, lessons, 35 miles of trails, waxing instruction, and videotaping. In 1978, it was the training site for the U.S. Cross-Country ski team. There is also a skating rink at the Snow Mountain downhill area—across the Valley from Tecumseh.

CHILDREN

The inns at the Valley are well-suited for children. A frequent and convenient shuttle to Mt. Tecumseh solves any transportation problem. There is a nursery at the mountain, $1 per hour, $5 per day. The mountain has no special children's ski school program and the village has no special facilities for children, but the inns all have game rooms. The village is a good area for outdoor play.

COSTS

Waterville is moderately priced. The 1-day lift ticket is $13; for juniors twelve and under, $8.50. A 5-day lift ticket is $45, or $65 with 5 lessons. The average cost of a 5-day package with lodging and lifts, but without meals, is $115 per person.

38

Gore Mountain

Gore Mountain is off the beaten track. It is a quiet backwater, left undisturbed by a current of skiers flowing past it on the way to more fashionable Vermont. We wish we could report that it is an undiscovered jewel, but alas we cannot. The mountain does have its virtues. It is a large (the largest in New York), predominantly intermediate mountain, offering a wide range of trails for intermediate and novice skiers. Once off the mountain, however, you'll find few diversions. The community around Gore is made up of an undistinguished collection of small towns and of adequate but inelegant lodges and motels. The neighboring town, North Creek, gives no signs of being a resort. You could drive through it and not know there was skiing nearby. During the week, the area is restful and uncrowded. As a place to retire for the week, Gore is good for all but the advanced skier.

ACCESSIBILITY

Gore is 235 miles north of New York City, about a 5-hour drive on the New York Thruway and the Northway. It is 85 miles north of Albany, 30 miles north of Lake George, a 40-minute drive. There is bus service from New York City to Lake George, the nearest major town, but no transportation in the area. A car is a necessity.

THE SKIING

Gore is included in this book because it does have a very respectable vertical of 2,100 feet. Unfortunately, that drop extends over a considerable horizontal distance, which means that much of the mountain has only intermediate or novice terrain. The showcase lift is an 11,000-foot gondola, going from bottom to top—the longest single span lift in the East. The bottom half of the gondola liftline, and the area around it, are not skiable. Rather, you ski off a ridge to the right of the top gondola terminal. The ridge has chairs in tandem: the Summit chair (4,000′ long; 800′ vertical), and the North chair (4,100′ long; 750′ vertical). As indicated by these figures, these chairs have long, not steep, intermediate and novice trails. Directly under the gondola at the top is the Straight Brook chair, an expert chair (3,000′ long; 900′ vertical) with two challenging runs, Chatiemac and Hawkeye. These are twisting trails that normally have moguls. Short stretches on these runs are steep, but no section exceeds an 8 in difficulty, and overall they are both 7's. These two trails are the entire expert terrain on the mountain except for a short stretch of Darby, a run on the Summit chair.

The intermediate and novice trails are long, often narrow, but not steep. The longest chair of all is a bottom chair (7,300′ long; 1,500′ vertical) parallel to the gondola. It serves intermediate and novice trails that are excellent for cruising. The Twister trail, marked "most difficult," is a long, pleasant run through the woods skiable by the weakest intermediate.

Novices can ski this long chair or the two chairs above it on the ridge. For beginners, the mountain also has a short chair, a T-bar, and a J-bar at the bottom.

Gore is likely to be empty during the week. On weekends in February or March, there are 15- to 20-minute lines, particularly on the long bottom chair and the gondola. The expert chair often has 10-minute lines.

Gore's snow conditions are similar to conditions in southern Vermont. The top of the mountain develops bare spots earlier in the season than its Green Mountain neighbors. There is snowmaking on the bottom beginner's slope and two of the trails off the long bottom chair. These trails have good cover all winter.

LIFE IN THE AREA

There is very little after-ski activity at Gore or in the town of North Creek at its base. The lodges are simple, the restaurants plain, and the entertainment strictly private. Forty minutes away, at Lake George, there are a few sparks of life, particularly on weekends, but it's not Las Vegas or even Albany for that matter. Many people who ski Gore stay in Lake George.

ACCOMMODATIONS

There are several lodges or motels on the access road two to five minutes by car from the lifts. None is fancy.

The **Inn on Gore Mountain** ($29) is plain but adequate and has a fireplace, lounge, a restaurant and a game room with ping-pong. The **Black Mountain Ski Lodge and Motel** has large rooms and a somewhat plastic lounge and dining room. Also on the access road is the **Valhaus Motel,** a basic motel without restaurant or lounge. Three other nearby motels are the **Alpine Motel,** the **Northwind,** and the **Gore Mt. Motor Lodge.** All have restaurants and the Motor Lodge has live entertainment on weekends. Also in North Creek is the **Highlands,** which has very inexpensive housekeeping apartments and rooms with kitchens for as little as $16 a day per room.

Somewhat more polished, but not a whole lot, are the motels of Lake George. The best of these are the **Holiday Inn** with a dinner-theatre, and the **Fort William Henry Motor Inn,** a two-story modern motel with a pleasant bar overlooking the lake.

The number for lodging reservations at Gore is 518-251-2612.

RESTAURANTS

The lodges mentioned above house the principal restaurants of the area. The **Inn on Gore Mountain** serves non-guests. The **Gore Mt. Motor Lodge** has a steak house restaurant. In North Creek, you can get a folksy, stick-to-your-ribs meal at **Smiths.** In Warrensberg, about halfway back to Lake George, is the **Grist Mill,** a better restaurant than those in North Creek.

Lake George adds some variety. The **East Cove Restaurant** is a good steak and lobster place. **Mario's** is Italian. **Theodore's** is a fish restaurant. There is even a Chinese restaurant south of Lake George on Route 9.

APRÈS-SKI AND NIGHT LIFE

Après-ski activity begins at the bar in the base lodge at the mountain. On weekends, there may be additional entertainment in North Creek at the **Alpine Motel** or the **Gore Mt. Motor Lodge.** The Motor Lodge also has a happy hour after skiing.

The more lively bars are in Lake George, but even there things are quiet during the week. There is a raunchy discoteque, **D.J.'s,** for the young. For the old, the **Holiday Inn** has a dinner-theater on Fridays and Saturdays. If you're looking for an active social scene, Gore is not the place for you.

DIVERSION

Gore has a spacious day lodge with a cocktail lounge and a large informal picnic area for those bringing lunch. Just outside is a large skating rink. There are also cross-country ski trails at the mountain, for novice, intermediate and advanced ski tourers.

CHILDREN

Gore is an excellent mountain for small children. There are three beginner lifts. All but one of the major chairs have some novice terrain. There is a nursery in the base lodge that charges 75 cents per hour. The inns near the mountain are also simple, have game rooms, and are in a rural setting so the children can go outside and play.

COSTS

Gore is an inexpensive area. The lift tickets are $11 on weekends, $9 during the week and $40 for a five-day week ticket. Lessons are $6. A five-day learn-to-ski week is $49. Food and accommodations in the area, particularly during the week, are also inexpensive. Rooms rent for $20 and less per night.

39

Hunter Mountain

Bringing skiing to the people; don't knock it. Hunter is not in the wilds of Montana or even in the lush Green Mountains of Vermont. In fact, it is just 20 minutes off the New York Thruway. It is, however, a substantial ski resort with a wide variety of terrain. It handles people with great efficiency, relying on its huge Base Lodge, its many lifts, and an uphill lift capacity of 14,000 people per hour. The resort is primarily a day or weekend skiing area, but it does have some attractive accommodations and restaurants suitable for a week's stay. The towns near Hunter and the facilities are generally simple and often ramshackle. Hunter is not stylish, but it does provide many of the essentials.

ACCESSIBILITY

The area is 2½ hours north of New York City and Newark, New Jersey, and only 35 minutes from Kingston, New York. From New York, take the Thruway to the Saugerties exit and travel west on Route 23A to Hunter. There is daily bus service to Hunter from New York.

THE SKIING

The resort advertises itself as three mountains: Hunter, the original development; Hunter One, the novice area; and Hunter West, the challenging backside. In fact, it is really one mountain with a respectible vertical of 1,600 feet. Future expansion may increase this to 1,900 feet. The vertical is not illusory. One lift alone, known as A, rises the 1,600 feet over a distance of 5,400 feet—a respectable ratio for an intermediate-advanced chair.

There is good expert terrain. As a result of the development of a new chair on the front of the mountain (known as Chair F), the expert can stay away from the central axis and ski K-27, which, while short, has good, steep pitch and deserves a 9 rating. The longer expert runs are found on Hunter West. Here, Clairs Run and Anapurna deserve 8 ratings, particularly if the snow is plentiful and the bumps build up. There are also some expert runs off the principal chair (Chair A). The Cliff, Racer's Edge, and Hellgate have short, steep sections which are 8's.

The intermediate can ski the broad open-slope skiing on the central part of the front of the mountain. The major trail in this area is often crowded and is appropriately known as 7th Avenue. The other runs are not long, or of great interest, but the pitch is consistent, and if people don't trouble you, there's excellent opportunity to practice. The intermediate can also ski Way Out, on Hunter West, which is marked expert but is suitable for less advanced skiers.

Hunter is not highly recommended for beginners though there are sufficient novice slopes. Hunter One is almost all novice. The runs are short but the biggest problem of all is, yes, people, people, people . . .

Of course, the people problem is limited to weekends, so if you can ski during the week, you'll find an area with a good variety of skiing and no congestion. The mountain really cannot be called charming, but the skiing is there and can be demanding.

Hunter has eight double chair lifts, a triple chair, one T-bar, 2 poma lifts, and two rope tows with an hourly lift capacity of 14,000 persons. That's capacity. Unfortunately, ski lifts are like roads: the more you build, the more people you attract. Lift lines on weekends on the principal chairs are likely to be 20–30 minutes. The old problem at Hunter was that it had too much uphill capacity for the downhill skiing area. The addition of the runs in the F chair lift area and on Hunter West may have helped a little on this. Some pressure has been taken off 7th Avenue and 42nd Street, though for those used to more rustic settings, these trails may still bring Times Square to mind.

Hunter West is less crowded and the lift is likely to have lines of 10 minutes even on crowded weekends. For the better skier, this is the place to ski.

Hunter has an average annual snowfall of 110 feet, but it makes its own snow everywhere on the mountain. It makes more snow than any other area. If the weather remains cold, Hunter will have good cover. Nonetheless, the snow at Hunter is tough. Perhaps because it is artificial or perhaps because of the volume of skiers, the snow tends to be scraped down and unforgivingly hard-packed. On the steep areas, and particularly on Hunter West, you'll need good edges, good body position, and icy confidence to maintain a fluid line. If you show up on a weekday after new snow, the combination of this snow and Hunter's reliable base will assure good skiing.

LIFE IN THE AREA

Hunter is for day-trippers, but it has an active after-ski life, particularly on Saturday afternoons and evenings. It's both a family and singles world (they mix without rancor).

The towns around Hunter Mountain—Hunter, Tannersville, and Haines Falls—are unpretentious villages of no distinction. On the main streets, there are old wood-framed, clapboard, two-story houses with beer signs in the front window. Ski shops are located in former pizza parlors. It's not classy, but it is relaxed.

ACCOMMODATIONS

There are two modern, first-class motels, several old rambling Victorian hotels, and many run-of-the-mill motels in the area. The hotels, while often not expensive, structure their rates to discourage one-night stays.

Right opposite the mountain with a fine view is the **Scribner Hollow Motel.** Scribner's is a multi-story, elegant, modern structure built up the side of a hill. The rooms are attractive, and the motel has a small indoor swimming pool and sauna plus a pleasant dining room. Another deluxe motel is **Villagio,** in Haines Falls, 8 miles from the mountain. It also has a large indoor pool, a night club, and an elegant dining room.

For those who like turn-of-the-century, faded-mansion style, there's **O'-Shea's Colonel's Table Inn** on the mountain (a half mile from the lifts); the **Hunter Village Inn,** in the center of Hunter (a quarter-mile from the lifts); and the **Great Escape** in town (about a mile or so from the lifts). All are large wood-frame hotels with game rooms, featuring pinball machines and low-lit bars with red upholstered furniture. Really, it's fun. In Hunter also is the old **Ritz Hotel,** on Main Street, and the inexpensive **Sun Land Farm Motel,** with home cooking, 3 miles west of town. There are other more conventional motels both in Hunter and in Tannersville, including the **Forester Motor Lodge,** the **Marichka Motel,** the **Terrace Garden Motel** in Hunter, and the **Hillside Lodge** and the **Sun View Motel** in Tannersville. Six miles from the mountain there is the **High Chaparral Ranch,** where you can ride horses or rent a snowmobile; it is sufficiently far away from Hunter so that there is a feeling of seclusion. The **Hunter Mountain Resort Ranch** in Haines Falls, about 8 miles from the mountain, also offers horseback riding. If you can't find housing right near Hunter, you can stay in Kingston or Woodstock (25–30 minutes).

The Hunter accommodations number is 518-263-4227.

RESTAURANTS

This is a world of Italian restaurants, including **Cibo Restaurant, Dominick's** in Tannersville, **Bruno's Continental, Cristy's Restaurant,** and **Trattoria Rinaldo** in Hunter, and **Antonio's** in Platt Cove. For variety, there's a **Weiner's Swiss Chalet,** and the **Blackhorse Pub** in Tannersville. You can also eat at most of the hotels or top motels mentioned above.

APRÈS-SKI AND NIGHT LIFE

There are lots of folks in Hunter on Saturday afternoons and at night, and sometimes even on Fridays. The Base Lodge itself is a huge singles bar from 4 to 7 P.M. Back in town, the **Hunter Village Inn** is a good bet for live hard rock after skiing and during the evening.

Saturday night there's usually action—live—at **O'Shea's** on the mountain or at the **Great Escape.** Also in town is a small, often crowded disco, the **Last Resort,** and further down the road is the **Mahogany Ridge,** which also has rock sound and caters to college-aged kids. Still other rock bands are found at the **Red Barn** and at the **First Run Inn** in Haines Falls. The First Run has a lively, inexpensive happy hour on Saturday afternoon.

Finally, for both night life and restaurants, one can go off to Woodstock.

DIVERSION

Two inns already mentioned have year-round horseback riding. In Windham, about 7 miles north, there is the **White Birches Ski Touring Center,** with a rental shop and lessons. If it's really cold, you can go skating on the river just below the town of Hunter. Beyond that, you can find a game room or two in the larger hotels.

CHILDREN

Hunter is big; don't let the kids get lost. There's a free toddler's ticket for children three and under, accompanied by a parent, and a nursery ($4.50 half-day, $8 all day), but you have to pick up the children for lunch. The novice area has two rope tows for beginners.

COSTS

Day tickets at Hunter are $12; $7, for juniors. The prices of food and drink are quite modest. Except for the posh motels, and the problem of reserving a room for two nights when you want only one, the accommodations are generally simple, modest, and inexpensive.

ɤ10

Whiteface—Lake Placid

Whiteface, 10 miles from Lake Placid, is a sleeper among Eastern Alpine areas—a sleeper that may never awake. With Lake Placid, it was the home of the 1936 Winter Olympics and will be the site once again for the 1980 games. Despite this, the area has yet to catch on. Even though it has the greatest vertical drop in the East, 3,216 feet, and is part of one of the most diverse winter resorts in the United States, it remains a second-class area. The reason appears to be that the mountain does not hold snow. Yet, when the snow is good, the mountain is very good. When the mountain is good, the area becomes first-class.

ACCESSIBILITY

Lake Placid is 300 miles north of New York City, 150 miles north of Albany, or 350 miles east of Buffalo. The 6-hour drive from New York starts on the Thruway, continues on the Northway, and finally ends with a 41-mile trip on twisting, two-lane Route 73. There are buses daily to Lake Placid from New York or Albany. You can also fly from New York to Lake Placid. From Montreal, it's about a 2-hour (100-mile) trip down Route 15, the Northway, and onto Route 9N at Keeseville.

THE SKIING

There are always great expectations when you find a big mountain you haven't skied and know little about. Whiteface, with its 3,200-foot vertical, sounds like an exciting prospect. The top chair has a vertical of 1,872 feet over a length of 4,820 feet, the steepest chair in the East and in the United States, second only to the bottom chair at Taos (4,000′ long; 1,800′ vertical) and equal to the bottom chair at Telluride (1,836'long; over 4,730'vertical), the steepest major lifts we know of in the West. This should be an expert's heaven, but alas the two trails on this chair do not maintain their cover. They ice up quickly and are almost always wind-blown. For the 1980 Olympics, snowmaking is being extended to the top and this may greatly improve recreational skiing. With snow, the two runs have continuous, challenging steep terrain (9's). Without snow, they are simply a struggle.

The top chair is reached by the long Chair #1 (6,420' long; 1,306' vertical), which goes up a narrow valley from the Base Lodge to the bottom of the top chair. The runs under this chair are novice-intermediate trails that stick closely, too closely, to the liftline itself. Halfway down this bottom lift, Chair #2 (4,740' long; 1,540' vertical) goes up almost parallel with the top chair. The runs off #2 are primarily expert runs, bumpy and twisty. In steepness, they are 7's, manageable by good intermediate skiers. However, even when the snows have been plentiful, these trails are usually icy at the top as well. There is one easy intermediate trail off the #2 lift. Intermediates can find challenge on this chair or take it easy on the runs on the Valley chair.

The novice can ski any of three lifts at the bottom: a short T-bar, J-bar, and a 2,200-foot chair, well segregated from the corridor served by Chair #1. This chair serves a good novice area, which is broken up into thin, twisting trails.

Whiteface is a balanced, challenging mountain when the snow is good. Unfortunately, the mountain seems to attract wind which hurdles over the shoulder of the mountain and sucks the snow off the trails. The bottom slopes keep their cover. The top slopes, generally, do not. The season as a result is shorter than that of New England.

Whiteface does have lift lines on weekends, but they are usually not longer than 10 minutes and are confined mostly to Chair #2. Lift lines on the top chair are rare and on the bottom chairs are usually short. During the week, lines are never a problem.

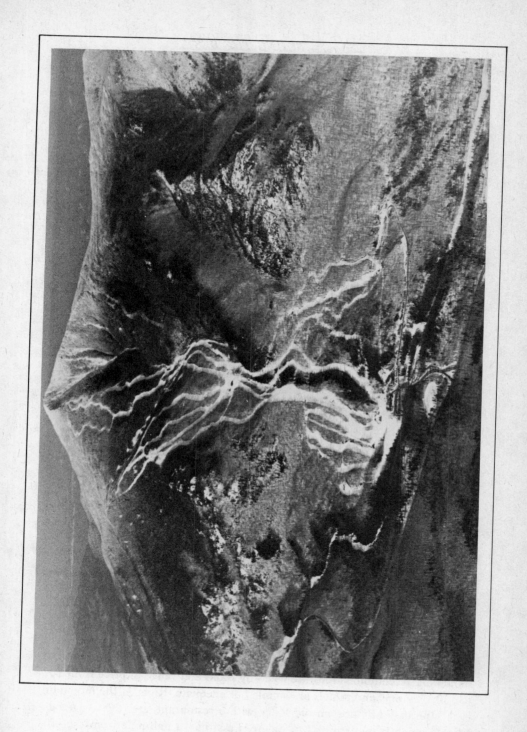

Whiteface Mountain   PHOTO BY J. GOERG. N.Y.S. DEPT. OF ENVIR. CONS.

LIFE IN THE AREA

The non-skiing activities are centered in Lake Placid, ten miles west of Whiteface. Lake Placid has everything from old inns to modern hotels, from 90-meter jumps to bobsled runs. On weekends, the town is alive, with bars and discotheques crowded by New York City singles who come in force, mostly from what New Yorkers call "the outer boros," the Bronx, Brooklyn and Queens. It is not uncommon on Saturday night to walk down a motel corridor and find doors open and parties in progress. It is the motel college dorm scene for the 25- to 30-year-olds.

ACCOMMODATIONS

The accommodations in the Lake Placid area are found mainly in new motels, most of them modern and attractive, but many a bit tacky. There are still several old inns. First among these is the **Lake Placid Club Resort,** a once grand hotel with large Victorian public rooms. The Club remains elegant. At the end of Main Street is the attractive **Mirror Lake Inn,** a wood-framed country inn with modern rooms overlooking the lake ($31–23 with meals). Also on Main Street is the **Homestead,** a large Victorian mansion.

In the middle of town are several modern motels including the **Holiday Motel,** with an indoor pool, sauna, and game room; the **Golden Arrow,** on the lake with indoor pool, pool table and ping-pong ($24–34); and, somewhat less plush than the others, the **Thunderbird Motel.** Above the ice arena, the town's central structure, is a **Holiday Inn** with two indoor tennis courts, open to the public. There is a modern **Ramada Inn** which has a pool, a game room featuring pinball machines, and a night club with live music on the weekends. There is also a modern **Howard Johnson's Motor Inn.**

This list includes the major inns of Lake Placid, but only a small portion of the many motels in the resort. There is no central reservations number at this writing, but for a more extensive list, you can call the Lake Placid Chamber of Commerce at 800-342-9561.

Nearer Whiteface itself there are additional inns and motels, none of them first-class. These are in the town of Wilmington, which is at the base of the mountain. Accommodations are listed by room and range in price from $12 to $30. The inns and motels are simple but adequate. Right at the mountain is the **Inn at Whiteface,** an old lodge with a restaurant, and the **Ledgerock Motel,** which is modern and mediocre. Less than a half-mile from the lifts there is the **Flume Motor Court,** also mediocre. Within a mile of the lifts are several other hotels including the **Wilderness Inn II,** with cabins, housekeeping units and a restaurant, the **Locust Inn and Cottages,** the **Whiteface Lodge,** the **Sportsman's Inn,** the **High Valley Motel,** and the **Landmark Motor Lodge.** Most of these have restaurants; most are adequate but by no means fancy.

RESTAURANTS

Restaurants in Lake Placid are inexpensive, serve large portions and can be good. Many of the major hotels have adequate to good restaurants, including the **Lake Placid Club Resort,** the **Mirror Lake Inn,** the **Ramada,** the **Howard Johnson's.** Of the restaurants, the **Steak and Stinger** is among the best known. It serves *French* food. The **Black Stallion** is inexpensive and has full-course Continental cuisine with an excellent salad bar. The **Villa Vespa** is an adequate Italian restaurant with a children's menu. The **Alpine Cellar** is a small restaurant serving German-American cuisine.

There are many other informal restaurants, both in Lake Placid and in Wilmington.

APRÈS-SKI AND NIGHT LIFE

There is lots of action in Lake Placid. Mostly it is oriented toward youthful singles but there is room for others as well. On the stuffy side is the **Adirondack Room** at the Lake Placid Club Resort. On the loud side is **Freddie's Inn,** a hard-rock place in town, **Sassafras,** a flashy disco, and **Tuckers** at the Ramada, a bar with live music on weekends. **Maxwells,** a bar, also has live music on weekends. There is country rock at the **Newman Opera House,** an old saloon down the hill from Main Street.

There is also music at the **Sportsman's Inn,** an after-ski bar (with pool tables) which is located in Wilmington near Whiteface. It attracts college-aged kids.

The real action is probably at the private parties but ignorance and decorum prevents us from telling the true story of these events.

DIVERSION

Lake Placid is a sports capital and as it prepares for the 1980 Olympics it will become an even more fully equipped center. It now has an outdoor speed skating oval in the middle of town, open without charge to the public. The indoor arena has college and semi-pro sporting events and is also open for free skating.

Cross-country skiing is found at the **Mount Van Hoevenberg Recreational Complex** about five miles from Lake Placid. This is also where the bobsled run is. The bobsled is open to the public for both participation and viewing. There is also a 90-meter ski jump, although the general public may not wish to participate in this.

Mt. Whitney, a small novice-intermediate Alpine area, has night skiing.

There is also a toboggan run, open to all, which shoots riders down the hill and out across the lake. On Sundays, they have toboggan distance contests. For those who want to watch but are tired of sports, there are three movie theaters. There is also cable television with choices of channels from New York, Albany and Montreal.

Finally, if you want to get away from all the activity, **Adirondack Ski Tours** in Saranac Lake offers a five-day wilderness ski tour. To be sure of a place, reservations should be made in advance.

CHILDREN

The skiing at Whiteface is acceptable for children. The choices of recreation help to keep them entertained. The resort is not compact, however, and you will have to ferry children about.

COSTS

Lake Placid is inexpensive. The State of New York, which runs the resort, has held lift tickets to $10. Accommodations are cheap and food at restaurants is very reasonable. It pays to ski away from the more popular and expensive Vermont resorts.

'41

Jay Peak

Jay Peak stands out all alone, high above the surrounding countryside in northernmost Vermont, near the Canadian border. Lacking the charm of more traditional Vermont, the area around Jay, while not unattractive, displays a sort of indifference to style which renders its restaurants and accommodations generally undistinguished. The resort itself is tasteful and the mountain has some real pluses. The bulk of the skiing is serviced by a tram, which is efficient, fast, and, most important, warm; the terrain on intermediate trails is more interesting than at many areas; and there is enough good expert terrain on the T-bar to keep strong skiers happy.

The appeal of the area tends to be to families and high school and college students who come because of Jay's modest prices and smaller crowds.

ACCESSIBILITY

Jay Peak is about 5 hours from Boston and 7 from New York. The best route from Boston is up Route 93 to Route 91, all the way to Orleans at the top of Vermont and then across Routes 5 and 100 to Jay. From New York, join Route 91 at New Haven or Hartford. Jay is only 90 miles from Montreal along good roads, Route 10 to Route 55 to Newport, Vermont. Burlington, Vermont, is the nearest airport, a little over 1 hour by car.

THE SKIING

Jay is a nice mountain for wandering. Like Smuggler's Notch, the trails on the principal mountain are cut not down the fall line but across the mountain, with short, steep drops ending in flat runout sections. The main lift is a modern aerial tramway with an 80-person capacity, which makes the trip to the top (7640' long; 2,100' vertical) in around 7 minutes. Skiing down on the left side, you take the Vermonter, an intermediate trail, along the narrow ridge of the mountain into an intermediate-novice area with twisting runs. Coming down off the right is Northway, a novice feeder trail that curves down and then back across the face of the mountain. Before you know it, you've lost 300 feet of vertical on a runout. Off Northway, there is one trail right under the tram, River Quai, which often does not hold snow but when open is steep and broad but short (8). The other trails off Northway to the right of the tram are intermediate on top and flat at the bottom. The bottom two-thirds of these trails are served by two chairs which start at the bottom and have 1,525- and 1,200-foot verticals. Intermediate adventurers or expert cruisers, who enjoy trails with constantly changing terrain, sometimes steep, then flat, will enjoy these runs.

The challenging part of the mountain is found on the Jet T-bar, a 3,600-foot-long lift with a 1,125-foot vertical. This lift ascends a short, steep hill with trails paralleling the lift coming down. Immediately to the left of the T-bar is U.N., steep, narrow (30–50'), and straight, with lots of bumps—not unlike the Mall at Sugarbush. This trail is a 9, with tough terrain at the top and tricky, sharp bumps at the bottom. Two other expert trails (8's) parallel U.N. These runs are challenging but, even by New England standards, are short. The T-bar is somewhat like the Valley chair at Sugarbush, both in steepness and length, and the trails are similar, though no trail is as broad or consistent as Stein's Run. The T-bar, which moves fast, gives Jay enough difficult expert terrain to keep the expert entertained.

There is ample novice skiing at Jay. Two lower T-bars provide access to good novice runs and good practice areas. For the somewhat more experienced novice, the two lower chairs have runs off them. Even the tram itself has a course designed for the daring novice.

On balance, Jay has something for all ranges of skiers but is particularly well-suited for the intermediate who enjoys the challenge of ever-changing terrain.

During the week, Jay rarely has lift lines. On weekends, Montreal visitors descend, and the line on the tram can be 30 minutes or more. The chairs are likely to have 10-minute lines on crowded weekends. The Jet T-bar has shorter lines and, in fact, is often uncrowded.

The mountain stands high above the surrounding area and is subject to heavy winds which can create a problem for the tram. Jay may also be a bit colder than its southern neighbors.

It has limited snowmaking capacity restricted to the lower slopes. Its northerly position, however, means it gets a little more snow, holds it a little longer, and is likely to have good conditions later in the season.

LIFE IN THE AREA

Jay is a family resort that is also very popular with college kids. It has lots of family inns with game rooms and bars with live and disco music.

ACCOMMODATIONS

Right at the tram is the **Hotel Jay.** It is modern with a Tyrolean decor and has large rooms with color TV, balconies, and like most of the other hotels in the area, a good game room, which includes a ping-pong and a pool table. A mile from Jay is the **Inglenook Lodge,** a pleasant, modern, chalet-type motel, which has a friendly lounge with an open hearth and game room, again with ping-pong and pool. This pattern dominates the area. About four miles down the mountain to the east is Jay, a rather bleak but not unattractive crossroads (it's not quite a town). In Jay, there is an older inn, the **Jay Barn Inn,** with bar, lounge, fireplace, and game room. Also there is the **Chateau Jaymont,** an intricate, elegantly designed modern hotel with a good French restaurant-bar, and the **Woodshed, Ltd.,** a simple building of the 1950 vintage which accommodates twenty guests.

Six miles west of the mountain are two towns, Montgomery Center and Montgomery, which predate skiing in the area. Toward Montgomery Center is the simple **Eagle Lodge,** an old charmless farmhouse with a game room, a b.y.o. bar, and dorm. The **Alpine Haven** is a chalet development having at its center a pseudo-Tyrolean modern lodge, the Waldhof, with lounge, sauna, and game room. The chalets can be rented for short stays and do provide maximum privacy.

In Montgomery Center there are two old inns: the pleasant and homey **Carinthia Inn,** with a good restaurant and bar, and the **Wedel Inn,** old, a bit run down, and inexpensive. Two miles north in the charming, quiet town of Montgomery is the small, old (1803) **Black Lantern Inn,** simply restored but attractive.

Jay also has three dormitories: the **Jay View Mountain Dorm,** a mile from the lift, with a good game room and bar (4–6 to a room); the **Schneehutte Ski Dorm,** a little over a mile from the lifts, with ping-pong and pool tables and a jukebox; and finally, in Montgomery Center, **Granny Grunt's Dorm,** a four-story, recently restored wood-built dorm with game room, skating rink and sauna. Granny's, with 16 rooms, sleeps 110 skiers, is well-run, popular, and provides a shuttle bus to the slopes. All of the dorms serve meals.

The lodging number for Jay is 802-988-2611, or, from Montreal, 866-2384.

RESTAURANTS

Jay is not for the jet set. Modified American Plans dominate the area and restaurants accordingly suffer. Montgomery Center has a couple of pleasant unpretentious restaurants, the **Swiss Chalet** and **On The Rocks.** Six miles from Jay to the east is the **Green Valley Restaurant,** which has a diner atmosphere, but good food. The best restaurants are found in the hotels, particularly at the **Black Lantern Inn** in Montgomery, the **Carinthia Inn** in Montgomery Center, or on the modern side, the **Chateau Jaymont.**

APRÈS-SKI AND NIGHT LIFE

Directly after skiing there is drink and sometimes music at the Tyrolean-designed base lodge right at the tram. For college or high school students activities center around the dorms or near them at places like the **Blue Bandana,** a pizza parlor with live music. In town or at the mountain, there are lounges with occasional dancing, and at **Granny Grunt's** there's a disco for college or high school students. The **Thirsty Boot,** a disco in Montgomery Center, is a low-ceilinged lounge which features loud music that goes on until 2 A.M. There is also live music at the **Golden Eagle Lounge** at the Hotel Jay on weekends.

DIVERSION

Ski touring at Jay is found at the **Chateau Jaymont,** which has 20 miles of marked trails, half of which are machine-groomed. There are rentals and instruction. **Granny Grunt's** offers free outdoor skating for its guests and charges a small fee to the public. At the **Waldhof Lodge** at Alpine Haven, you can take a country sleigh ride for a touch of fresh air.

CHILDREN

Jay is a good area for children. Despite its size, the mountain is not overwhelming and kids will not get lost or caught in areas they cannot handle. There is a nursery at the mountain for children 2 to 7, $2 per hour or $10 per day with lunch. The inns almost all have Modified American Plans, house play rooms, and are mostly located in places where the children can go outside and play.

COSTS

Jay is a moderately priced area. The weekend day lift ticket is $13, $10 for children 12 and under. On weekdays, the lift ticket is $10. A 5½-day ticket with lessons costs $60 during the Christmas and February vacation periods, and $45 in January and early February. At the Hotel Jay, a five-day MAP plan, double occupancy, costs $225 per person. A similar package costs $150 at other hotels, and at Granny Grunt's ski dorm, a 5½-day lift ticket with all meals included costs $120. Jay may be an extra couple of hours' drive further away, but as far as cost is concerned, it's worth it.

42

Killington

Four mountains, 10 chair lifts, a 3½-mile-long gondola and a season that lasts from late October to mid-May. That is the rough outline of the resort at Killington, the largest ski complex in the East. It was built by one of the most aggressive ski corporations in America, which has been a leader in ski promotion and imaginative ski programming. Killington was the home of the GLM*accelerated teaching method which produced the instant intermediate skier. The resort has out-done all others, except for Hunter Mountain, in its use of snowmaking equipment. It has organized racing programs and teaching training camps.

The area has reaped the advantages and disadvantages of bigness: it has a huge choice of skiing terrain and is active after skiing, but it can be quite crowded both on and off the mountain. Killington is not a retreat; it is an operation, but one that offers a lot of skiing and a lot of activity.

ACCESSIBILITY

Killington is a 5-hour drive from New York and a 3-hour drive from Boston. From New York, take the New York Thruway to the Northway, then at the Fort Anne exit, take Route 49 to Route 4 through Rutland to Killington. Alternatively, you can take Route 91 from New Haven or Hartford and exit at Bellows Falls onto Route 103 and Route 100, or stay on Route 91 to White River Junction, changing to Route 89 to Woodstock, and then across Route 4 to Killington. The New York Thruway is the fastest and most direct route. From Boston, the most direct route is Route 93, into Route 89 at Concord, New Hampshire, and then onto Route 4 at Woodstock. Albany, 2 hours away, is the closest major airport, with Boston and Springfield (3-hour drives) as

*See footnote, p. 26.

alternatives. There is limited air service to Rutland, 20 miles from Killington, or Lebanon, New Hampshire, 40 miles away. On weekends, there is also direct bus service from New York to the resort. During the week, there is daily bus service to Rutland or White River Junction, where you must hire a cab.

THE SKIING

Killington is a wanderer's mountain *par excellence.* There is unlimited, tricky intermediate terrain running throughout the resort, which has six distinct skiing areas interconnected by trails.

At the center of the mountain complex is the Killington chair lift, which goes to the summit of Killington Mountain at 4,250 feet, the second highest point in Vermont. Off this chair (6,100' long; 1,680' vertical), there are several expert trails including Escapade, Cascade, and East Fall, each of which has a gradual top section, then a very steep, bumpy middle area, and finally a long, flat runoff at the bottom. The steep sections have about 500 feet of vertical and are 9's for these stretches.

The Killington chair also takes intermediates to their point of departure. To the right of this chair on the north face of Killington Mountain at the summit are three trails of average intermediate steepness, with occasional short bump sections, served by a triple chair lift. This chair, the Glades Triple, has snowmaking, is very high, and can be skied from October to May. After skiing the Glades, the intermediate can ski down to the Snowden area to the north of the Killington chair. Snowden has about six trails, all criss-crossing and intersecting. Snowden is a busy area. It has a double and triple chair, and a lower and upper poma lift. The triple has a steep expert liftline and a racing trail to its left, but the other Snowden runs are all intermediate. Snowden is the most popular area at Killington and suffers from the Killington malady, too many and too much—too many people and too much uphill lift capacity. On a crowded Sunday with icy conditions, the intersections on Snowden, the top of the Killington chair, and parts of a third area, Needle's Eye, can look like an Italian traffic interchange without stop lights. This increased uphill lift capacity has greatly reduced lift lines but has created new problems. Even on weekends, the Killington chair and the Snowden chairs will have only short lines (10 minutes). The other chairs may have none. But the trails, particularly on Snowden, may be jammed.

To continue the tour, the intermediate can go beyond Snowden to a third area, Ramshead Mountain. Ramshead has a 6,450-foot-long chair with three intermediate narrow runs coming down closely paralleling the liftline. Ramshead is an area to itself, is often uncrowded, and has its own base lodge.

Killington seen from Route 4; right to left, peaks of Ramshead, Snowden, Killington, and Needle's Eye   KILLINGTON SKI RESORT PHOTO

From the top of Ramshead, the intermediate can return to the area at the bottom of the Killington and Snowden chairs (where there is another base lodge). Ascending again on the Killington chair, the intermediate can adventure to the left of the lift (the east face of Killington) to an area served by the 3½-mile-long gondola, the longest ski lift in the world (what we like to call the "cross-county" gondola) and another double chair lift.

The top section on this east side starts with a narrow flat ridge. Along the top of the ridge runs the Great Eastern, a novice trail, going more than 4 miles from the top to the bottom of the gondola. Dropping off the ridge on the north side, back toward the Killington chair, are two steep expert trails, Superstar and Skye Lark (8.5), which have a continuous steep pitch over a 1,000-foot vertical distance. With bumps, these provide the best expert terrain at Killington.

Continuing east along the Great Eastern, you come to the Needle's Eye area, the liftline for the middle section of the gondola. Needle's Eye has a double chair lift (4,400′ long; 1,200′ vertical). The liftline is an intermediate-expert slope, a 7 at the top. Great Eastern crosses Needle's Eye and runs in and out of the Four Mile Trail, a gentle intermediate run that parallels Great Eastern, from the top down. These two trails continue along the last gentle section of the gondola, coming down to the gondola terminal on Route 4 at 1,160 feet above sea level, a total drop of 3,060 feet. The intermediate will have fun cruising this entire 4-mile stretch on these narrow and occasionally tricky trails. For the novice, Great Eastern can be an interesting trip and a bit of a challenge, depending on conditions. The ride back on the gondola takes 45 minutes. There is a restaurant at both the top and the bottom of the gondola.

The south face at the top of Killington has a new triple chair dropping 900 feet and serving three gladed areas without traditional trails. This new south chair is triangular: the first section going up to a mid-station is steep. The chair then turns and ascends along a gradual slope designed for advanced novice and intermediate skiers. The returning chairs go down an entirely different liftline of intermediate steepness. The bottom leg of the chair is for experts, the top leg is for novices, and the returning leg is designed for intermediates.

"Enough, enough," you say, but there's more. In fact, we've left out the guts of the Killington operation. There are three double chairs on a 400-foot-wide beginner's practice slope, the Snowshed area. Snowshed has its own base lodge, a nursery, an après-ski bar, ski shops, and a formal restaurant. The bottom of Snowshed is just across the access road from Ramshead; the top is just above the bottom of the Killington chair. Snowshed sits in a basin formed by the peaks on Ramshead, Snowden, Killington and Needle's Eye. We think Snowshed is altogether too crowded, but it is the area where Killington's 140-member ski school operates.

Killington has the longest season in the East and one of the longest in the United States. It opens in late October and closes in May. It has snowmaking capacity on most of the Killington chair trails, all of Snowden, and, of course, Snowshed. It has a high elevation, makes snow all the time, and receives more natural snow than any area in the East (averaging 275 inches a year).

In keeping with its size and the length of its season, Killington offers many special programs. In addition to its accelerated (GLM) week's learning package, it runs ski tuning clinics, learn-to-race weekends (in December), learn-to-be-a-ski-instructor, ski patroller, or racing coach programs (November), and a free-style program with a fall, spring and summer camp.

LIFE IN THE AREA

Killington has an active non-skiing life with many, many lodges and motels, several good restaurants and many nightspots, and other diversions. The lodging area is spread out over a four-mile access road which comes into the basin from Route 4. Most of the lodges are traditional and simple. There is no central town serving the area (and no public transportation), and the access road provides the only focus.

ACCOMMODATIONS

There are two inns and two modern condominiums about 5 to 10 minutes' walk from the Snowshed lifts. The closest of these are the two inns, the brand-new **Mountain Inn** (opening in 1978), which has a game room, sauna, and an elaborate dining room and bar (MAP, $42 per person), and the less elaborate **Killington Village,** which is modern but has few accessories. The two condominiums, **Whiffletree** and **Edgemont,** are also modern and attractive but have no extra facilities such as a game room or sauna. They are a 10-minute walk from the lifts.

On the 4-mile access road coming in from Route 4, there are another 25 inns. In general, these lodges are simple and comfortable, but not luxurious. The **Basin Lodge, Red Rob Inn** (good piano-bar lounge), **Chalet Killington, Pikes Lodge, Alpenhof, Killington Village Inn, Little Buckhorn, Whispering Pines Lodge,** and **Chalet Salisbury** are inns with restaurants. These are well-suited to families. Except for the last two, they all have dormitory accommodations in addition to their rooms. The **Chalet Kristin, Brindlehof, Skol Haus Motor-Lodge, Fractured Rooster, Chalet International,** and **Chalet Roedig** are informal and have b.y.o. bars but do not have restaurants.

Above the access road with splendid views of the ski mountain is the **Summit Lodge,** an old inn with large fireplaces, relaxed common rooms, a large whirlpool bath, and ping-pong tables (with meals, $32–40 per person).

The most luxurious of all inns at Killington is the modern **Cortina Inn,** about 10 miles from the resort on Route 4. The Cortina has a handsome lobby, a heated indoor pool, game room, resident masseur, a ski touring center, ice skating, and live entertainment in its bar. Less luxurious than the Cortina is the **Grey Bonnet Inn** on Route 100 north of Route 4, 6 miles from the resort. The Grey Bonnet has attractive rooms, a whirlpool bath, and a pleasant bar. On Route 4 a few minutes' walk from the gondola Base Lodge is the **Turn of the River Lodge,** which is informal, inexpensive, and has a nice lounge and b.y.o. bar.

In Rutland, there are several large modern motels including a **Holiday Inn** and a **Travelodge Motel.**

For reservations, the Killington Lodging Bureau's number is 802-422-3333.

RESTAURANTS

The major inns have restaurants. The **Summit Lodge** and **Cortina Inn** are Continental; the **Alpine Inn** is Italian; the **Grey Bonnet** has steak, Continental food, and a salad bar.

On the access road is an attractive pub, **Charities 1887 Tavern,** with a pub menu. There are two informal pizza places, **Bilbos** and **Zorba's,** both with music. **Churchill's,** on Route 4 west of the resort, is a gourmet restaurant serving Continental food. East of Killington on Route 4 in an old Vermont home is **Laurens Gracious Country Dining,** also with a Continental menu. (Alas for the disappearance of New England home cooking!) The **Basin Lodge** very near the lifts serves inexpensive, all-you-can-eat meals.

APRÈS-SKI AND NIGHT LIFE

Killington has a wide choice of nightspots. There are two bars at the Snowshed base area, the **Angus Tavern** and **Snowshed Lounge.** The latter has guitar music after skiing in a large convention center room. The liveliest action, however, is at the **Pickel Barrell** and the **Wobbly Barn** after skiing and at night. Both have rock groups and happy hours and direct their appeal to the under-thirty crowd. The Pickel Barrell has an attractive upstairs area with a large fireplace. Drinks are very inexpensive during the happy hour.

Locals hang out at the quieter **Kings Four,** a restaurant-bar with live entertainment at night. **Bilbos** and **Zorba's** also have live music and are informal. Zorba's has pool tables, pinball and TV.

For the elderly (those over thirty), the cozy **Red Rob Inn** has a quiet, elegant lounge, often with guitar music late at night. The **Cortina** and the **Grey Bonnet Inn** may also have piano or group music in their bars. Several other inns on the access road may on any weekend have music in their lounges.

DIVERSION

There is cross-country skiing at Killington just across Route 4 at the **Mountain Meadows Ski Touring Center** and a cross-country center at the **Cortina Inn.** There are two indoor tennis centers, both in Rutland, 20 miles from the mountain. The **Brookside/Tennis** has four hard-surface courts, a bar, and a sauna. **Rutland Indoor Tennis** has four Hartru courts.

CHILDREN

Killington is just adequate for children. Its sheer size and the number of day lodges (five, including one at the top of the gondola) can make it a confusing place. The beginners' slope, Snowshed, can be very crowded, detracting from its quality as a learning area. Furthermore, there is no public transportation on the access road and limited accommodations at the lifts, so you must drive the children back and forth to your lodge.

There is a nursery at the Snowshed base area and a ski school program for small children.

COSTS

Killington is a moderately priced area. Weekend day lift tickets are $14. A two-day ticket is $24. A five-weekday ticket is $55, $75 with lessons. Lodges sell five-day per-person packages with meals for $100 to $195 (most below $150). The same package with dorm accommodations costs as little as $75. Without meals, the five-night cost ranges from $50 to $90. Restaurants in general are both informal and reasonably priced.

'43

Mount Snow

Mount Snow appears to have successfully combined the traditional setting and architecture of New England with the modern social style and pace of middle-class New York. The nearby towns, with their white clapboard wood-frame homes, inns, and churches, lend the feeling of a traditional Vermont village. The skiers are young professional singles from the City and families from the suburbs. The mountain is an excellent intermediate and novice area, with two or three challenging trails on the back that are as tough as any in southern New England.

ACCESSIBILITY

There is a choice of routes from New York, each of which is a 4½-hour drive. The longer but easier course is up Route 91 through Hartford to Brattleboro and then across Route 9 to Wilmington. The shortest route is up the Taconic Parkway, exiting at Chatham on Route 295. From Route 295, you can take back roads through West Lebanon and Garfield to Route 22. Then you go up Route 22 to Route 7, to Route 9 to Bennington, and from Bennington, on Route 9 to Wilmington. As a variation on this, you can take the New York Thruway to Albany and pick up Route 7 at Troy. By air, Albany is the closest airport, about a 1½-hour drive. The airport at Hartford-Springfield is about 2 hours away by car.

THE SKIING

Mount Snow has a broad, smooth east face with a moderate slope, not unlike its neighbor, Stratton. This face has a vertical of 1,900 feet over a distance of about 7,200 feet, and is made up entirely of intermediate or novice terrain. Many trails that extend from top to bottom, such as Canyon, Lodge, and Exhibition, are narrow with some tricky intermediate terrain at the top and broad with gentle novice-intermediate terrain at the bottom. These trails are served by two enclosed bubble chair lifts (skis-on gondolas), one of which goes all the way to the top; by two double chairs that go up two-thirds of the mountain; and by several other short chairs at the bottom. The area, which was purchased by the corporation which owns Killington, plans to build a new top-to-bottom triple chair lift up the middle of the east face.

Novices can ski the bottom sections of the east face on the shorter chairs or, with a little trail experience, can go to the top and ski down the extreme left side of the face on very gradual trails, Deer Run and Long Run, which curve languidly through the woods.

Experts will find their challenge on the north face, which has two trails with steep, narrow, bump sections: P.D.F. and Jaws of Death. Jaws is an 8 and is as tough as any trail you can find south of Killington, except possibly for a run or two at Hunter Mountain. The other trails on the north side are 7's, similar in steepness and terrain to Spruce at Stratton. There is one double chair serving these trails (3,650' long; 1,025' vertical). This North Face chair generally has short lines (10 minutes) on weekends. The chairs on the east face, particularly the gondolas, often have 20- to 30-minute lines.

Mount Snow has an average annual snowfall of 130 inches. It has snowmaking on the lower portions of the central trails on the east face and on the entire Canyon trail to the top. This capacity is being expanded. Snow's more southerly location can make snow preservation difficult.

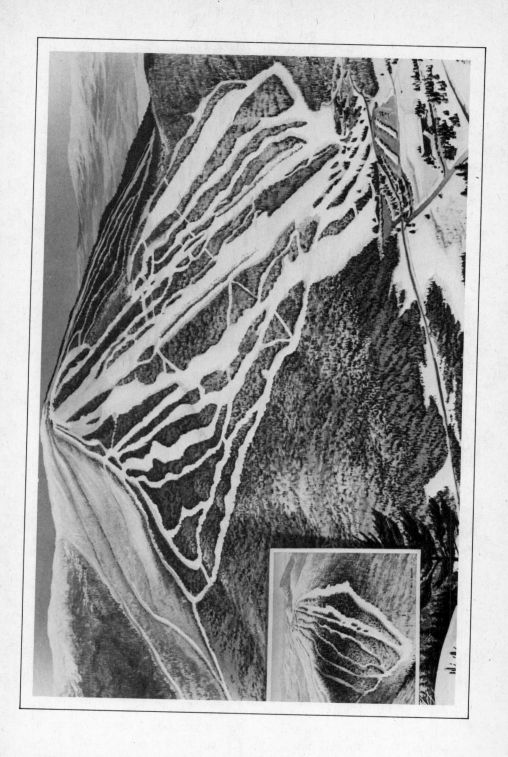

Mount Snow: north face in background, top right   COURTESY MOUNT SNOW SKI AREA

LIFE IN THE AREA

Mount Snow has a full range of accommodations and entertainment. It is a lively center, particularly on weekends. There are several good restaurants, a variety of entertainment, a raucous singles' scene and, sedate, "adult" (over 30) entertainment.

ACCOMMODATIONS

The majority of lodges at Snow function on the Modified American Plan. Rates listed below all include meals and are all based on a daily, per person, double occupancy rate.

There is a small grouping of lodges at the mountain about five minutes' walk from the lifts. The largest and most luxurious of these inns is the **Snow Lake Lodge,** a six-story wood and glass structure, with a handsome lounge and bar, an indoor heated pool, and a game room ($36–48). The **Snow Lake** provides Mercedes shuttle service to the mountain, one minute's drive away. The three modern but not luxurious hotels next to the Snow Lake are the **Lodge,** with a heated indoor-outdoor pool, a whirlpool and a bar ($22–30); the **Ironstone** with a sauna and cocktail lounge ($21–27); and the **Thunderbird** with an outdoor heated pool and a b.y.o. bar ($19–24).

North of the Snow Lake Lodge and almost on the slopes are two smaller, more rustic inns: the **North Branch Club** and the **Snowbrook.** The North Branch Club has rooms with fireplaces, a sauna, and an indoor pool ($36). The Snowbrook is older and cozier and has modern chalets ($15–25). Nearby is the **Tamarack,** which has a b.y.o. bar and an attractive, informal, modern lounge ($19–27).

Three inns located just south of the lifts about a seven-minute walk away are the **Mountaineer Lodge,** the **Alp-hof Lodge,** and **Encore** at the slopes. The Mountaineer and Alp-hof are informal, with b.y.o. bars ($17–24). The Encore is more luxurious and has an indoor pool, cocktail lounge and game room ($20–29).

Once away from the mountain, there are many motels and some old inns. Reservations can be made through the area association at 802-464-8501.

RESTAURANTS

The Snow area has many restaurants in addition to those at the inns. The most elegant of these is the **Inn at Sawmill Farm,** which has a Continental menu. In West Dover, 3 miles from the mountain, there is a good, small French restaurant, **Le Petit Chef.** There are several restaurants serving hearty

American food, including the **Roadhouse** in West Dover and the **Old Red Mill,** located in Wilmington. The **Deacon's Den** is a very inexpensive steak house.

APRÈS-SKI AND NIGHT LIFE

Après-ski life starts as a mixer at the bar on the top floor of the Base Lodge. Other bars, **Sister Kate's, North Country Fair,** and the **Snow Lake Lodge,** may have after-ski entertainment.

At night, those over thirty drift to the Snow Lake for dancing to "popular music." **Le Disco,** on the Mount Snow entry road, 500 yards from the lifts, is the disco-rock music place in town and draws the whole crowd of young couples and singles to its huge, plush surroundings. There are several other bars with live or disco music, including **Andirons,** Sister Kate's, the **Deacon's Den,** the **Dover Forge,** the **Old Red Mill, Sitzmark Lodge,** and others. To find the spots that are currently in vogue, ask around at the Base Lodge bar.

DIVERSION

There are two cross-country centers at Snow. The **Sitzmark** in Wilmington has 20 miles of gentle trails. The **Mount Snow Cross Country Touring Center** has 50 miles of trails with greater variation among them. Beyond cross-country, diversion is found in the lodges and inns, with their swimming pools and game rooms.

CHILDREN

Mount Snow is a good area and mountain for kids. There is a nursery on the slopes. The mountain is very manageable. However, small children may have difficulty walking to and from the lifts. Many of the inns do have swimming pools and game rooms.

COSTS

Snow is moderately priced. Inns charge on a MAP basis, with five-day packages costing $90 to $150 except at the Snow Lake or North Branch Club, which have rooms up to $200 or $175, respectively. Lift tickets are $14 per day or $50 for a five-day ticket during the week. There are reduced prices for any multi-day ticket.

44

Okemo Mountain

The shy sister, overshadowed by her aggressive siblings, may be the jewel of the group. Okemo, located between hard-selling Killington to her north and high-class Stratton to her south, is generally overlooked despite a vertical drop of 2,100 feet (the fourth or fifth longest in the state) and an uphill lift capacity of 8,000 persons per hour. Okemo is skied by families with young children who enjoy the unpretentiousness of the ski resort and the inexpensive simplicity of the surrounding community. The town of Ludlow, at the base of the mountain, while not charming, is a quiet Vermont town, unspoiled by the pressures brought on by large ski developments. Okemo is not glamorous, but it is as solid as a Vermont maple.

ACCESSIBILITY

Okemo is a 4½-hour drive from New York via Route 91 to Bellows Falls, then Route 103 to Ludlow, and a 3-hour drive from Boston, out Route 2 and either up Route 91 to Bellows Falls or across Route 12 from Fitchburg, Massachusetts, to Bellows Falls. Alternatively, you can take Route 93 to Concord, New Hampshire, and then travel east across Route 89 to Route 103. The closest air service is through Rutland, 18 miles away, or Lebanon, New Hampshire, 40 miles northeast. The area is only 16 miles north of the Bromley-Magic crossroad, Route 11, so those skiing Okemo who want a change can readily go south to Stratton. Similarly, it is only 20 miles south of Killington.

THE SKIING

Okemo is a young family ski area. As is largely true of all areas in southern Vermont (with the principal exception of the north side of Mt. Snow), the mountain is predominantly an intermediate skier's area. The upper trails are rated expert, but they are easily managed by a good intermediate. There is no sustained steep vertical anywhere on the mountain. Trails such as Upper War Dance, Upper Chief, and Geronimo have narrow, twisty patches near the top of the mountain and can have tricky moguled stretches, but none rates higher than a 7. The steepest lifts on the mountain are the top chair (length, 3,895'; vertical, 1,032') and the major poma lift (length, 6,207'; vertical, 1,520'), ratios of about 4 to 1.

Okemo's strength, then, is its intermediate and novice terrain. For the intermediate, there are the bumpy trails at the top and broad, rolling, well-groomed trails at the bottom. The entire top right side of the mountain, served by two short poma lifts, has wandering intermediate runs.

Chief and Geronimo trails are long and good for cruising by strong intermediates. They extend nearly from top to bottom directly down the center of the mountain for a distance of 7,400 feet or more (1,900' vertical). These runs will appeal to juniors who like to fly down the mountain.

The novice trails start at the top and wander about all over. One trail, Mountain Road, is 4½ miles long. The bottom slopes, with two poma lifts and a chair lift, are a bit flat and crowded, but trails off the top and off to the left side on Chair #2, particularly the Sachem trail, have just the right pitch for novices and are pleasantly removed from the central bustle.

The lift system at Okemo is unusual but will appeal to young people in particular. Okemo started as an area with no lifts other than poma lifts. It still has six pomas, one of them 6,200 feet long. Pomas can be fun, especially for kids. They are fast; the 6,200-foot poma takes about 7 minutes to pull you to the top, about half the time of the trip in an equivalently long chair lift. The poma lift area is designed in such a way that you're not jerked off your feet as you get in the lift. Of course, you can get pretty tired skiing pomas all day, but you can also cover an awful lot of ground.

The area has now added three chairs, two in tandem going to the top of the mountain (#2, length 4,415', vertical 961'; #3, length 3,895', vertical 1,032'). Chair #1 traverses the foot of the mountain and services novice practice slopes and some of the other lower lifts.

Okemo is a good bet for lines. They won't be short on big weekends, but on other weekends they'll be manageable (10–15 minutes or less on the major lifts). There are many lifts, so you can hunt and pick with some success.

Okemo has the *relatively* mild southern Vermont weather and the predictable 125 inches of snow per season. It makes snow on the lower slopes and does extensive grooming.

LIFE IN THE AREA

Okemo is out of the way, is oriented toward families and their children, and has an atmosphere of semi-rural New England. It is only 30 minutes from Stratton, but it is as different from Stratton as Peoria is from Grosse Pointe. The town of Ludlow, at the base of the mountain, has a few shops, a few gas stations, a shopping center and several inns on the periphery, but it remains a small, modern Vermont town.

ACCOMMODATIONS

Tips on lodging near Okemo must start with **Castle Inn,** a 1904 large Victorian stone mansion with wide, long stately hallways, huge fireplaces, a sombre, elegant dining room, and cavernous Victorian bedrooms. Once owned and lived in by a governor of the state, the mansion rests on a hill above Route 103 in Proctorsville, five miles from the mountain. In the backyard of the Inn is the Castle Tennis Club with two indoor clay courts. Also in Proctorsville are the **Okemo Lantern Lodge,** an old farmhouse inn, and the **Golden Stage Inn,** a renovated inn with a lounge, game room, and cable TV. In Ludlow, 5 minutes from the mountain, is the **Winchester,** a village inn built as a colonial home in 1813; the Winchester has old rooms, a charming dining room, and good food.

Also in Ludlow is the inexpensive, simple **Inn Towne Motel.** East of town is a plain, modern motel, the **Hideaway Motel,** an old (1810) former farmhouse; the **Okemo Inn,** with an informal, rambling homelike friendliness; and a still more simple inexpensive inn, the **Farm House Lodge,** which has dormitories. Back off Route 103, two miles from the mountain, is the modern **Fox Run,** a resort accommodating up to 150 persons, with ice skating, cross-country skiing, sauna, a bright, high-ceilinged dining room facing the mountain, and nightly entertainment, at least on weekends. Like the other accommodations near Okemo, the Fox Run is informal and inexpensive during the week and attracts families.

Farther north on Route 100 five miles from the mountain is the **Echo Lake Inn,** a restored Colonial inn with restaurant, lounge, and a quiet country air.

If you want to hedge your bets and ski the Triangle (Stratton, Bromley, or Magic) to the south, you can stay 12 miles south of Ludlow on Route 100 in Weston at the **Inn at Weston,** an old on-the-green country inn, or at the **Black Shutters,** an inn—private home, alone off Route 100 a half-mile north of Weston.

The number for reservations at Okemo is 802-228-2982.

RESTAURANTS

The most interesting dining room in the area is again at **Castle Inn,** featuring Continental food in a sombre, intriguing, Victorian atmosphere (entrées, $7–10). The **Winchester,** just east of Ludlow, is also good and serves a large Continental menu featuring veal, fish, and Caesar salad (entrées, $5–9). **Fox Run** serves pleasant, plain American food (entrées, $6–9). **Diamond Jim's** in Ludlow is unpretentious and features steaks and fish. The **Chopping Block** in Proctorsville (sandwiches, $1–3) and the **Farm House Lodge and Lounge** in Ludlow (sandwiches and pizza) are informal (the former has live music). **Nikki's** in Ludlow is also informal and has a menu of salads, chili, teriaki steak and sandwiches ($1.50–3.00). For the younger kids, there is **Seward's Family Restaurant** right in the heart of the Ludlow Shopping Plaza.

APRÈS-SKI AND NIGHT LIFE

Okemo appeals to families with young children, and as a result guests lead a quiet après-ski life. Foot-loose teenagers may wander off to the **Mill** in Londonderry 20 miles south or **Haigs,** still further south in Bondsville, both associated with the Triangle resorts, or north to the **Wobbly Barn** at Killington. However, Okemo does have the rock sound at the **Chopping Block,** an old but solid barn in Proctorsville, which appeals to those in their late teens and early twenties. It also has a seven-foot TV screen.

In Ludlow, the **Pot Belly Pub,** advertised as "The Place to go in Ludlow," is a small, old-tavern-like bar with folk or bluegrass music après-ski or at night. You can also find entertainment in the lounge at **Fox Run.**

For those who want quiet but don't want to stay home, there is a movie theater in Ludlow, but don't expect a first-run flick.

DIVERSION

Okemo offers cross-country skiing at the mountain (class lessons, $5), and **Fox Run Resort** has its own center with groomed trails open to the public.

There is indoor tennis at the **Castle Tennis Club,** right behind the Castle Inn at Proctorsville, 5 miles from the mountain; Castle Tennis has two clay courts in a bubble and rents to the public at rates ranging from $10 to $14 per hour.

CHILDREN

Okemo is for kids. The pomas have a sort of amusement park quality for them, and there is a day-care center, **Wahoo Nursery,** at the slopes for those who do not ski ($1 per hour, $5 all day). There is also a **Little Wahoo** ski school for the youngest kids, lessons starting at $2.75 per hour. The area even has a family day ticket, $28.50 for 2 parents and a junior, $7 for each junior thereafter. During the week, children under six ski free. There is one central base lodge, so kids should be easy to find at least when they are not skiing.

COSTS

One of the real contrasts between the neighboring Stratton and Okemo areas is the price differences. Day care as stated is $1 per hour at Okemo, $2 at Stratton. The weekend day ticket at Okemo is $12 to Stratton's $15, and the weekday ticket at Okemo is $9 ($40 for 5 days). Except for the somewhat more expensive rate at Fox Run on weekends, rates at the lodges on weekends run $15 to $25 per day per person with meals or around $100–160 per person for 5 days with meals *and* lifts. In Vermont, that's about as inexpensive as you are likely to find.

'45

Smuggler's Notch

As if to prove its name true, Smuggler's Notch is tucked away in a small valley just a stone's throw from the East's foremost resort, Stowe. In fact, thousands of skiers ski Stowe and have never even heard of its neighbor. Yet Smuggler's is a major resort, with one of the most compact but complete ski village developments in the East. The village, modeled after the newer Western resorts (and claiming to be the Sun Valley of the East), has condominiums, restaurants, bars and sports facilities at the base of the mountain. The skiing itself is mixed, with good intermediate and novice terrain.

ACCESSIBILITY

Smuggler's is just north of Stowe, but don't be misled. You can get off the lift at Spruce Peak and in 10 minutes ski across to Smuggler's, but the same trip by car, in the winter when the pass between the mountain is closed, takes almost an hour. From New York, the best route is up Route 91 to White River Junction, up Route 89 to Exit 11 near Burlington, then up 2A to Essex Junction, and finally along Route 15 north to Jeffersonville. From Boston, you can join this route by taking Route 93 to Route 89. As an alternative after joining Route 89, you can exit at Stowe and follow Route 100 to Route 15 and then west to Jeffersonville. From New York, the time is almost 7 hours; from Boston, around 4½ hours. From Montreal, Smuggler's is quite accessible by coming down Route 89 and taking Route 104 to Jeffersonville, a trip of about 1¾ hours. By air, you can reach Smuggler's by flying to Burlington, which is about a half-hour drive from the resort. Also, Amtrak's train from New York to Montreal, leaving Penn Station in the evening, arrives early in the morning at Essex Junction, which is only about 25 minutes from Jeffersonville. The resort will meet trains or planes if given advance notice.

THE SKIING

Smuggler's has three mountains which break down more or less (perhaps less) into novice, intermediate, and expert areas. The novice area begins right above the village a few feet from the condominiums. It has a medium-length chair and two wandering, gentle trails just suited to giving the novice confidence. This area is well segregated from the more demanding slopes found at the other chairs. Once the novice feels secure, he can begin adventuring, starting from the top of the novice chair and skiing across a pretty trail to the day lodge and the bottom of the two other chairs. The novice can continue up the Sterling chair and come down Rumrunner, a twisting trail of advanced novice difficulty. Most of the other runs on Sterling are intermediate. Our favorites are Black Shake and Treasure Run, which we found narrow and, from time to time, challenging. With only a 1,500-foot vertical, Sterling also has an expert run, the liftline (7), which has bump sections and steep sections. From the top of Sterling, you can also ski across to Stowe's Spruce Peak area. You ski along a picturesque trail which crosses a small lake and then drops through the woods until it joins Stowe's intermediate Sterling trail. Beware: there are no interchangeable lift tickets and the return up the Spruce lift will cost $4.

The blood and guts of Smuggler's is its big mountain, Madonna (2,100′ vertical), which, incidentally, was the mountain after which the resort was formerly named. If Madonna's trails were as well cut and skiable as Sterling's, Smuggler's would be a first-class area. Unfortunately, the entire right side of Madonna has nothing but catwalks that traverse the mountain. One trail, the Glade, which supposedly comes down the right side, in fact exists only on the trail map. The two principal trails down the left side, F.I.S. and Dempsey's Run, are very tough at the top. The area claims that F.I.S. has a 45° slope, but this steepness is found only at the very top. F.I.S. is, in any case, a 9 at the top. Dempsey's Run is a glade which is both demanding and fun (8). The problem with each of these trails is that they flatten out halfway down and become intermediate runouts. Somehow, the 2,100-foot vertical of Madonna gets lost. Beyond these expert trails, there are several intermediate runs off Madonna, complementing the ample intermediate terrain on Sterling.

Smuggler's Notch, while not well known outside Vermont, does have lift lines on weekends, though they're not long like those at Mt. Mansfield or areas further south. During the week, you'll have no problem with lines.

LIFE IN THE AREA

The central attraction of Smuggler's is the village itself and the life it offers. It is a nicely designed, modern condominium complex that has most of the amenities vacationers would want, including a ski shop, restaurants, bars, a pool, sauna, and, at a distance of 5 miles, indoor tennis. The real advantage is that you can throw away your car keys, disconnect the telephone, and forget about the outside world.

ACCOMMODATIONS

In the village, the condominiums have apartments of all sizes, including single rooms. The village is small, so all the condominiums are within a minute's walk of the shops and restaurants and the lift at Morse. Those renting these apartments have the right to use the indoor pool and saunas.

A half-mile from the village is the **Red Fox Ski Lodge and Dorm,** which caters to college students and is inexpensive. In the town of Jeffersonville, 5 miles away, is the **Windbridge Inn,** a classic New England town inn that is not luxurious but is pleasant. Beyond Jeffersonville on Route 15 there are several moderately priced motels.

Most skiers who come for the week, however, stay in the village. Reservations there can be made through a toll-free number, 800-451-3222 or 802-844-8851.

RESTAURANTS

The village itself has several restaurants. If you stay in the condominiums, you can take a meal plan with standard American fare at the **Village Barn.** Next-door is the **Village Steak House.** A third restaurant, the **Crown and Anchor,** has the style of an old English pub and is a bit more elegant than the others.

Near the Red Fox Lodge, a quarter-mile from the village, is the **Salty Dog,** with salad bar, steak, and fish in an informal atmosphere. A mile or so away from the village is a Swiss fondue–snack spot, **L'Auberge Chez Moustache,** where the chef plays dinner music on the piano. In Jeffersonville, you can eat at the **Windbridge Inn,** which has a traditional New England menu served in a restored eighteenth-century dining room.

APRÈS-SKI AND NIGHT LIFE

You'll find folk music and drink after skiing at **Snow Snake Lounge** or soft-rock music, live on weekends, recorded during the week, at the **Barn.** The

Barn also has a game room with darts, electric pong games, and the like. Both Snow Lake Lounge and the Barn are open in the evening, as is the **Crown and Anchor.** College students and others who like hard rock will have an excellent, loud evening at the **Salty Dog,** where music is also live on weekends.

DIVERSION

The resort management has carefully planned alternative sports activities for you in the village. Cross-country equipment can be rented at the sport shop, and trails, some of which are lighted for night adventurers, begin at the village. There are saunas and an indoor swimming pool in its own bubble close to the condominiums. Five miles from the resort is the **Windbridge Tennis Center,** which has two indoor clay courts that rent for $12 per hour. The resort provides transportation to and from the courts without charge. There is also a skating rink in the village.

CHILDREN

The village and its facilities make Smuggler's an excellent area for a week's family retreat. Children can be very self-sufficient. There is a nursery immediately adjacent to the bottom chair. For $1.50 per hour, the nursery will give ski instructions to those with equipment. You can also arrange for baby-sitters through the front office.

COSTS

Smuggler's is moderately priced. Packages for a five-day week with lifts and lessons in the village range from $125 to $150 per person without food but with extras like tennis time and equipment. The one-day lift ticket is $15. The five-day ticket with lessons is $74. A five-day MAP eating plan for lunch and dinner at the Village Barn and the Crown and Anchor is $70.50, $74 for children.

46
Stowe

Stowe, the self-proclaimed ski capital of the East, is just that. The skiing it offers is the most challenging in the East and, on balance, rivals all but the very toughest areas of the West. Its community, centered around a charming, nineteenth-century Vermont town, is as lively, varied, and complete as any in the East. Since the authors admit —almost assert—a strong bias for Stowe, these comments should be somewhat discounted. But for the advanced skier Stowe is simply a little bit better than the competition. It is not the best area for the beginner or the family, and it is not inexpensive. It is not without crowds, but for sheer hill and thrill, or food or dance, you'll have to go quite a distance (2,000 miles west) to find its equal.

ACCESSIBILITY

Stowe is 6 solid hours by car from New York (330 miles), a 4-hour drive from Boston (210 miles), and just under 3 hours by car from Montreal. From New York, the preferred route is up Route 91 from Hartford to White River Junction, across Route 89 to Waterbury and then 10 miles up Route 100 to the village. From Boston, take Route 93 to Route 89 and repeat the New York formula. The alternative from New York is the New York Thruway to Glens Falls or further north, and then by two-lane twisters across and up—mostly on Route 100 to Stowe. This route is a similar distance to the Route 91–89 course, but the roads are narrow, two-lane highways almost all the way after leaving the Thruway.

Stowe is accessible by air through the Burlington airport, about 30 minutes away. Also, Amtrak has service from New York to Waterbury, leaving Pennsylvania Station at 9 P.M., arriving at Waterbury at 6:45 A.M. The train stops at Stamford, Hartford, and Springfield for those in between. You can avoid a night's lodging and be at the slopes early in the morning. A berth for sleeping is recommended. Stowe also is served by bus from New York, Boston, Burlington, and intermediary cities.

THE SKIING

For the Eastern skiing devotee who rises to the challenge of ice and an occasional rock, Stowe's Mt. Mansfield is Mecca. Mansfield has two quite independent sets of lifts—the chair lifts, a single (dating back to 1940) and double, and a gondola, all with more than 2,000 feet of vertical. But the chair lifts are the spot. Just looking up from the parking lot at the chairs ascending causes a feeling of challenge or of terror to swell in one's chest or stomach. About 10 separate trails going from top to bottom fan off the chairs. Four of these trails are rated by the mountain as super-expert, and super indeed they are.

Most famous of these is the steep and broad National (50–100′), with a true fall line. This run is normally a mogul field top to bottom, steep at the top, steep again near the bottom, somewhat more moderate in the middle, but averaging about 20–25° all the way. The top of the National is a 9. Unsung, but demanding, is the Liftline, an 8 overall, very steep at parts, moderate at others, and broad. It was rated by *Ski Holiday* magazine as one of the top 20 steep and long trails in North America, but in fact it's the fourth toughest at Stowe.

Then there's the Goat and the Star. Of the four, the Goat is the only one that does not itself go all the way to the bottom. The top of the Goat is narrow, very steep (30°) and sloped off to the left. The trail is cut about 40 feet wide, but the right side rarely holds snow, leaving a slanted, moguled 20-foot strip to work down. After the top, it is twisting and moguled with high rocks in the middle at the bottom. The Goat must rate a 9. The Star, as steep at the top as the Headwall at Mt. Washington, is a 10. The top is also narrow, about 40 feet wide, 20 of it usually covered with rock. After a drop of about 400 feet, the trail "flattens out," with a few tough drops and a few thousand moguls to the bottom. The Star, which is crossed by no other trail and allows no escape, is a challenge top to bottom.

Each of these four runs compares favorably with anything on Aspen Mountain for length, steepness, or terrain, is equal to and longer than Lime-light or Exhibition at Sun Valley, and is perhaps less challenging but is longer than Al's Run or Snakedance at Taos. In the East, only the top of the liftline at Mad River, White Cloud at Whiteface when open, and perhaps (only perhaps) the Snowfields at Sugarloaf (when open) can really be placed in the same league. There are other tough runs, Polly's Folly at Cannon, Bobby's Run at Waterville, Superstar at Killington, Stein's Run and the Mall at Sugarbush, U.N. at Jay Peak, Jaws of Death at Mt. Snow, and La S at Mont

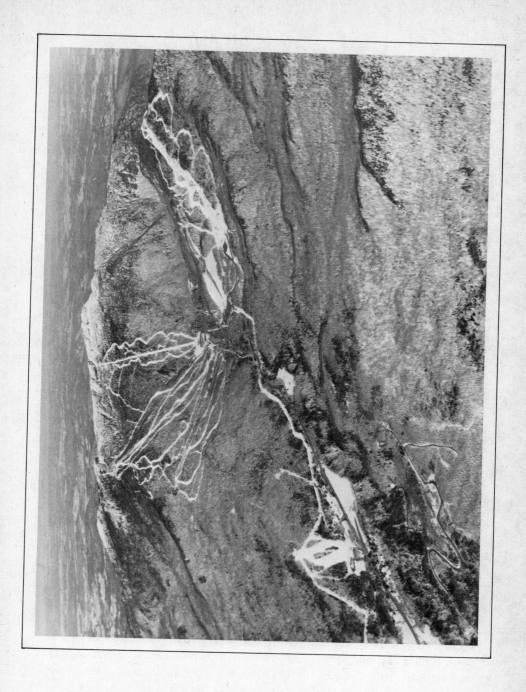

Stowe: tollhouse slope at bottom left; Mansfield chair area with gondola to the right; spruce Peak on extreme right   STOWE, VERMONT; SKI CAPITAL OF THE EAST

Ste-Anne, but none of these have the steepness, terrain, and *length* of Stowe's four top runs.

The chair lift area does not stop with these runs. Two other expert-intermediate runs, the Nosedive (perhaps the most famous trail in the East), and Hayride, have steep sections and cruising areas. As Eastern ski buffs know, the Nosedive has had several turns taken out of it, but it is still narrow and tricky on top. The bottom three-quarters of this mile-and-a-half trail is broad and generally well-groomed, providing intermediates with a solid challenge. To the far right on the mountain are long, curving, challenging intermediate runs: Center Line, Skimeister, and Charlie Lord. Finally, the chair has a novice descent, the Toll Road, a 4½-mile road that permits a return to the bottom of the chairs or goes to a separate novice area, the Toll House T-bar, a mile from the bottom of the chairs. The Toll Road is narrow but enjoyable for the novice. It is a nice adventure for less advanced skiers who want to see the top of the mountain and eat there at the Octagon.

If the chair lift area on Mansfield is primarily an expert area, the 7,000-foot gondola, with a 2,100-foot vertical, is primarily an intermediate area. The trails, Gondola, Switchback, Perry Merril, are gradual, even-sloped, well-groomed, long intermediate runs. Farthest to the right is Chin Clip, an expert trail (7) with several tough drops and many areas of intermediate terrain. Chin Clip is as hard as anything at Stratton. It ranks about sixth in difficulty at Stowe.

Mt. Mansfield is not entirely unsympathetic to the novice-intermediate. Stuck in a corner, but a very picturesque one, is a 4,000-foot-long, 1,000-foot vertical T-bar with five trails ranging from novice-intermediate to intermediate-advanced. The terrain is consistent. The novice-intermediate trails are usually uncrowded, broad, and are sufficiently smooth to permit practice.

Across the road from Mt. Mansfield, but an integral part of Stowe, is Spruce Peak, a not entirely successful experiment in open-slope skiing. Facing south, and most visible from the Mountain Road as you approach the ski area from the village, Spruce has an open central slope running top to bottom (1,750′ vertical). This slope, Main Street, was an attempt at Western open skiing, but facing south toward the sun and the wind, Main Street rarely holds snow and is often closed. The principal chair does serve three other runs: Sterling, a rolling, banked, fun "novice-intermediate" trail (fully intermediate anywhere else), Whirlaway, and Smugglers—more intermediate-advanced terrain, narrow, twisting, tricky. At the bottom of Spruce is a shorter chair (4,000′ long; 1,000′ vertical) and a T-bar (1,800′ long; 450′ vertical) which are steep for intermediates or novices (as evidenced by the 4:1 ratios) but which have runs off to the side that can be handled by an advanced novice. At the top of the Spruce chair, you can take marked trails over the back and ski Smugglers. (See SMUGGLER'S NOTCH, p. 276.) The trip is about a 10-minute walk over on skis and about 10 minutes back. Smugglers does not honor a Stowe lift ticket, so don't get caught broke.

Finally, there is the Toll House area, about a mile from the Mt. Mansfield area, with a 1,500-foot T-bar. This is the "novice area," though it's not recommended for those just starting. It has two broad slopes, one on either side.

As would appear, skiing at Stowe is not designed for everyone. By Eastern standards, the area has inexhaustible expert and intermediate-advanced terrain. An intermediate will have fun; a novice should go forewarned.

Stowe is not without lines. On major weekends, you must expect lines from 20 to 40 minutes at the gondola or the Mansfield chairs. If you're willing to give up the big runs, you'll find mostly short lines at the Mansfield T-bar and no lines at all at the major lift at Spruce.

One feature deserving mention is that the resort provides blankets on the chair lifts for the ride up. This is a most civilized practice, and, while labor-consumptive for the area, it makes skiing on very cold days almost pleasant.

Stowe usually gets as much snow as any area in the East. The Mansfield chair area, tucked behind the mountain with a northeast exposure, is about as well sheltered from the sun and prevailing wind as any mountain could be. The result is excellent snow preservation in the chair area of Mansfield. The gondola area is more open to wind and sun. Spruce flaunts itself to wind and sun and accordingly suffers. The area has little snowmaking capacity, limited principally to the lower slopes of Spruce.

There is a problem at Stowe that must be pointed out to skiers with families. Stowe is really three separate areas, arguably four. One lift ticket serves all, but otherwise the transition from one area to another can be difficult. The chairs and gondola on Mt. Mansfield have separate base lodges and restaurants at the top. Transition between these chairs, the gondola, and the T-bar is not difficult, but getting to Spruce and Toll House is hard work; they are a half-mile and a mile, respectively, from the base at Mansfield. There is bus transportation among these four centers (the gondola being the fourth), but it can be time-consuming. This segregation can be particularly difficult for those wishing to go into ski school. For novices, the school meets at Toll House; for intermediates who do not parallel well, at Spruce; and for experts, at the Mansfield T-bar.

The area provides bus services up and down the Mountain Road during the day, but the trip from hotel to restaurant can be burdensome. Stowe is definitely an area which you can get about without a car, but there will be moments of long waits and difficulties in the evening.

LIFE IN THE AREA

The village of Stowe has preserved its small-town, old New England appearance. A single-spired church stands at its center, surrounded by wood-framed buildings and homes. Extending from the town along the 8-mile access road to the mountain are the many inns, motels, restaurants, and nightspots that provide the area with as broad a range of social activities as can be found in the East.

ACCOMMODATIONS

Starting at the mountain, at the Toll House novice area, are two rather formal, well-kept inns: the **Lodge at Smugglers Notch,** traditional and stuffy, with small bedrooms and an excellent dining room, and the **Toll House Motor Lodge,** an elegant, modern inn with deluxe rooms and an excellent *haute cuisine* dining room. Neither is inexpensive.

Down the Mountain Road is the **Topnotch** at Stowe, a deluxe lodge with luxurious rooms and many services including Jacuzzi, sauna, massage, color TV, and more. The Topnotch has an excellent restaurant and an elegant bar. Off the Mountain Road, up a hill about 8 minutes from the slope, is a condominium development, **Notch Brook Resort;** it has attractive units, an unpretentious restaurant, sauna, outdoor heated pool (open at least in holiday weeks), and a quiet site among the trees with a sweeping view of Mt. Mansfield.

Also off the Mountain Road, about 10 minutes from the mountain, is the famous **Trapp Family Lodge.** Established by the family that fled Austria in the face of the Nazi occupation, the Lodge is a spacious inn situated above the valley by itself, with panoramic views and empty fields surrounding it. The rooms are not luxurious but are pleasant, clean, and warm. Some have fireplaces. Many of the rooms are across the road in a two-story unit that is less charming than the inn. The food is excellent; the desserts, better. The Lodge has its own cross-country ski center, with a wilderness shop serving lunch and pastries.

The Trapp Family Lodge is the best known and perhaps the most elegant of several family-type inns at Stowe. These inns try to achieve a homey atmosphere. They have common rooms, game rooms, central fireplaces, b.y.o. bars. **Edison Hill Manor,** located off the Mountain Road above the valley, is similar in feel; it is small, familial, with pleasant common rooms, and has its own cross-country trails that tie into the trails of Topnotch and finally into the Trapp Family Lodge trails. On the Mountain Road there is the **Scandinavia Inn,** which has excellent food served at tables for 10 persons, a sauna, whirlpool, and a large downstairs lounge and game room. The rooms in the Inn are small, but there are several modern chalets that have larger rooms. The **Logwood Inn** has a comfortable library, common room, game room, and some seclusion, being off the Mountain Road. The **Ski Inn,** 5 minutes from the slopes, is small, friendly, simpler than the Scandinavia, and more like a private home; it also has cross-country trails that connect to the Stowe cross-country complex. Of the same vintage, but simpler, are the **Sieberness Lodge, Andersons',** the **Ski-Mor Lodge,** and the **Grey Fox Inn.** Located on or just off the Mountain Road no more than 10 minutes from the slopes, all these inns have an informal, homey feeling. Off the Mountain Road, situated on its own 90 acres, is the **Ten Acres Lodge,** a farmhouse inn with a library and common rooms.

Stowe also has several modern motels. The **Alpine Motor Lodge** is good, with a restaurant, common room, and game room—a bit of the old and new. With indoor swimming pool and in good taste, though understated, is the **Town & Country Motor Lodge.** Less attractive, even tacky, but with large rooms and also with an indoor pool is the **Salzburg Inn,** formerly the Grand Motor Inn. Similar is the **Mountaineer Motor Inn,** with a heated indoor pool. The **Golden Eagle Motor Inn,** about 10 minutes from the mountain, is a pleasant motel that has "efficiency apartments" and chalets with kitchens that are good for family accommodations. Other motels are the **Innsbruck Motor Inn, Die Alpenrose,** and the **Stowe Motel.** More elaborate and pleasing is the **Holm,** an apartment resort, with swimming pool, saunas, and whirlpool. Also, there is the **Hob Nob,** a motel-inn done in good taste, with a pleasant bar and dining room.

Inns which are quite simple, but adequate, are the **Mile Away,** sleeping 10 persons in close quarters, the **Golden Kitz Lodge and Motel** (friendly, small rooms), and, perhaps a step better, the **Gables Inn and Motel.**

Two inns that appeal more to adult singles and have game rooms, b.y.o. bars, and the like, are the simple **Sans Souci** and, somewhat more pretentious, the **Yodler,** which has a clientele consisting mainly of young professionals from New York.

Finally, for high school students, there are two inns with dormitories, communally served meals, jukeboxes, and games. These are the **Round Hearth** and **Winterhaus.** At the mountain is the **State of Vermont Ski Dorm,** which is inexpensive and requires lights out at 10:30, no liquor permitted.

This summary by no means includes all the inns or motels. Others are listed with the area association. Stowe has a toll-free number: 800-451-5100 (from Canada or not toll-free, the number is 802-253-7321). Almost all the inns mentioned above are between the mountain and the village. There are hotels in the village, among them the **Victorian Green Mountain Inn,** and others south of the village: **Nichols Lodge,** an informal, family-oriented simple inn;

the **Spruce Pond Inn and Motel,** a modern motel; the **Stowe-Bound Lodge,** Colonial in appearance, inexpensive, simple with dorms. One mile above the village, on its own hill, is an old mansion, the **Four Winds,** which has a handsome living room and great windows overlooking the view. A word of caution should be given to those not staying on the mountain side of the village. Terrible traffic jams develop on the Mountain Road, particularly on weekends at the point where the Mountain Road enters the village. Often, it will take 20 minutes or more to cover the last mile of the Mountain Road.

One final comment. The inns at Stowe are in general not elegant or luxurious, with the possible exception of the Toll House Motor Lodge, the Lodge, and the Topnotch. But there are many inns that have an atmosphere which is tasteful, communal, and lively. They achieve a friendly New England togetherness.

RESTAURANTS

Stowe has many restaurants, some of which are excellent. The most formal and most expensive are those at the more elegant inns, the **Toll House Motor Inn,** the **Lodge,** and the **Topnotch,** all Continental, and at the **Trapp Family Lodge,** Austrian with notorious desserts. Perhaps the best is the relatively new **Golden Horn East,** south of the village on Route 100; this restaurant, the sister of a restaurant in Aspen, is also Continental. Less elegant but with excellent American cuisine is the **Partridge Inn Restaurant.** The **Scandinavia** serves large homemade meals. **Three Green Doors** is a cozy restaurant featuring steak and Alaskan king crab. More formal *haute cuisine* is provided at the **Chateaubriand** on the Mountain Road at the Stowe Center. Rather simple but pleasant are the **SHED** and **Sister Kate's,** done in 1890's saloon style with a piano bar serving informal American meals. In the cellar of the **Baggy Knees** is a steak house. In the village, you'll find a small informal French restaurant, **La Bicoque,** and an informal Swiss fondue restaurant, the **Swisspot;** north of the village is an Austrian-Hungarian restaurant, the **Charda.** On the mountain road, informal but simple and pleasant, is **Whiskers,** serving sandwiches, prime ribs, and wine.

APRÈS-SKI AND NIGHT LIFE

Stowe has perhaps the most lively après-ski life found in the East. It all starts at the **Matahorn,** a bar on the Mountain Road a mile from Mansfield; mobbed by college kids and persons in their twenties and thirties, the Matahorn has a pool table, disco music, and, on weekends or during the week of holiday periods, dancing from 4 to about 8 P.M. Different but lively in the afternoon is **Sister Kate's,** a beer-and-peanuts 1890's saloon with piano bar and a light-hearted accompanist.

At night, Stowe swings to different beats. For the youngest and loudest, there is the **Rusty Nail,** a high school–college hangout featuring hard rock.

The **Baggy Knees** follows closely for loud sounds, but its music appeals to a slightly older crowd.

In the Stowe Center on the Mountain Road, there is the **Jaxon Restaurant and Jazz Club,** with, as one might guess, jazz and contemporary music. At Sister Kate's, Rocky King entertains with limericks set to music. Then there's drink at many small bars, such as the very fancy **Buttertub Bar** at Topnotch, **Hob Nob,** and the **Three Green Doors.** You should have no trouble making it through the evening.

DIVERSION

Cross-country skiing centers can be found at the **Trapp Family Lodge,** the **Edison Hill Manor,** and **Topnotch,** all of which are interconnected by trails. The Lodge, well separated from the Mountain Road, has greater isolation and a renowned coffee shop with pastries. Adventurous cross-country skiers can take the chair or gondola to the top of Mansfield and go through Smuggler's Notch to the ski area of that name on the opposite side of Spruce Peak. This is a day's trip and should be attempted only by experienced skiers.

There is covered skating in the village. There are also ski movies each night at the village auditorium. Filmed and personally narrated by Victor Coty, the movies provide an invariably amusing and enjoyable evening.

Snowmobiles can be rented at the **Nichols Farm,** and there is indoor tennis on the Mountain Road. Indoor riding is provided at the **Ryder Brook Stables,** north of Stowe on Route 100. There are also some novelty shops around Stowe.

CHILDREN

Stowe does not go out of its way for families with small children. The mountain itself, lacking any good novice practice slopes (even the Toll House area is not good for very young children) and being divided up into three separate lift complexes, in part segregating skiers by ability, does not lend itself to easy rendezvous for children and their parents. There is now a good nursery at the Toll House area and a program for club skiers. Meeting the kids during the day, if you ski Mansfield, is still difficult. Even the prices—$10 for a child's all-day ticket—are not encouraging to the parents' pocketbooks. All this is not to say that kids and Stowe don't mix. Take them to Stowe, but expect to work a little harder to make them happy.

COSTS

The Stowe area, and particularly the Mt. Mansfield Corporation, thinks it's the best and charges accordingly. Day lift tickets are $15 per day, weekdays or weekends. Stowe does have a very good $75 6-day package that includes lifts and unlimited lessons. Lessons are 1½ hours long, so you can take 3 a day for 6 days if you want.

The lodges at Stowe are moderate to expensive. The inns with Modified American Plans charge from $15 to $40 per day per person, most somewhere in the higher range. Motel room prices range from $25 to $35 per day.

Other prices around the area—entertainment, shopping—are comparable to the other more expensive resorts (Stratton and Sugarbush) of Vermont.

47

Stratton, Bromley, Magic

Stratton is the classiest of these areas, and in a way, the classiest resort in New England. At Stratton, stylish New York has driven out informal New England. The Stratton skier has it all together. The Bogner parka matches not only his pants, but his boots and skis. This is not to say it is a singles scene. Stratton attracts the East Hampton, Fairfield County, Upper East Side family. After all, it's as good a place as any to meet your children when they come "home" from prep school. Kidding aside, the resort is well groomed throughout, the facilities are well kept, and the clientele is select. Bromley is less pretentious and Magic is still less so, but the aura of Stratton dominates the area. The skiing complements the ambience of the area: the gentle mountain helps to give even the novice the feeling and appearance of competence and style. However, while the expert terrain is unchallenging, Stratton does have one of the best racing programs in the East.

ACCESSIBILITY

One of the reasons for the area's popularity is its accessibility to the New York area. It is 4½ hours from the City by way of several routes. You can go through Connecticut, up Route 91 to Brattleboro and across on Route 31, or stay in New York State, take the Taconic to Route 22, to Route 7 to Manchester, or finally, take the New York Thruway, cutting across to Bennington through Troy, New York, and then up Route 7. Take your pick; they're all about the same. From Boston, it's about a 3½-hour drive out Route 2 to Route 91. By air, the closest service is Albany, about 2 hours away.

THE SKIING

Stratton. The largest of these three downhill areas, Stratton has an abundance of manicured intermediate and novice trails and limited expert terrain. The entire range of intermediate skiers should enjoy the area. The whole mountain has a constant gradual slope from top to bottom. It is like a tailored mountain: no steep drops, no sharp cornices, no ridges, no unexpected changes of terrain. To supplement nature's smooth hand, the resort grooms most of the trails continually. The trails at the top are marked expert, but in general a strong intermediate can handle them.

The steepest terrain on the mountain is a short drop (400′) at the bottom of Slalom Glade on the Snow Bowl chair, the most efficient lift at Stratton (4,922′ long; 1,390′ vertical; 16°). This stretch might rate an 8–9 but for its shortness. The most difficult run on the mountain is Spruce (7), which is fun, has varying terrain, but can be run by a solid expert without much struggle. Upper Standard and Rimeline can be tricky at the top because their exposure creates icy conditions. Three other runs from the top, Tamarack, Grizzly Bear, and Polar Bear, are intermediate trails, *par excellence,* although they are also marked "expert." Novices can ski the entire bottom of the mountain and the trails down from the top on the extreme right or left. All of these trails are long, as Stratton spreads its 1,900-foot vertical over a lift-length distance from the bottom to the top of more than 7,000 feet.

Stratton is popular and does have lift lines. It takes two chairs to reach the top, and on a crowded day the trip can be time-consuming. To avoid this problem, you can ski the upper chairs, which are long (around 4,800′).

Bromley. In terms of skiing, Bromley is largely duplicative of Stratton, but the Stargazer chair lift (3,285′ long; 919′ vertical) on the back of the mountain adds terrain that is more challenging than the terrain at Stratton and, while having only moderate vertical, can keep the expert fully occupied. Bromley's vertical is only 1,300 feet.

Bromley is one of the oldest developments in New England. Its original lift, a J-bar, dates back to 1941. Its front side, which faces south, is, like Stratton, gradual and even. The trails are broad, and the snow is well groomed to prevent extensive moguling and to preserve it against the direct sunlight. The very top is intermediate. The bottom is novice. At the bottom are the East Meadow and Plaza, which are two wide-open, short slopes served by chair lifts. A broad novice trail, Thruway, extends to the three-quarters point on the mountain.

The trails on the Stargazer chair, Blue Ribbon, Papst, Peril, and Ava-

The face of Stratton   STRATTON MOUNTAIN; PHOTO BY HUBERT SCHRIEBL

lanche, while short, have real steepness and tough terrain (8's). There is no chair at Stratton which is as demanding.

Bromley's lines are likely to be somewhat shorter than Stratton's. In fact, the Stargazer chair is an excellent bet to be uncrowded, even on weekends. Bromley also has extensive snowmaking capacity, though this capacity is used largely to make up for the difficulties which result from the southern exposure.

Magic. Magic is the third sister, with a respectable vertical of 1,600 feet. Again, Magic is predominantly an intermediate-novice area. Unlike Stratton or Bromley, the mountain is irregular, having short, steep drops on the liftline followed by flat areas. Expert trails, Magician and Witch, provide short, uneven challenges. The fun at Magic starts at the top with Magic Carpet, a novice trail which is broad and curves 2 miles to the bottom. A short chair at the bottom (1,500') affords practice slope skiing well segregated from the central access.

LIFE IN THE AREA

The Triangle covers an area 15 miles on three sides, and includes the three ski areas, the large town of Manchester, and several small towns. To understand the location of inns, it may be helpful to set out the location of the ski resorts. Stratton is on the southern point of the Triangle; Bromley, on the northwest corner; Magic, on the northeast corner. Route 11 runs across the north side of the Triangle from Bromley to Magic. Route 100 runs between Magic and Stratton, and Route 30 runs from Stratton to Bromley. Manchester is 5 miles west of Bromley on Route 11. Londonderry is on Route 11 between Bromley and Magic. The ski resorts are about 10 miles apart. Each has its own community at or near the mountain, but skiers stay at inns throughout the area.

ACCOMMODATIONS

Accommodations consist primarily of modern lodges with an occasional older inn. Having several towns, the area has innumerable lodges. Reservations are best made through the area housing associations (Stratton: 800-451-4261; Bromley: 802-824-5224).

At the mountain at Stratton, there are four first-class inns built in a Tyrolean style. The **Stratton Mountain Inn** (capacity, 140 persons) has an elegant dining room, a recreation room, a sauna, entertainment in the bar, and special-priority access to the John Newcombe Tennis Center 200 yards away. The **Birkenhaus,** the **Lift Line Lodge,** and the **Glockenhoff** are modern Tyrolean inns with sauna, bunk rooms, and entertainment, all 200 or 300 yards from the lift. Also near the lift is the simpler, smaller **Chalet Wendland,** with a capacity of 6 persons.

At the foot of the Stratton access road is the small hamlet of Bondville, which has a store or two and a nicely restored inn, **Haigs,** with its own restaurant, elaborate disco and breakfast-only plan. Just up Winhall Hollow Road is the secluded **Red Fox Inn,** with the style of an old country inn but also having disco music and dancing.

A mile east of Bondville on Route 30 is the **Fundador,** which is modern, looks somewhat like a motel, but has the communal aspects of an inn and one of the best restaurants in the area. In Jamaica, 5 miles east of the Stratton access road, are several old Vermont inns or houses, including the somewhat run-down **Jamaica House,** with a bar populated by locals; the small **Robinson House; Doughty's Three Mountain Inn,** guaranteeing transportation to Stratton; and the simple **Sunny Brook Lodge.**

To the west of the Stratton access road on Route 30 is the modern **Wake Robin Lodge,** with bunks, two dining rooms, and a night club, and, at the intersection of Routes 30 and 11, 2 miles west of Bromley, the **Kandahar Lodge Resort Motel,** with modern rooms, a pool table, and a pleasant bar.

One motel, the **Bromley Sun Lodge,** sits at the foot of Bromley. A six-story structure opened for the 1976–77 year, the lodge has a bright, spacious lobby, rooms with decks facing the sun, kitchens, a game room, and an indoor pool. Bromley also has, at the mountain, a "village" with condominiums which can be rented for the week. Two lodges, the **Mountaineer Lodge,** which is modern, and **Johnny Seesaw's,** an older inn, are within walking distance of Bromley. Johnny Seesaw's has a special children's meal served at 6 P.M. and a game room where children can play while adults eat. The **Wiley Inn** is a mile from Bromley and offers a country flavor, a b.y.o. bar, pool table and traditional lounge.

In Manchester, 5 miles west of Bromley, or about 20 minutes from Stratton, there are many middle-price range motels such as the **Four Winds, Chalet Motel, Track Fore Motor Lodge, Skylight Lodge,** and **Toll Road Motor Inn,** and older inns such as the **1811 House,** an authentic old New England home, and the **Hillcrest Inn.**

Five miles to the east of Bromley (20 minutes from Stratton) along Route 11 toward Magic Mountain is the **Village Inn** at Landgrove, which is an old rambling inn ideally suited to families and situated in an absolutely quiet setting with cross-country skiing at its door. Close by is the small **White Pine Lodge,** which has night skating, kitchens, and private fireplaces in the rooms. Also nearby is the **Swiss Inn,** a plain but pleasant inn with game room. Off Route 11 is the **Nordic Inn,** which sleeps 16 persons and has good inn food and cross-country trails at its door. South of Route 11, in the little village of South Londonderry 10 minutes from Stratton, is the old **Londonderry Inn,** with an excellent game room including ping-pong and pool, and two outdoor paddle tennis courts.

Returning to Route 11, 9 miles east of Bromley and right near the entrance to Magic is the plain **Magic View Motel.** At the foot of Magic, 9 miles from Bromley, 12 from Stratton, is the elegant, first-class Tyrolean inn-motel, the **Dostal,** with heated indoor pool, whirlpool bath, and lounge with live music. Also at the base of Magic is the **Christie Inn,** again Tyrolean, with a ping-pong–pool table game room, and the simpler **Blue Gentian Lodge** and **Post-Horn Inn.**

Four miles north of Route 11 on Route 100 is the small village of Weston. At the center of the village is the **Inn at Weston,** an old (1848) vintage Vermont inn with small rooms, a bar, and game room. Just north of town, by itself, is an old private home, the **Black Shutters,** which accommodates about 10 persons in a homelike atmosphere.

This list does not exhaust the inns near the ski areas or even touch on the more distant lodges. One inn, the **Newfane Inn** in Newfane, 20 miles southeast of Stratton, deserves mention, however. It is one of the old distinguished village inns found in Vermont, situated right on the Village Green. While not well located for skiing, it has style, history, and atmosphere.

RESTAURANTS

The most highly recommended of the area's many restaurants is that at the **Fundador Lodge,** just south of the Stratton access road on Route 30 in Rawsonville, serving top Continental cuisine with an emphasis on excellent vegetables and salads. There are two French restaurants, **Pierre's,** on Route 7 in Manchester, and the very small, old **Three Clock Inn** in South Londonderry. **Haigs,** in Bondville, is an excellent, atypical steak house found in a remodeled inn. The **Mill,** formerly an old mill with rough beams and floors, is also a good steak house with an appealing informal atmosphere. Manchester has other good restaurants, including the **Track Fore Motor Lodge,** Continental; the **Chantecleer,** also Continental; and the **Palace,** a steak or pasta place. Of a more rural nature are the **Nordic Inn,** with Scandinavian food, and, at a distance in Chester, Vermont, the old restored **Chester Inn,** serving, appropriately, an American fare.

You should remember that Stratton is very much like New York in that people eat out often, and reservations are a necessity on Saturday night or, at the smaller restaurants, on Friday night.

APRÈS-SKI AND NIGHT LIFE

Stratton is elegant. **Haigs,** *the* place for nightlife, fits its style to a T. It is not a squeaky, lopsided barn, nor an old farmhouse, but rather a vibrant disco with strobe lights, pictures flashing on the walls, artificial fog filling the air, and loud records played back to back. The bar has a large video machine for watching the weekend's sports events. The crowd is twenties and thirties. The dress is casual but classy.

For those seeking less gloss and live sound, there is the large barnlike **Roundhouse,** once a railroad roundhouse, with a huge undivided interior space, several bars, a band and an informal blue jeans ambience. Smaller, more human in scale, are the **Red Fox Inn,** a disco near Bondville, and the **Wake Robin Inn,** a night club spot. On Route 11 in Londonderry is the **Mill,** which has live rock music in an authentic mill with hewn beams and barn siding for walls and a small low-ceiling dance floor. The Mill is as authentically Vermont as Haigs' disco is authentically modern and chic.

DIVERSION

The area's cross-country ski centers are the **Stratton Ski Touring Center** at Stratton and the **Viking Touring Centre.** Both offer equipment rental and group lessons; each charges $1 for use of the trails. The Stratton Center is located on the access road to Stratton. Its trails are short. Viking offers 30 miles of trails, most of them gentle. Viking is located just north of Route 11 near Magic, and maintains and patrols 10 miles of its 30 miles of trails.

There is indoor tennis at the mountain at Stratton, at the **John Newcombe Tennis Center,** which has two hard-surface courts in a fixed structure. Prime time (weekends and weekly evenings) is $18 per hour; non-prime is $15.

CHILDREN

All three areas have nurseries. Stratton charges $2 per hour, $12 per day, for children one year and up. Children three years and older can join the **Little Cub Ski School** to start their training. Bromley has a superb nursery which combines supervision with ski school classes for kids three and up. Stratton also has an excellent racing program for juniors.

COSTS

Prices in the Triangle are moderate to expensive. Stratton and facilities near Stratton are expensive, while those connected with Magic are not. Lift tickets at Stratton are $15 per day on weekends, $13 during the week. Bromley is one dollar cheaper, and Magic is $12 and $10, respectively. Day care at Stratton is $2 per hour. The better inns charge $32 to $40 per person per night with two meals.

48

Sugarbush, Mad River, Glen Ellen

There ought to be a collective name for these three resorts strung together (over a 6-mile stretch of mountains) above the valley that surrounds the small town of Waitsfield. We would like to suggest "Mad Sugarglen." The reason one name has not caught on is that while the three resorts are close to one another, each mountain has maintained its own image. Sugarbush, called "Mascara Mountain" by some, is social and slick. It attracts New York's young East Side professionals to a mountain that has some of the most demanding skiing in the East. Mad River is rugged and satisfies a New England skier's dream of grueling challenges and difficult terrain. Glen Ellen is thought of as a family retreat—unpressured, uncrowded and uneven in terrain. Together they provide excellent ski recreation for a valley with facilities ranging from the most posh in New England to the most ascetic. In terms of the challenge and variety of the skiing, the areas combined rate second in the East only to Stowe.

ACCESSIBILITY

The valley is 6 hours from New York and 4 hours from Boston. From New York, there are two choices: one is to go up Route 91 to White River Junction, across Route 89 to Middlesex, west of Montpelier, and then south on Route 100 (about 320 miles). The second is to take the New York Thruway to Glens Falls, coming across Route 149 and Route 4 to Rutland and then going up Route 100 about 1 hour's distance to the valley (300 miles). From Boston, the route is simpler. Take Interstate 93, then 89, to Middlesex and then go south on Route 100 (200 miles). The area is just under an hour from the Burlington airport. It is also accessible by train from New York. Amtrak leaves Penn Station in the late evening and arrives at Waterbury (about 25 minutes from Waitsfield) at 6:30 A.M. You save a night's rooming cost and can get a pretty good rest.

THE SKIING

Sugarbush. The biggest of the three, Sugarbush sprawls out across a broad basin. There are four quite distinct areas of skiing.

At the center of the Sugarbush complex is the gondola, the longest single span lift in New England (9,300′ long; 2,400′ vertical). Experts and advanced intermediates can ski the narrow trails to the right of the gondola, which are marked expert but none of which are very steep (7's). Intermediates and good novices will enjoy Jester, a curvy, advanced novice trail with banked turns. Jester leads to an excellent glade with an intermediate pitch. The trails off the gondola are few, but they are long and are good cruising runs for intermediates and experts.

The second area, located on the extreme right of the basin, is a well-segregated intermediate-novice area with a chair and poma lift running in tandem. This is principally an intermediate area, but adventurous novices can ski the upper slopes off the poma or can go through the woods on Sleeper Run on the chair. To the right of the chair, there is a novice practice area, served by a double chair. This is an adequate beginner's slope.

The third area is the Castlerock chair, which starts halfway up the mountain in between the gondola and the chair-poma area. Castlerock is an expert chair. The runs are narrow, twisting and tricky. Two trails, Lift Line and Rumble, have steep sections (8's), but in general the difficulty ranges between 7 and 8 and results from bumpy terrain, not from sustained vertical or even extended mogul patches. Rumble, to the right of Lift Line, is very narrow, at times about 15 feet wide. It demands continuous control.

Finally, there is the Valley chair (3,500′ long; 1,250′ vertical), which serves further intermediate and expert terrain. Unlike the runs on Castlerock, the two expert trails on the Valley chair, the Mall and Stein's Run, have a consistent pitch, a true fall line, and a profusion of moguls. Stein's, named after Stein Erikson, the former head of the ski school, has a 1,200-foot vertical over 3,000 feet, a 24° slope, and with big bumps is an 8.5. These runs are not long, but they provide the most damaging bump punishment found in New England except for the liftline at Mad River, the major runs at Stowe, and possibly Polly's Folly at Cannon. The Valley chair also has two expert-intermediate trails with bumps at the top and glades at the bottom as well as one broad intermediate run. For a short chair, this one has a lot of life.

Sugarbush is a tough mountain, but it has good balance. Both the Castlerock and Valley chairs are well designed to take advantage of the vertical they serve.

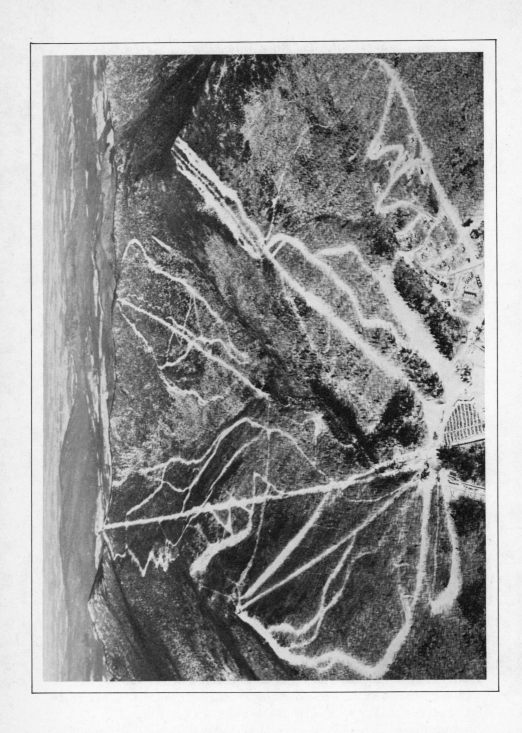

Sugarbush: Valley chair, gondola, Castlerock chair, and intermediate chair area rising from left to right   SUGARBUSH VALLEY, INC.; PHOTO BY CHAN WELLER

Mad River. Mad River is *the* skier's mountain in New England. Before 1962, when a double chair was added, the mountain had one single chair that served two super-expert trails (9's) and two expert-intermediate trails, and a T-bar going up the "novice" area, the bottom of which was suitable for slalom racing. Mad River has added more varied lifts, but for the true skier it still has its uncompromising single chair (meditate, don't talk on the way up, for improved concentration).

The single chair (6,000' long; 1,900' vertical) has two of the toughest trails found anywhere (9's). At the top of the liftline is Chute, which true to its name is of average New England width (70 feet or so), has good pitch (25°), and usually has moguls that make you crave the friendly challenge of the National at Stowe. Once destroyed by the bumps of the Chute, you can take on the truly steep, narrow glade of Fall Line to the right of the chair off the top. With a touch of ice, this steep, tree strewn slalom can really be one hell of a challenge. Unfortunately for real experts, the steep terrain on both trails comes down only a third of the distance from the top. After that, the trails flatten out. Two other trails off the single chair, Catamount and Antelope, are marked intermediate but parts of them are steep and narrow.

The new double chair, the Sunnyside chair, adds wandering, intermediate and novice trails to the resort. The liftline of this chair is steep at the top. The trails are mainly intermediate. Novices can come down two trails which snake back and forth across the mountain. At the halfway point, they will find the Birdland chair, which serves short, very gentle novice runs. Birdland is almost always uncrowded. Novices don't hang out at Mad River.

Glen Ellen. Glen Ellen is the one in-between that is often overlooked. It does have a legitimate 2,600-foot vertical, the highest in the state excluding Killington's cross-county gondola. However, Glen Ellen simply doesn't work. The first of two tandem chairs going to the top is flat for three-quarters of its distance and then rises sharply to its end (6,250' long; 1,600' vertical). The top chair is then of gradual steepness for one-half its length and steep for the last half (3,600'; 1,045'). These chairs are like a roller coaster, with excessively long, flat sections. The novice skier will like the bottom chair. Many of the trails are marked intermediate and do have a steep spot on them, but in general they are long, gentle trails, too gentle at the bottom. Novices can also ski a short bottom chair and T-bar. Intermediates can practice on the long runs off the bottom chair or ski an intermediate chair off to the right.

The experts are mostly confined to the top chair, which has one very steep and one very bumpy expert run. The first of these is Upper F.I.S., which is one of the steepest trails in New England (35° at the top; a 9). Upper F.I.S. is broad, and has its share of large moguls, but it is short. The other, High Road, is of average steepness for an expert trail, but is narrow and has tough, bumpy terrain (8). Beyond these two trails, there is nothing at Glen Ellen to sustain an expert's interest.

The real advantage of Glen Ellen is that its lift lines are short in contrast to those at Sugarbush or Mad River. A 10-minute line at Glen Ellen is long. Sugarbush, on the other hand, is not a well-kept secret. It draws large crowds and its lifts, particularly the gondola, can have 30-minute lines on weekends. The Castlerock lift has a limited uphill capacity and even a short line can be a time-consuming one. The Valley chair is a better bet, but lines there can easily be 15 minutes for a run that is not long.

Mad River has the same problem. Its uphill capacity is limited. In the past, the area's appeal to the inveterate skier has kept lines down, but on February and March weekends one can expect 30-minute lines on the single, 20 minutes on the double. The Birdland chair and the practice slope virtually never have lines. If you want to give a novice a lesson on weekends, Birdland is perfect.

The three resorts receive an average of only 120 inches of snow annually but preserve the snow well. Keep in mind that Mad River has had a record of giving the most accurate snow condition reports in New England. If its conditions are reported as less favorable than others, it usually reflects greater honesty and not less snow. None of the three resorts makes snow outside of the novice-intermediate areas, only a small percentage of the skiing area of each.

LIFE IN THE AREA

The Warren-Waitsfield valley has a full range of social facilities and life-style choices. There are elegant condominiums with indoor tennis courts or sleeping-bag loft accommodations with hooks for your clothes. Restaurants range from elaborate *haute cuisine* to greasy spoon snack bars. Sugarbush attracts an affluent singles set mostly from New York. Mad River appeals to the New England college student skiing in blue jeans out of the back of a van. Glen Ellen attracts the family skier who seeks quieter surroundings. While the ski areas appeal to different crowds, the mountains are close together and the after-ski life is fully integrated.

ACCOMMODATIONS

The valley has innumerable inns and the best access to available accommodations is through the areas' lodging bureaus: Sugarbush, 802-583-2381; Mad River, 802-496-3551; and Glen Ellen, 800-451-5020.

It probably makes sense to choose a hotel nearest the area you intend to ski. If you wish to wake up right at the edge of the slope, Sugarbush has a small modern condominium village at the slopes with shops and restaurants. If you stay there, you really do not need a car. The Village includes the modern **Hotel Sugarbush** (not to be confused with the Sugarbush Inn), which is part of the small mall. The hotel has good motel-like rooms, a bunk room, a pleasant lobby and game room. Also at the mountain is the **Trail's End,** which has a small bar, pleasant lounge, small rooms, and a dorm. Glen Ellen and Mad River have condominiums available within walking distance of their lifts but without such supporting facilities as restaurants or shops.

The choices away from the slopes are many. The most luxurious accommodation is the **Bridges,** a condominium complex located about a mile from Sugarbush. It has an indoor recreation center that includes a pool, sauna, tennis, squash and heated paddle tennis courts. Equally elegant is the **Sugarbush Inn,** a handsome Colonial inn with a good restaurant, a bar with live music and dancing, and a cross-country ski center. Also on the Sugarbush access road are smaller, simpler inns such as the **Gamble Inn,** Swiss chalet-like; the **Focus Inn,** inexpensive and modern; the **Golden Horse Lodge,** with a pleasant lounge and bar; and the **Kehoe Inn,** which is also simple and pleasant. At the base of the access road is the **Christmas Tree Inn,** which is traditional outside, modern inside, and open to the public for breakfast. The **Lodge,** near the Bridges, has tiny, unsoundproofed rooms and a large common room.

Along Route 100 between the Sugarbush access road and Waitsfield there are several modern motels, all pleasant but undistinguished, including the **Madbush Chalet Motor Inn** (sauna, game room with pool table, b.y.o. bar), the **Seasons Motel** (restaurant and lounge) and the **Alpine Inn** (Tyrolean appearance with skating pond, cross-country skiing and a game room).

In Waitsfield and along Route 17 leading to Glen Ellen and Mad River (about 5 miles from Sugarbush, 3 miles from Mad River), there are inexpensive accommodations such as the **Ark,** an old farmhouse with inexpensive meals; the **High & Dry Motel,** a second-rate motel; the **Mad River Barn,** an old, informal and comfortable inn with full bar. Nearby is the **Snuggery,** with a cozy, old-farmhouse style, a bar and a game room. The **Mountain View Inn** is small, accommodating only 13 guests. Also just outside Waitsfield is the more traditional **Tucker Hill Lodge,** with paddle tennis, cross-country trails, and a good restaurant. Nearby is the **Garrison,** a curious, inelegant, wood-framed building with small condominium apartments surrounding an indoor pool. Above Waitsfield, off the beaten track, is the very small **Knoll Farm** for those who wish greater privacy and fields for cross-country skiing. Above Mad River on Route 17 is **Quittner's Stark View Lodge,** on 140 acres with cross-country trails. It is inexpensive, close to the ski area, and has dorms, small rooms, and two lounges.

Special mention goes to the **Bagatelle Ski Lodge** in Waitsfield. The Bagatelle has some private rooms, some dorm rooms, and an attic dorm which sleeps about 30 persons on a floor covered with thin mats lined up along either wall ($4.25 per night). If you want to save a buck, this is it, but do not stay there unless you can sleep soundly despite noisy distractions.

RESTAURANTS

Sugarbush particularly seems to sustain a number of good restaurants. In Sugarbush Village at the mountain is a good bistro, **Chez Henri,** which serves quiches and pâté at lunch and good dinners (entrées, $6–10), and the **Phoenix,** a *haute cuisine* Continental restaurant with extraordinary desserts (entrées, $6–9). The Village also has a pizza joint, the **Odyssey.** On the Sugarbush access road a mile from the mountain is **Sam Rupert's,** which is charming inside and serves good Continental food and an assortment of salads and vegetable dishes (entrées, $4.50–7). On German Flat's Road, which goes north off the Sugarbush access road toward Glen Ellen near the Sugarbush Inn, is the **Common Man,** a handsome two-story, 1881 barn with hand-hewn rafters. It serves excellent Continental food to a background of classical music (entrées, $4–10). Back on the Sugarbush access road below the Sugarbush Inn together in one farmhouse are **Little John's Pub,** a cellar pub with sandwiches and salads ($2–3), and **La Bocca Grazia,** a quiet Italian restaurant (entrées, $4–8).

In Waitsfield there are several good restaurants: the **Azteca Sun,** Mexican; the **China Barn,** Chinese; **Gallaghers,** an informal steak house ($4–8) (the Waitsfield romping and stomping hangout); and the **Den,** serving steaks and chicken ($4–8).

In addition, there are restaurants within the inns: the Sugarbush Inn has a traditional dining room and a steak and lobster restaurant, the **Beef & Bottle** ($5–9); the **Golden Horse Lodge** dining room is Swiss; and in Waitsfield, the **Valley Inn** restaurant is German ($5–8). The **Ark** serves seafood ($5–8). The **High and Dry** offers steaks and sandwiches ($2–7). In general, the restaurants in Waitsfield are less formal and less expensive than those in Sugarbush, where reservations on weekends are necessary.

APRÈS-SKI AND NIGHT LIFE

Mad Sugarglen is one of the liveliest after-ski centers in New England, with rock music centers that compete with Vermont's best. These are the **Blue Tooth** on the Sugarbush access road, which adds ski flicks to the entertainment, and **Gallaghers** at the crossroads in Waitsfield. Both appeal to a predominantly college set. There is a new disco-restaurant, the **Downstreet** on the Sugarbush access road, which caters to those over thirty. Dancing and live music are offered at the bar downstairs at the **Sugarbush Inn.** There is a disco at the **Alpine Inn,** guitar music at **Little John's Pub,** and other entertainment elsewhere in the valley.

DIVERSION

The valley has an assortment of cross-country skiing. The principal center is at the **Sugarbush Inn,** with 32 miles of marked and 15 miles of unmarked trails. There are cross-country trails at Glen Ellen. The **Alpen Inn** and **Tucker Hill Lodge** have a cross-country center. Also, you can start at the top of the Mad River double chair and ski back into the valley on marked trails.

Sugarbush has an unparalleled racket center at the **Bridges,** with facilities for tennis, squash, and platform tennis (two lighted courts) as well as a pool and sauna. It is open to the public, except on Saturdays and during the Christmas and George Washington's birthday weeks.

CHILDREN

Mad River has a junior club and junior racing program for kids six to eighteen. It also has a nursery at the slopes for infants three weeks and up ($1.50 per hour; $9 per day).

Sugarbush has an excellent nursery in the Village about three minutes' walk from the central base lodge.

The areas are all quite compact (Sugarbush being a bit spread out), so that supervision and meeting is relatively easy. Hotels are near the slope and older kids can be self-sufficient, depending, of course, on where you stay. Of the three resorts, Glen Ellen is the best for young children.

COSTS

The valley is big and thus has accommodations and restaurants that range across the full economic spectrum. Most facilities near Sugarbush are more elegant than those in Waitsfield or near Mad River and are often more expensive. In general, the area is slightly less costly than the Triangle area or Stowe, although Sugarbush is comparable. Sugarbush lift tickets cost $15 per day, with reductions for three or more days. Mad River's lift ticket is $11 per day weekdays, $14 weekends, and $45 for a five-weekday ticket. The Glen Ellen rates correspond closely to the Mad River rates (weekends, $13), except that in early December, January and April weeks, lessons are even cheaper.

'49

Mont Ste-Anne

As far north and east as you will want to go (perhaps further) is Mont Ste-Anne, a tough, well-balanced mountain offering a rather special vacation. The area is about 25 miles east of Quebec City, and the combination of the mountain and the city makes vacationing at Mont Ste-Anne unique and exciting. The mountain has good terrain for skiers of all abilities. Quebec City feels very much like a small European city. By preserving and restoring many of its old sections, it has maintained a strong sense of history. It has narrow, curved streets, stone houses, and handsome ornate structures. If your travel companion tires easily of skiing at Ste-Anne, he or she can enjoy marvelous sightseeing in town.

ACCESSIBILITY

Mont Ste-Anne is not a hop, skip, and a jump away. The area itself is 30 minutes east of Quebec City, which is a 3-hour drive northeast of Montreal, or about 600 miles from New York and 450 miles from Boston. The most comfortable travel plan is to fly to Quebec City, by way of either Montreal or Boston.

The better accommodations for all purposes are in Quebec City, so it's useful to have a car. Some tours that sell packages for Mont Ste-Anne provide bus transportation each morning. If you can avoid this, do—especially if you're an impatient skier. The 30-minute drive from the City to the slopes, with inevitable delays resulting from group travel, can end up being twice or three times as long.

THE SKIING

Mont Ste-Anne is a first-class mountain. It lacks the scope of Stowe and its variety of difficult runs, but it does have four top expert runs and extensive intermediate and novice skiing.

The mountain's vertical is 2,050 feet over a length of 7,700 feet. Like Mont Tremblant, Mont Ste-Anne is developed on both the north and south sides of the mountain, the south being the principal side with a greater variation of terrain. Unlike Tremblant, Ste-Anne is nicely spread out away from the central axis.

The expert terrain is on the south side on the top three-quarters of the mountain. The top of the gondola–double chair lift (both lifts go top to bottom and are 7,700 feet long) is of moderate steepness and has wicked, twisted moguled terrain. To the left is an area reserved for experts with three steep, moguled runs. Two of them, side by side, La S and La Super S, are broad, steep and straight, have true fall lines (the fall line goes straight down, not directed to the right or left of the trail) and are reminiscent of the National at Stowe or Stein's Run at Sugarbush. These two runs have overall verticals of 1,325 feet over a length of only 3,400 feet, and in the steeper parts vary between 25 and 30°. Like the top of the National, they combine steepness and terrain for a 9 rating. Two additional expert trails are found still further to the right. These runs are served by a 4,500-foot poma lift with a 1,465-foot vertical. This is pure, steep, mogul-field, no-nonsense skiing at its best. If you can run four runs down La S or La Super S in an hour (5,300' total vertical) while riding a poma up and still feel strong in the thighs, you've really got it made.

On the right of the mountain on the south side is one cruising expert trail, La Pionniere (7), with an 8,100-foot run. The balance of the right side is reserved to intermediates and novices. There is a novice T-bar on top and a novice J-bar at the bottom. There are also two chairs which serve intermediate and novice runs. The novice run from top to bottom is 3 miles long.

The north side is almost entirely intermediate or novice, though some trails are marked expert. These trails are generally broad and straight with continuous, even terrain. This side has a double chair and poma which run parallel to one another with a vertical of 1,000 feet over a length of 4,500 feet. There is also a T-bar on the north face which adds a little advanced-intermediate skiing.

All in all, Mont Ste-Anne is a well-balanced, well-laid-out alpine area.

Despite its distance from the massive population centers of the U.S.A., Mont Ste-Anne is not undiscovered or uncrowded. There will be lines on weekends, though they will be shorter than those at Vermont's major areas. The expert poma is likely to have short lines, even on weekends.

The weather at Ste-Anne is similar to Vermont's but a bit windier. Mont Ste-Anne has an average annual snowfall of 155 inches, equivalent to that of central Vermont. The principal exposure is southern, so that conditions are less stable than at other Eastern areas. While the area advertises skiing until May, Mont Ste-Anne is not likely to have good late skiing.

LIFE IN THE AREA

Skiing Mont Ste-Anne offers one of the most unique skiing-tourist packages in North America, particularly because of Quebec City. The mountain has excellent skiing, but the town of Beaupré, located at the base, is drab. In fact, the area around the mountain, except for the views of the massive St. Lawrence River running a few miles from its base, is quite unattractive. However, Quebec City adds all the necessary spice. It sits on the northern shore of the St. Lawrence at a point where the river narrows. About 200 feet to a quarter of a mile back from the river is a high 300-foot rock face. The area between the foot of the rock and the river, centered around the Place Royale, was first settled as a fur-trading center in 1608. The structures built at that time were entirely destroyed by fire in 1682. Houses built thereafter in the early eighteenth century still stand and are now being renovated. The fortress constructed at the top of the rock and since replaced was the site of the famous Battle of the Plains of Abraham in 1759, when General Wolf at the head of the English army unsuccessfully laid siege to the city. Benedict Arnold attacked the city in 1775, again to no avail. The city next to the fortress remains intact. At its center is the Chateau Frontenac, a magnificent Gothic hotel built in the 1890's, the scene of two Roosevelt-Churchill World War II meetings.

Removed from the center of the City is the elegant late-nineteenth-century French Rennaissance Parliament Building and grounds, the home of the independent, outspoken Quebec provincial government. Two minutes' walk from Parliament are space-age hotels and modern boulevards.

ACCOMMODATIONS

At Mont Ste-Anne, you must make a basic choice before picking a hotel. Quebec City is 30 minutes from the mountain. Normally, we would recommend that you stay at the slopes and drive to the big city for occasional diversion. At Mont Ste-Anne, the opposite is recommended.

There are motels in Beaupré at the foot of the mountain. However, Beaupré is a one-road town and the motels on that road, Boulevard Sainte-

Anne, are mediocre, class B motels: the **Central, Zenith, Joanne, Bellevue Hotel,** and **Le Lucern.** Each is simple, cheap, uninteresting but adequately clean. Also in Beaupré off the main drag is the **Chalets Hobec,** a cottage development slightly better than the motels, with a kitchen. The only advantage to these motels is their accessibility to the slopes.

A second choice is to stay at a motel just east of Quebec City. This allows easy escape to the mountain in the morning, easy access to the city at night, and easy parking. Again, there are modern motels, tacky but a step above those in Beaupré. Better among these are the **Hotel Motel** [*sic*], **Des Laurentides,** the **Motel Orleans,** and the **Motel Le Chatelet.** This area itself offers nothing, has no charm, but is convenient.

The third choice, and perhaps the best, although certainly the most expensive, is to stay in Quebec City itself. At the center, on the heights above the river, is the old, historic **Chateau Frontenac.** Offering Victorian grandeur and sobriety and a striking location above the river, it is centrally situated near the best restaurants and entertainment.

By contrast, there are two wonderfully modern, elegant, deluxe hotels five minutes' walk from the center of town. The most elegant and architecturally successful is the **Auberge des Gouveneurs,** a multi-story plush structure with restaurants, an outdoor heated pool (open in winter) and a piano bar. Equally elegant is the **Quebec Hilton,** with a spectacular roof restaurant, heated indoor-outdoor pool, and deluxe service. One rung down on the elegance scale is a Loews hotel, **Le Concorde,** which also has a pool and, most notably, a roof restaurant which revolves and provides a view of the entire city. Quebec City also has guest houses *(pensions)* which are less expensive and very French.

Reservations can be made through Hospitalité Quebec: 418-694-0457.

RESTAURANTS

The choice and quality of restaurants in Quebec City is the best you will find in any ski area, including Aspen. In the Place Royale, below the Chateau Frontenac, are four very small *haute cuisine* restaurants situated in eighteenth- or even seventeenth-century houses. Most charming are **La Traite du Roy,** serving French food; **L'Hatelet,** also French; **L'Eperlan,** seafood; and the **Auberge de La Fine Guele,** Quebeçois food. Near the Frontenac and within the eighteenth-century walls of the upper city above the Place Royale are **Au Vieux Quebec,** Continental; **Chez Guido,** Italian; **Aux Anciens Canadiens,** Quebeçois and charming; and the **Continental,** French. All of these restaurants have excellent food, are small and have a warm atmosphere.

This does not exhaust the list by any means. Restaurant guides to the City are available. There are also restaurants in each of the major hotels and restaurants outside the walls of the old city.

APRÈS-SKI AND NIGHT LIFE

Quebec City provides exciting after-ski life. There is a bar upstairs in the base lodge at the mountain which attracts college students and adults in their twenties. It is comfortable but has no music, and is good for a quick drink after a day on the slopes.

The many night clubs, bars and discos vary from the formal, modern, roof-restaurant bars at the **Hotel Hilton,** or the **L'Astral** at Le Concorde, to intimate, dark, petite discotheques in the area around the Place Royale. The City has the atmosphere of Montmartre at night. This mood is found principally in the smaller discos. Right near the Chateau Frontenac is **Le Grenadier,** a simple piano bar. Close by is **Le Gaulois,** a "boîte à chansons," small with live singing groups and music. The **Eglantine,** in the Place Royale, is an intimate and elegant eighteenth-century disco, with high, plush stuffed chairs. There are also modern discos at the newest hotels and small bars or piano bars at the older hotels. In all, Quebec City offers lots of choices for night people for whom the day's activities are not enough. It is pleasant just to walk about the narrow streets and to eat in one of the many Quebeçois restaurants.

DIVERSION

The principal diversion is sightseeing and shopping in the old city.

In Quebec City, in front of the Chateau Frontenac and above the river, is an outdoor rink and an ice toboggan run. You can snowshoe and cross-country ski right in the park near the hotel or at Mont Ste-Anne itself, which has 60 kilometers of marked trails. We were unable to find indoor tennis, but how long can that last in a city this size?

CHILDREN

The mountain is compact. There is one base lodge and no difficulty moving from one part of the mountain to another to rendezvous with skiers of different abilities. The base lodge has a nursery for children three years of age and older.

The motels and hotels both in and out of Quebec City are not well suited for children. Most of the motels are situated on a highway and as a result do not have good outdoor play areas. Two of the city hotels have swimming pools and the **Chateau Frontenac** has a skating rink and toboggan slide for recreation.

Children are not discouraged, but the surroundings of Quebec City are better suited to adults.

COSTS

Prices, of course, vary with the exchange rate. Assuming relative dollar parity, prices at Ste-Anne are moderate. Lift tickets are $9 per day on weekends and $8 during the week. Five-day tickets are $32 non-holiday. Lessons are on the inexpensive side, starting at $4, $16 for 5 consecutive days of 2-hour lessons. Motel prices range from $16 per day to $30. The Quebec Hilton, one of the two most deluxe hotels, is $90 per person, double occupancy, for 5 days during the week. Meals at good French restaurants range from $10 to $15 per person with liquor.

It's not a steal, but it *is* a good value.

50
Mont Tremblant

Mont Tremblant is the oldest of the major Canadian resorts and the crown of eastern Canadian skiing. The mountain has a vertical drop of 2,300 feet, comparable to almost any resort in the East. The area is a full-scale resort with large hotels, some good restaurants, a French Canadian atmosphere, and a lively ambience. Is it worth traveling from afar to ski 2 hours' drive north of Montreal? For the skiing, no; for the weather, certainly not; for *la différence,* perhaps.

ACCESSIBILITY

Mont Tremblant is 80 miles northwest of Montreal, effectively 2 hours by car. Montreal itself is a 6-hour drive from New York, or a 5-hour drive from Boston, and is, of course, served daily by air from all major Eastern and Midwestern cities in the United States. Bus and limousine transportation is available from the airport or from downtown Montreal to the resort. Service from downtown Montreal by bus is frequent (5 times per day), but from the airport it is infrequent. Rental cars are available at the airport. A car is by no means necessary at Mont Tremblant, particularly if you stay at the mountain at the Mont Tremblant Lodge or at several of the other major resort hotels, which provide transportation to the lifts.

THE SKIING

The mountain is developed along a central access which goes up both the south and north sides. Each side has two tandem lifts to the top. On the south side, the total vertical is 2,300 feet, rising from 700 feet above sea level to 3,000 feet. This vertical is extended over a distance of about 6,500 feet. The north side is similarly structured with tandem chairs but with a total vertical of only 1,850 feet over a similar lateral distance.

Mont Tremblant has no extended, steep, challenging expert runs. Flying Mile and Expo, trails that do have some steep, moguled terrain, are open and broad, with the steep portion extending no more than 700 feet. These are located at the top of the liftlines on the bottom chairs on both the north and south sides. The top lift on the south side, with a 1,300-foot vertical, has two narrow expert trails with short steep parts, Kandahar and Grand Prix, but these are principally 7's. Experts and strong intermediates can cruise on two trails, Ryan on the south, and Devit's River on the north, which have tricky terrain and run from top to bottom. However, skiing at Mont Tremblant suffers not only from the lack of extended expert trails, but from an excess of lift concentration up the central axis on each side, which diminishes the aesthetic quality of the area. Also, only a small portion of the mountain has been developed and as a result skiers tend to be crowded together.

Intermediates will find a full range of terrain designed to meet their needs. Those who want more challenge can ski the narrow trails of Nansen, Ryan, and Charron on the top chair on the south side. Those who want a more relaxed experience can stick to the trails on the north face. Particularly attractive, scenic, and broad is the trail named after Lowell Thomas, who skied often at Tremblant. There are really only two novice runs, one on the bottom chair of each side, but the intermediate trails on the north side can be skied by the trail-wise novice.

Mont Tremblant is not the place to get away from crowds. Montreal skiers are an enthusiastic group and Tremblant is very accessible to them. On weekends, lines can be 15 to 20 minutes long. The lift line problem is aggravated by the relative shortness of the lifts and the need to take two lifts to go from bottom to top.

Mont Tremblant's snowfall is roughly equivalent to New England's (about 160"). The southern exposure of more than half the trails and the low elevation results in bare spots and ice and tends to shorten the season. The south central axis of the mountain now has snowmaking facilities which cover an area that includes some terrain for skiers of all abilities. The weather at Tremblant is colder and windier than that in New England, and the cold can be quite bitter.

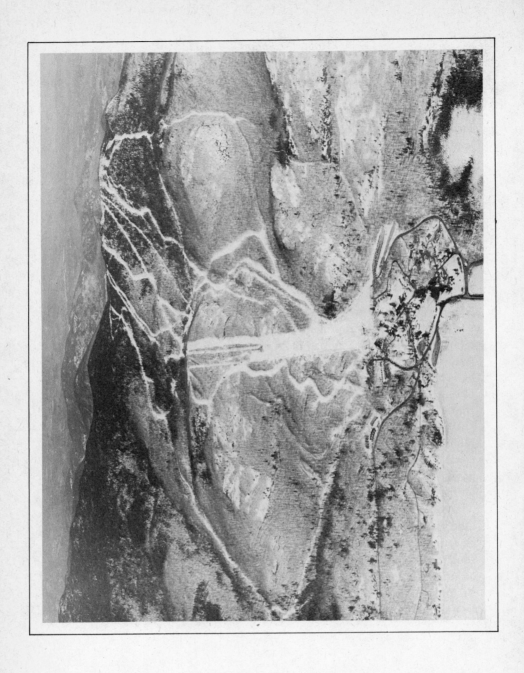

The south side of Mont Tremblant, with Mont Tremblant Lodge at base   JACK
MARKOW & CO., PHOTOGRAPHERS

LIFE IN THE AREA

Mont Tremblant has huge, old resort hotels, small out-of-the-way inns, and some good restaurants. It is not, however, truly "French," or "quaintly European," or "wonderfully exotic." But for the Canadian currency, an occasional non-English-speaking innkeeper, and excessive cigarette smoking in the base lodges, the area could just as well be set in New Hampshire.

ACCOMMODATIONS

At the base of the mountain is the **Mont Tremblant Lodge.** Comprising two main buildings, an annex, and small cottages that can be shared, the Lodge is an old inn with boutiques, restaurants, and bars. It is attractive and warm but not luxurious. Dormitory accommodations are available, as well as ample double rooms. Ski week packages for $200 and up include lifts, 4 hours of lessons per day, and three meals. The Lodge is, as it advertises itself to be, a little village at the slope. For those without a car, it is ideal.

Next in popularity is the **Grey Rocks Inn,** a huge Victorian hotel that accommodates 450 persons and has two restaurants, a large bar with live music, and its own ski area with five lifts (vertical drop, 600 feet). It's about 5 miles from Mont Tremblant but has a shuttle bus to the mountain. Grey Rocks is informal, lively, and plain but pleasant. Ski week packages are available but include lift tickets for Grey Rocks, not Tremblant.

Most elegant among the resorts at Mont Tremblant is **Cuttle's Tremblant Club,** a smaller inn, secluded on the edge of the lake with a view across the lake to the mountain. Cuttle's is quiet, attractive, and well-managed, though not luxurious. Its dining room is small, well-appointed, and first-rate, and there's a piano bar for entertainment. Again, it provides shuttle service to the slopes. Cuttle's is the class of the area, although the Lodge gives it some close competition.

Within 2 miles of Mont Tremblant there are numerous other inns, including the first-class **Villa Bellevue,** with an attractive disco and dining room, and its own ski school; the **Manoir Pinoteau,** an old country home facing the mountain, with a simple ambience, good food, a game room, and its own ski school; and the **Chateau Beauvallon,** a small, inexpensive chalet hotel with a cozy lounge and a family atmosphere. There are also modern motels: the attractive **Chalet** and **Chutes;** the **Mont Tremblant Motel,** which is plain; and **Schmidt's Gasthaus,** which has a Tyrolean style.

Three inns are located about 10 minutes away from the north side of Mont Tremblant. This side of the mountain is very rustic and quiet. Particularly rural is the **Auberg de la Boulé,** a small simple inn in an isolated setting. The other two, the **Chalet Caribu Lodge** and the **Hotel Motel Rustique,** are on the edge of the tiny town of Lac Supérieur. They have a hunting lodge quality.

Finally, there are motels in the town of St Jovite, 10 miles from the mountain.

RESTAURANTS

Dining at Mont Tremblant is largely confined to the inns and hotels of the area. This, in part, results from the widespread reliance of the hotels on the American Plan. Perhaps the best restaurant is **Cuttle's,** which serves high French cuisine in a quiet, elegant dining room. Also good is the **Mont Tremblant Lodge,** which is Continental, and the **Manoir Pinoteau,** which serves less formal French-Canadian food. In the small village of Mont Tremblant there is a French-Canadian restaurant, **L'Auberge 1896.**

In St Jovite, the only large town in the area, there are several undistinguished restaurants, including a Chinese restaurant, a steak house, and a brasserie. More interesting and authentic is **L'Auberge Enchantée,** a French-Canadian (Quebeçoise) restaurant north of St Jovite. Seventeen miles south of St Jovite, on the road to Montreal, in the town of Ste Agathe des Monts, is the highly recommended **Chatel Vienna,** with a Continental menu.

APRÈS-SKI AND NIGHT LIFE

Again, the centers of après-ski life are the large resorts. Particularly raucous is the **Grey Rocks,** with a huge dance floor and, on most weekends, a loud band. The Villa Bellevue has an attractive disco, the **Alenden. Cuttle's** has a piano bar that is relaxed and pleasant. There is also live entertainment at the **Mont Tremblant Lodge.**

DIVERSION

The principal diversion of the area is cross-country skiing. Trails extend throughout the entire area, connecting most of the principal inns. There are over 60 miles of marked trails with warming huts or access to inns, so you can stop for refreshments. Trail maps are available at the major inns or at the tourist bureau in St Jovite (819-425-3300).

The area encourages shopping, and there are boutiques at the mountain or in St Jovite. There is also an art center at Mont Tremblant featuring work by French-Canadian artists.

COSTS

For Americans, the prices at Mont Tremblant can change with currency fluctuations. With this caveat, it is fair to say that the area is cheaper than its

New England counterparts. In Canadian dollars, day tickets are $7.50 on weekdays and $10 on weekends. Packages are available for a room, two meals per day, and all lifts at $200 to $250 per week per person, double occupancy, at the best hotels. The lesser inns offer the same package for as little as $150, again in Canadian currency.

The Skier's Chart

	VERTICAL (IN FEET)	NOVICE	INTERMEDIATE	EXPERT	SNOW	ACCOMMODATIONS	RESTAURANTS	ENTERTAINMENT	FAMILY AREA	UNCROWDED & QUIET	DIVERSION	INEXPENSIVE
California												
Alpine Meadows	1700	3	4	2	3	2	3	1	4	4	2	3
Bear Valley (Mt. Reba)	2100	3	4	3	3	3	2	2	4	4	2	3
Heavenly Valley	4000	3	3	4	3	3	2	5	1	1	3	3
June Mountain	2562	4	4	2	3	1	2	2	4	4	2	4
Mammoth Mountain	3000	4	5	3	3	4	4	4	3	1	4	2
Squaw Valley	2700	3	3	5	3	3	3	3	2	1	3	2
Sugar Bowl	1500	3	3	2	3	3	3	1	1	5	2	2
Oregon												
Mt. Bachelor	1400	3	4	3	2	5	3	3	2	3	3	3
Washington												
Crystal Mountain	2430	3	4	4	2	2	2	2	4	3	2	4
Canada												
(British Columbia)												
Whistler Mountain	4000	1	4	5	2	2	2	3	1	3	3	3
Colorado												
Aspen	3000	4	5	4	3	5	5	5	1	1	5	1
Crested Butte	2150	3	4	2	3	2	3	2	4	3	2	4
Purgatory	1600	5	3	1	3	3	2	3	3	3	3	3
Snowmass	3500	3	5	2	3	4	3	4	4	2	4	1
Steamboat Springs	3600	3	4	3	3	3	3	4	3	2	3	2
The Summit Areas												
—A-Basin	1700	2	4	3	3	1	1	1	2	3	1	4
—Breckinridge	2200	4	3	4	3	3	3	4	3	2	3	2
—Copper Mountain	2450	2	4	3	3	4	3	2	4	3	2	3
—Keystone	2350	4	4	1	3	5	4	4	5	3	4	1
Telluride	3200	5	2	4	4	2	3	2	3	5	2	4
Vail	3050	4	5	5	3	5	3	4	3	1	4	1
Winter Park	2100	3	4	4	3	2	3	2	3	3	2	3
Idaho												
Sun Valley	3400	2	4	4	2	4	2	4	2	2	5	1

	VERTICAL (IN FEET)	NOVICE	INTERMEDIATE	EXPERT	SNOW	ACCOMMODATIONS	RESTAURANTS	ENTERTAINMENT	FAMILY AREA	UNCROWDED & QUIET	DIVERSION	INEXPENSIVE
Montana												
The Big Mountain	2000	4	3	2	2	2	2	2	5	4	2	5
Big Sky	2260	3	4	1	5	4	4	2	4	5	3	2
New Mexico												
Taos	2600	1	2	5	3	4	3	2	4	4	4	3
Utah												
Alta	2000	3	4	4	5	3	3	2	3	3	3	3
Park City	3000	4	5	3	4	3	3	4	3	3	3	3
Snowbird	3100	2	2	5	5	4	3	2	2	3	3	2
Wyoming												
Grand Targhee	2000	3	4	2	5	2	1	1	5	5	1	4
Jackson Hole	4100	3	3	5	3	3	2	2	5	3	4	4
Canada (Alberta)												
Banff—Lake Louise	3300	3	4	3	3	3	2	3	2	3	3	3
The Bugaboos— Helicopter Skiing	5000	–	–	5	5	2	2	1	1	5	1	1
Maine												
Sugarloaf	2600	4	5	4	3	3	2	2	5	5	2	4
New Hampshire												
Cannon Mountain	2000	3	4	3	2	2	2	2	3	4	2	4
Washington Ski Valley	2000	3	4	2	2	3	3	3	3	3	5	3
Waterville Valley	2000	3	4	2	2	3	2	2	4	3	2	3
New York												
Gore Mountain	2100	4	4	3	2	1	1	1	3	4	1	5
Hunter Mountain	1600	2	3	3	3	2	2	3	2	1	2	3
Whiteface—Lake Placid	3200	3	2	4	1	2	3	3	2	2	5	4
Vermont												
Jay Peak	2100	4	4	3	3	2	1	1	4	4	1	4
Killington	3000	3	5	3	3	3	3	4	2	1	3	2
Mount Snow	1900	3	4	2	3	4	3	4	3	2	2	2
Okemo Mountain	2100	4	5	1	3	2	2	2	4	4	2	5
Smuggler's Notch	2100	3	4	3	3	3	1	2	5	4	3	3

	VERTICAL (IN FEET)	NOVICE	INTERMEDIATE	EXPERT	SNOW	ACCOMMODATIONS	RESTAURANTS	ENTERTAINMENT	FAMILY AREA	UNCROWDED & QUIET	DIVERSION	INEXPENSIVE
Stowe	2100	1	4	5	3	4	4	4	2	2	4	1
Stratton, Bromely, Magic	1900	4	5	1	3	4	4	4	4	2	3	1
Sugarbush, Mad River, Glen Ellen	2400	3	4	4	3	5	3	4	4	2	3	1
Canada (Quebec)												
Mont Ste-Anne	2050	4	3	4	3	3	5	3	2	2	4	3
Mont Tremblant	2300	2	3	2	3	4	4	3	4	2	3	3

About the Authors

MILES JAFFE and DENNIS KRIEGER are two young
New York City attorneys who have skied
throughout the United States and Canada. Both are
expert skiers.